THE MAN WHO THOUGHT LIKE A SHIP

ED RACHAL FOUNDATION

NAUTICAL ARCHAEOLOGY

SERIES

THE MAN WHO THOUGHT LIKE A SHIP

LOREN C. STEFFY

TEXAS A&M UNIVERSITY PRESS

College Station

This paper meets the requirements of ANSI/NISO z39.48-1992
(Permanence of Paper).
Binding materials have been chosen for durability.
♾ ♻

Library of Congress Cataloging-in-Publication Data
Steffy, Loren C.
The man who thought like a ship / Loren C. Steffy.—1st ed.
p. cm.—(Ed Rachal Foundation nautical archaeology series)
Includes bibliographical references and index.
ISBN 978-1-60344-664-8 (cloth : alk. paper)—ISBN 1-60344-664-8 (cloth : alk.
paper)—ISBN 978-1-60344-058-5 (e-book)—ISBN 1-60344-058-5 (e-book)
1. Steffy, J. Richard (John Richard), 1924–2007. 2. Institute of Nautical
Archaeology (U.S.)—History—20th century. 3. Institute of Nautical Archaeology
(U.S.)—History—21st century. 4. American Institute of Nautical Archaeology—
History. 5. Marine archaeologists—Texas—Biography. 6. Underwater
archaeology. I. Title. II. Series: Ed Rachal Foundation nautical
archaeology series.
CC115.S74S74 2012
930.1028′04092—dc23
[B]
2011049776

To Ben, Daniel, and Annie,

in hopes that the past may illuminate the future

And a boat, above all other inanimate things,
is personified in man's mind. . . . Man, building
this greatest and most personal of all tools, has
in turn received a boat-shaped mind, and the boat,
a man-shaped soul.

—John Steinbeck, *The Log from the Sea of Cortez*

CONTENTS

AUTHOR'S NOTE

Perhaps it's no longer appropriate to refer to ships as "she." Editorial stricture demands that an inanimate object is an "it." Nevertheless, I have chosen to keep with the long-standing nautical tradition of assigning a feminine pronoun to these ancient vessels. For my father, ships were always something more than simple objects; they inspired a reverence bordering on affection. My mother always said that ships were his first love. She was wrong about that. They were a close second. I ask that you overlook the editorial and social incorrectness and indulge this minor anthropomorphism.

THE MAN
WHO THOUGHT
LIKE A SHIP

The wood, dark as obsidian, is harder than I remember it, and heavier. For more than three decades, it had existed in my memory as a fragile thing, the object of warnings to a young boy to be careful in its presence. It's irreplaceable and old beyond belief—older than the ancient castle walls that surround it, older than Christ—older, perhaps, than Alexander the Great.

In this moment, as I hold a piece of the ancient wood, transformed to a rock-like heft by chemical preservation, the millennia seem less significant than the mere thirty-five years that have passed since I last saw these timbers. It was my father who reassembled them like some massive jigsaw puzzle into the hull of the merchant ship they had been before they spent centuries rotting and forgotten on the sea floor.

Near the battered bow, my children stand alongside the restored planks, touching for the first time a history they've known only through pictures and stories. We all agree we can feel my father's presence here as we stand before his greatest achievement. My mind wanders over the decades like a river flowing backward.

For more than a year in the early 1970s, my father handled these same timbers, positioning them on scaffolding that would hold them in their original shape. Rotted and broken and eaten through by parasites, the wood nevertheless forms a thing of beauty, an elegant arch from shattered bow to broken stern, a vessel transporting knowledge of its ancient world into the future.

I look at the frames, or ribs, spread like strips of licorice across the inside of the hull planking. I remember him squeezing between them, attaching one piece or another. He stood over them on ladders, squinted with one eye as he looked along the length of the keel, and lay suspended above the entire ship on a cradle, placing some of the innermost pieces.

I can see him standing to one side, lost in thought, stepping back from the half-assembled wood as he mulled why a piece didn't seem to line up and made calculations anew as he compensated for some discrepancy. The ship, he would say, talked to him. She would tell him when he'd misplaced a particular piece.

His face was weatherworn, almost craggy by then, and his hands were rough and scarred from half a lifetime spent doing physical labor. His hair was black and slicked back from his face. He was about 6 feet tall, slender and muscular from climbing ladders and working on heavy machinery. It was a physique leftover from an earlier part of his life, a life that by then was changing because of the ancient hull. Even here, in the sweltering Mediterranean heat, he usually wore dress pants. Sometimes, he would talk softly to himself as he tried to decipher the latest problem, yet he never seemed to grow discouraged. It was almost as if he rejoiced in each setback, eager at the chance of unraveling the latest mystery that confronted him. Each problem was telling him something new. The lines on his forehead would furrow ever so slightly, and if you spoke to him then, he probably wouldn't hear you, even if he grunted in acknowledgment.

He wasn't just solving an archaeological puzzle. He was laying the foundation for a new life, a new field of study, a method of unlocking the lessons of history. He lacked any formal training, yet in a harborside castle in northern Cyprus, J. Richard Steffy, known to all his friends as Dick, became the first person to ever reconstruct an ancient ship from its sunken fragments, to take its flattened hull from the sea floor and piece it together in its original form. Today, the darkened timbers stand as a monument to history, a window into the ancient world, but they also stand as the culmination of a dream. For an electrician from a tiny Pennsylvania town, this rotted wood changed everything.

The Kyrenia Ship was the first ship in human history to be built twice. She rests aloft on black iron stanchions, giving her the illusion of sailing on air. During Dick's "reconstruction" process, though, the fragments were supported by a cradle of wooden battens that were really his analytical equations expressed in wood. The whole thing could be adjusted as he corrected his calculations, which was inevitable because he was trying to realign several thousand broken nail shafts and mortise joints.

Before she sank, the ship probably had traded at the Greek islands of Samos, Rhodes, and Nisyros, then headed to Cyprus. A "tramp trader" of her day, the merchantman probably picked up cargo in one port and dropped it off in another, hopping around the eastern Mediterranean on a perpetual voyage of commerce. When she sank, she was hauling wine, millstones, and almonds, whose shells, miraculously, also survived their long, watery sleep. By the time of her final voyage, she was a grizzled old lady of the sea, bearing signs of three major overhauls and many minor repairs.[1]

How she sank remains unclear. The waters about a half-mile from the Kyrenia Harbor are typically smooth sailing, without any reefs or obstructions or a history of severe storms—the most common threats to sailing ships of that era. She may have been attacked by pirates and scuttled to hide the crime. Divers uncovered spearheads under the hull, indicating a possible attack, and they found few coins or other signs of payment that should have been present on a commercial trader. Also onboard was a "curse tablet," a folded piece of lead driven through with a copper spike. It contained no writing, but such tablets were used by the ancient Greeks and Romans to bring harm to enemies. Part of the starboard hull was missing, rotted away during the almost twenty-three centuries since the ship sank, perhaps concealing the place where the hull was scuttled. One of the few representations of an ancient Greek merchant ship is a painted cup that depicts a pirate ship approaching the merchantman, seemingly about to ram her starboard bow,[2] the same section missing from the Kyrenia Ship. Small coves to the east of the harbor could have served as hiding places for bandits, who could have swiftly rowed toward the old, cargo-laden ship and overtaken her.[3]

A less dramatic but perhaps more likely theory is simply that the ship's captain overloaded her, perhaps hoping to take on a little more cargo to shore up his profits on that particular trip, and the old vessel, dangerously top-heavy, succumbed to rough seas. She was sailing in autumn, after the almond harvest, when the chance of storms was greater than in the summer. No matter the cause, she sank to the sandy bottom about 90 feet below the surface, where the weight of her cargo and shifting currents pressed many of her hull timbers into the sea floor, sealing them in a protective layer of silt for more than two thousand years.

She was found in 1965, the year I was born, by Andreas Cariolou, a Cypriot sponge diver who also served on the Kyrenia town council. The discovery came by accident. In those days, sponge divers scouring the sea floor for their wares were the primary source for discovering shipwrecks in the Mediterranean. Cariolou, who had a tangle of graying hair, a mustache, and an easy smile, had been diving since he was a boy. He was among the first to use scuba gear on Cyprus, once emerging from the water to startle unsuspecting beach-goers. The day he first found the ship, he was diving about 90 feet down when he noticed the anchor of his boat dragging along the bottom. The winds had picked up on the surface, pulling the anchor loose. As he followed it, desperately trying to save his boat, he swam upon a mound of clay jars piled up like an ancient underwater burial mound. Cariolou knew he'd made a spectacular find. "When I saw that pile of amphorae, the hair stood up on my neck like a hedgehog's."[4]

The choppy waters prevented him from taking note of the location when he returned to the surface. He would spend the next several years trying to find the site again. When he finally did, he took readings to record its location, then notified the Cypriot government, adamant that the site must be preserved and studied. Eventually, Michael and Susan Katzev, pioneers in the fledgling field of nautical archaeology, learned of Cariolou's discovery, and he led them to it.

"She's yours now," Cariolou told them. "Only archaeologists must touch her. I've kept the secret for just such a group as yours, and to assure proper honor to my town. You must not forget that she's part of Kyrenia's history." Michael Katzev quickly decided that whatever discovery his team unearthed would be called the Kyrenia Ship.[5]

With a team of fifty-two people, the Katzevs began an excavation the following year. More than four hundred amphoras, the giant clay jugs that the ancient Greeks used for transporting wine and foods, filled the ship's open hold. They were soon dated to the fourth century B.C., making this the oldest Greek ship found at the time.

As divers removed more of the cargo, they began seeing the wood of the hull remarkably preserved underneath, pressed deep into the sand and mud, which helped preserve it from erosion and shipworms. In all, almost three-fourths of the hull remained. Divers carefully removed the wood in pieces and transported them inside the thick walls of Kyrenia's harbor-side castle. Built by Richard the Lionheart in the late twelfth century as a staging area for his assault on the Holy Land in the Third Crusade, the castle now became home to an astonishing piece of antiquity.

When Dick first saw the fragments, they were beyond anything he'd imagined. An amateur ship modeler and self-taught student of naval architecture, he had boldly suggested to one of the world's first nautical archaeologists that he could build research models based on data gathered from shipwrecks. A mere seven years later, he stood in the castle, the wood arrayed before him, as he prepared to put his homespun theories to the test. Could this centuries old, waterlogged "Humpty Dumpty" be put back together again?

This was no salvage operation, no treasure-hunting exercise. The Kyrenia Ship's most valuable cargo was knowledge. Few discoveries, Dick believed, could carry as much information about the past as a wrecked ship. "When wooden merchantmen sailed the seven seas, they carried two kinds of cargo—material and intellectual," he explained years later. "The intellectual cargo is information that was stored in the material cargo as well as in the artifacts, ballast, chandlery, hull timbers, and anything else that survived. If a project is properly conducted, the material cargo can never be as valuable as its intellectual counterpart. Even if that material consists of tons of gold objects or fine statuary, its importance can never match that of the knowledge gleaned from a well-researched, well-disseminated shipwreck study. That knowledge grows and spreads over the years, and its dividends can be priceless."[6]

With thousands of hours of scrutiny, Dick began to unlock the ship's mysteries, to loosen her long-buried narrative that offered a glimpse of seafaring in the ancient world. She was 47 feet on the waterline, and 15 feet across the beam, drawing about 4 feet of water.

A square sail, about 26 feet on each side, powered the ship, and her four-man crew steered her with two large oars, one on either side of the stern. Most of the hull was undecked, allowing a large open area for cargo. She was made almost entirely of an eastern Mediterranean pine, and the craftsmanship was exquisite down to the minutest detail. The hull was held together with four thousand oak tenons—resembling short, fat tongue depressors—that slipped into mortises, or deep grooves carved into the edges of the planks. The tenons, in turn, were locked in place by wooden pegs driven through them and the surrounding plank. From these mortise-and-tenon joints, spaced about 12 centimeters, or 5 inches, apart, the hull derived most of its strength. The frames were added later, after most of the planks had been joined, the reverse of the way wooden ships were built in more modern times. Also unlike more recent vessels, the Kyrenia ship's frames didn't extend all the way to the base of the hull to join with the keel.[7]

I run my fingers along the hull planking. It feels waxy from the preservatives, but surprisingly solid. The reassembled hull is a marvel to behold, but the memories flooding back to me are of a work in progress. Until now, I'd seen only pictures of the completed reconstruction.

When I last left Cyprus, the ship was half finished. For much of my stay, the wood was still in various stages of conservation, some baking in the molasses-like goo of preservatives, others still soaking in fresh-water tanks. As a seven-year-old boy, I stepped gingerly across boards laid over the freshwater tanks, my arms outstretched as if I were on a balance beam. "Don't fall," I'd tell myself. One slip of the foot and the wood below would be crushed to pulp.

My senses come alive with memories from the past. Once again, I can smell the waxy treatment solution, like an oven that needs cleaning, and feel the heat of the liquid as the wood was lifted from the preservation tanks. The thick, dark solution could burn your fingers then dry quickly like candle wax. I remember standing by the ship's conservator as she scooped up a beaker of the stuff to check its consistency, then allowed me to empty it back into the tank. It poured like old motor oil. Mostly, though, I remember the sense of quiet excitement among the small band of archaeologists as Dick began easing those preserved fragments onto the wooden cradle of battens and scaffolding.

I recall him on a stepladder, standing over the lip of the partially rebuilt hull, using an electric drill to drive stainless steel wires through the ancient timbers to secure them. I can see his head peering through an opening as he placed a stubborn piece. During the course of that year, starting with the keel just as the original shipwright had done centuries earlier, Dick pieced each rotted fragment back into its original position—more than 5 tons of wood—one shard at a time.

I walk alone to the stern and touch the ragged end of the keel, protruding from its pedestal. The keel is the spine of a ship, spanning the lowest point of the hull and steadying it in the water. On the Kyrenia Ship, the keel was also the most stunning timber. It had survived in one solid, flowing piece, stretching 33 feet along the seabed for two thousand three hundred years under the weight of the millstones, iron ingots, and amphoras filled with 20 tons of wine.

For Dick, the keel was the foundation of his reconstruction, the starting point from which all his calculations evolved. As a sort of mathematical keystone, the keel represented a bond between him and the shipwright who almost two dozen centuries earlier had originally carved and set it, using it as the basis for his own calculations from which to build the rest of the hull. Dick spent hours toiling over those lines, trying to understand what the ship was telling him, what the shipwright, reaching across the ages, wanted him to understand. He studied the grain of the wood and the tool marks still visible on each piece, trying to grasp the messages being telegraphed in the ship's timbers. He often spent twenty or thirty nonstop hours determining the shape of a single part of a frame or plank. In those hours, he developed a kinship with the long-dead shipwright whose hands had converted trees into transport. By studying the woodworking marks, he could tell in which hand the craftsman held his tools, whereas changes in the striking angles suggested the height of an apprentice.

The longer he worked on the ship, the better he felt he knew this shipwright, whom he eventually named Aristides — "man of pride." He didn't tell even his closest colleagues about this for fear they might think he was losing his mind, but it helped to put a name to the person he'd felt he'd come to know.

"We spent many long hours in the castle, he and I. Sometimes, we would work right around the clock, with me trying to fathom the reason for fastening two timbers a certain way and he standing somewhere in the shadows of the vaulted stone ceiling, grinning at the ignorance of this modern, supposedly educated man," he wrote years later.[8]

My fingers trace the knobby end of the keel where the stempost, lost millennia ago to rot and shipworms, was torn away, perhaps from the impact of the ship hitting the seabed. If the keel of any ship is special, this one is more so, at least for my father and me. Just as he gave a name to the ancient shipwright, so too did he and I share a name for the keel. I stare down the length of the timber as it stretches before me, like some long black highway connecting the present to the past.

"Hello, Crooked Aleppo," I whisper to myself. I can't help but smile. My father made up that name for a bedtime story he wrote for me during our year in Kyrenia. It was the story of a pine tree that "grew first one way, then the other" in a zigzag fashion. All the other trees made fun of the crooked one, which they said was destined to be cut for firewood. In my father's imaginary world, trees all aspired to be useful, to be made into something beautiful. Crooked Aleppo, the forest laughing stock, is chosen for the keel of the Kyrenia Ship. No tree, of course, could have a greater honor. Later studies have found the wood wasn't aleppo pine, it was *pinus brutia,* another species native to the eastern Mediterranean. The keel, it turns out, wasn't carved from a crooked tree either. Dick later determined the original shipwright had used a straight timber. It doesn't matter. To me, the keel will always be Crooked Aleppo.

That story, never published, cemented a bond among my father, this ancient ship, and myself. It was a magical tale that inspired me to become a writer, an unexpected gift from a vessel that would give so much to the modern world in the form of insight and knowledge. The Kyrenia Ship, standing to this day in its castle home more than forty years after archaeologists raised her, continues to be studied and continues to reveal new secrets.

Somewhere in the shadows, as I gaze once again upon her blackened hull, Aristides lingers still, guiding his modern counterparts to new clues. My father is there too, perhaps sharing a laugh with his old friend or simply talking about ships forever. The bond spans the generations, from my children to me to my father and back across the centuries to the ancient shipwright, all of us connected through this one vessel.

Dick went on to work on many other ships, from Roman vessels to ferry boats in the southern United States, but this ship was always the most special. Stretching across the Crusader hall in all her splendor, she's the embodiment of his dream, of a journey from whimsy to genius. That dream took him from electrician to professor, from blue-collar worker with just a few years of trade school to world-renowned expert who taught doctoral students. Perhaps most important, though, the dream enabled him to unlock the secrets of the past for all to see.

Susan Katzev describes how the Kyrenia Ship, decades later, still captivates visitors:

> It is in a vaulted sandstone gallery which visitors enter on a balcony. They look down in this darkened room onto the lighted ship. I have observed that time and time again, people who have been chatting away enter this room and become suddenly silent. I believe this is out of respect for the drama of seeing the ship so amazingly preserved and so magically made whole after its long centuries in the sea. Of course, the magician was Dick Steffy.[9]

Societies, Dick believed, leave testaments to their achievement not just in great works of art or buildings but in their everyday tools. Ships reflect a society's ingenuity, its values, its relationships with other cultures. To understand shipbuilding is to understand people who lived centuries ago.

"I like to think that shipbuilding was the most important early everyday technology," Dick once said. "The Greeks and Romans built big and beautiful temples, but I think there's really nothing like a ship, their ships."[10]

And of all of their ships, none compare to the Kyrenia Ship. Amid her well-preserved timbers, though, resides a deeper story, a story not mentioned on the displays that discuss the ancient vessel and her journey. The Kyrenia Ship's final voyage took her from the sea floor to the castle hall, but she carried my father much farther, from a hobbyist's basement to a scholar's dream. Those who look down upon the reconstructed hull from the castle catwalk aren't seeing magic. They're seeing proof that sometimes the best ideas come from the most unlikely places.

2 : DREAMS IN PAPER AND PASTE

The dream began on a corner of Main Street in the smallest of small-town America. The six-year-old boy who would become my father folded pieces of paper to form hulls and decks, gluing them together with homemade paste. In time, he built enough paper boats to turn the living room floor into a busy harbor. Though young Richard Steffy, whom everyone called Dickie, grew up in the landlocked town of Denver, Pennsylvania, 60 miles west of Philadelphia, he was captivated by boats at an early age. By the time he started elementary school, he was building models out of the only materials he had available. The Great Depression was at its apex, and though his family was getting by, things like paste were in short supply. His mother would mix flour and water for him, which he used as an adhesive. Even with such crude materials, the boats he built were detailed, reflecting hours of meticulous work.

"There was something really artistic about it, the way he would sit there studiously," his sister, Muriel, said. "It wasn't just a toy to him; it was something more than that."

He never really knew what sparked his fascination with ships or what gave rise to his paper-boat-building enterprise. Ships and maps always seemed to hold his attention. His sister suggested it may have been a picture of the USS *Princess Matoika* that hung for decades behind the chair of their father, Milton G. Steffy. Milt served in the Navy during World War I, aboard the captured German passenger liner, which had been pressed into service as a troop transport. He was a fireman, spending most of his time below decks shoveling coal into the boilers. The ship made at least a dozen crossings of the Atlantic, shuttling thousands of troops to and from the war zone in Europe.[1] As youngsters, Dickie and his brother and sister would look at the picture of the ship and ask their father what it was like. During battles, he told them, he and other firemen were locked in the engine room to ensure they kept

John Steffy and Eliza Grill Steffy.
(From the author's family collection)

Milt Steffy in the Navy during World War I.
(From the author's family collection)

The USS Princes Matoika *underway in 1919. (From the author's family collection)*

(left) Dickie Steffy in 1931, the year his flour paste boats won the school art show. (From the author's family collection)

(right) Dick, soon after entering the Navy in 1942. (From the author's family collection)

Dick marries Lucille Koch in 1951. (From the author's family collection)

The Egyptian ship model that won Best of Show in Lancaster, 1963. (Courtesy Reading Eagle)

Milt and Zoe in the electrical store, just before Milt's retirement. (Courtesy Ephrata Review*)*

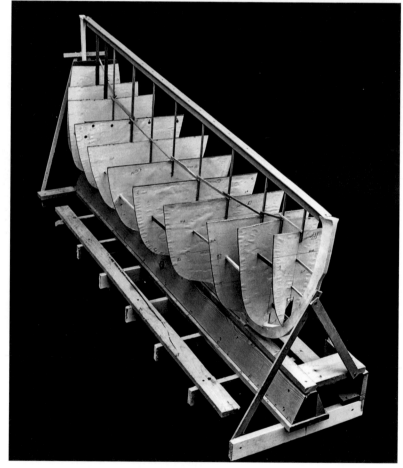

An early mold model. (From the author's family collection)

The original, unfinished mold and batten model of the 7th century Byzantine wreck at Yassi Ada. (From the author's family collection)

Susan Katzev swims over the pile of amphoras that covers the wreck of the Kyrenia Ship in 1968. (Courtesy Susan Katzev, Kyrenia Ship Excavation)

Divers work on logging details about each piece of wood on the sea floor.
(Courtesy Robin Piercy)

Uncovering the hull on the bottom. (Courtesy Susan Katzev, Kyrenia Ship Excavation)

A diver records an amphora. (Courtesy Susan Katzev, Kyrenia Ship Excavation)

(opposite) The hull on the sea floor. (Courtesy Susan Katzev, Kyrenia Ship Excavation)

The Kyrenia ship expedition. (Courtesy Susan Katzev, Kyrenia Ship Excavation)

David, Lucille, Dick, and Loren in Cyprus, 1972. (From the author's family collection)

Kyrenia Castle and harbor. (Photo by David Steffy)

The "ship room," modified Lusignan barracks. (From the author's family collection)

Manifold House in the 1970s, viewed from the castle. (Courtesy Robin Piercy)

Placing a strake on the 1:5 model. (Courtesy Susan Katzev, Kyrenia Ship Excavation)

David and Loren testing the 1:5 fiberglass replica of the Kyrenia ship. (Courtesy Susan Katzev, Kyrenia Ship Excavation)

Setting the first piece of the Kyrenia ship's keel. (Courtesy Susan Katzev, Kyrenia Ship Excavation)

Dick placing wooden battens on the scaffolding to conform for the curvature of the hull. (Courtesy Susan Katzev, Kyrenia Ship Excavation)

(opposite) The port side frames, looking like a beached whale carcass. (Courtesy Susan Katzev, Kyrenia Ship Excavation)

(top) Adding the port side planking. (Courtesy Susan Katzev, Kyrenia Ship Excavation)

(left) An example of the damage from teredo worms on the Kyrenia ship. (Courtesy Susan Katzev, Kyrenia Ship Excavation)

(right) Drilling stainless steel wires into the timbers to hold them in place.
(Courtesy Susan Katzev, Kyrenia Ship Excavation)

Making adjustments near the mast step. (Courtesy Susan Katzev, Kyrenia Ship Excavation)

Beginning work on the shattered bow. (Courtesy Susan Katzev, Kyrenia Ship Excavation)

Finishing the starboard side. (Courtesy Susan Katzev, Kyrenia Ship Excavation)

The finished hull reconstruction. (Courtesy Susan Katzev, Kyrenia Ship Excavation)

The professor. (Courtesy Kevin Crisman)

Dick's model of the Brown's Ferry ship. (From the author's family collection)

INA's first headquarters at Texas A&M University. Dick was given the far end of the building for a ship lab. (From the author's family collection)

George Bass and Fred van Doorninck. (Courtesy Institute of Nautical Archaeology)

Dick examines the charred, overturned hull of the Herculaneum boat. (Courtesy Institute of Nautical Archaeology)

(top) The half model of the 7th century Byzantine wreck from Yassi Ada. (Photo by Don Frey, courtesy Institute of Nautical Archaeology)

(left) An example of Islamic glass found on the Serçe Limani wreck. (Photo by Don Frey, courtesy Institute of Nautical Archaeology)

(right) The puzzle still in the box, pieces of wreck waiting to be reassembled. (Photo by Don Frey, courtesy Institute of Nautical Archaeology)

Robin Piercy removing a piece of the Serçe Limani wood from the polyethylene glycol tank. (Photo by Don Frey, courtesy Institute of Nautical Archaeology)

Placing the frames on the Serçe Limani reconstruction. (Photo by Don Frey, courtesy Institute of Nautical Archaeology)

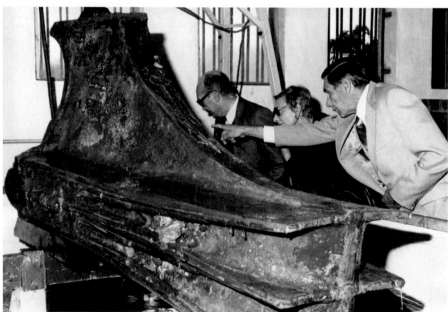

(top left) Sheila Matthews working on the Serçe Limani reconstruction.
(Photo by Don Frey, courtesy Institute of Nautical Archaeology)
(top right) The completed Serçe Limani reconstruction on display in Bodrum Castle.
(Photo by Don Frey, courtesy Institute of Nautical Archaeology)
(bottom) Studying the Athlit ram. (Photo by Merav Dror, courtesy of the Leon Recanati Institute)

Examining the Sea of Galilee in situ *with Shelley Wachsmann pointing at right. (Photo from the collection of the Yigal Allon Center)*

The excavated Sea of Galilee Boat in its museum cradle. (Photo from the collection of the Yigal Allon Center)

Dick with Michael Katzev in front of Kyrenia II. (Courtesy Susan Katzev, Kyrenia Ship Excavation)

Kyrenia II *hull interior. (Courtesy Susan Katzev, Kyrenia Ship Excavation)*

Smoothing the exterior hull of Kyrenia II *with an adze. (Courtesy Susan Katzev, Kyrenia Ship Excavation)*

A worker hammers a copper spike through the outer hull and the frame of Kyrenia II.
(Courtesy Susan Katzev, Kyrenia Ship Excavation)

Kyernia II *underway. (Courtesy Susan Katzev, Kyrenia Ship Excavation)*

Laina Swiny, Michael Katzev, Dick, and Susan Katzev with the Kyrenia II *before her launch. (Courtesy Stuart Swiny)*

Dick in 2004 outside Texas A&M University ship lab that now bears his name. (Courtesy Institute of Nautical Archaeology)

The Kyrenia ship in 2008, more than 30 years after the reconstruction. (Courtesy Susan Katzev)

Dick and George Bass at a book signing in 2004. (From the author's family collection)

the engines running no matter what was happening above. The stories terrified Muriel, but they seemed to capture the imagination of young Dickie, and may have inspired the fleet of paper boats. Ironically, Milt Steffy had no love of the sea. Whereas Dickie would grow up enticed by the salt spray and the pull of the tides, Milt frequently got seasick. He much preferred the outdoors, walking the woods of northern Lancaster County in central Pennsylvania, as he'd done all his life. He had a habit of making his own way, eschewing paths, even in dense woods. His normally quiet nature gave way to a talkative tour guide in the woods, and he would often point out flowers and trees by the names he'd known growing up—names spoken in the region's Pennsylvania Dutch dialect that combined German and English.[2]

Some of Milt's ancestors had been living in the area for almost two centuries. They came as part of a wave of German immigrants seeking a better life and religious freedom, and settled in small farms around the county. Milt's grandfather, Henry Steffy, was born in Germany in 1825 and immigrated to the area as a young man. A lifelong farmer whose grandchildren gave him the nickname "Dawdy," Henry could neither read nor write, and he never learned English.[3] So many in the area spoke German, he didn't need to. Henry married Fietta Steffy, a distant cousin his same age. Fietta was born and grew up in nearby Berks County, the eldest of nine children. Her great-grandfather, Philip Steffy, emigrated to the United States in 1737 from Hirschthal, in the Rhineland-Palatinate region of southwestern Germany.[4] Henry and Fietta had four children, two girls and two boys. Fietta died in 1905, at the age of seventy-nine, and Henry in 1917, when he was ninety-two. Their graves are among a small group of family tombstones in the cemetery in Denver.

Henry and Fietta's youngest child, John Steffy Steffy—his middle name was taken from his mother's maiden name, which was also Steffy—grew up on the family farm near Denver. For much of his life was a successful businessman. He was stern and quiet, known for his long white mustache that drooped around the corners of his mouth and twitched when he became annoyed. He rarely smiled and never hugged his grandchildren, yet he surrounded himself with family, taking in relatives when tragedy struck and caring for his own father later in life.

A stonemason by trade, John built a house about a half-mile north of Denver that still stands, the intricate interlocking four-stone pattern a trademark of his craft. Some of the stones were reused from Henry and Fietta's home nearby.[5] The stone masonry business did well, at one time employing as many as eighty masons working simultaneously to build churches, houses, and walls that can still be seen around the county.

John Steffy owned about a hundred acres of land, part of which was farmed by sharecroppers and contained an orchard that grew apples, pears, and peaches. Woods lined the property, which spanned the Cocalico Creek and included a mill. John also grew tobacco, a common crop in the area during the 1800s, and he owned a small cigar factory that employed men, women and even children rolling the tobacco leaves. Such family-run factories were typical of farms across Lancaster County at the time, but like most of them, John's factory didn't produce enough to ever be much more than a side business, selling its wares to local customers.[6]

John was a devout Protestant and helped found St. John's Reformed Church in 1890. He always sat at the right end of the fourth pew on the right side of the sanctuary every Sunday, and later in life, with his health failing after a series of heart attacks, he still insisted on making his way to the communion rail, even though he could barely walk.[7]

Despite his business success, John favored a simple lifestyle. He was one of the last homeowners in the area to get indoor plumbing, believing that toilets didn't belong inside the home. Even after his wife convinced him to install one, he continued to use the outdoor privy for years. He saw electricity as an extravagance that should be used only when necessary. Talking in the living room with family, though, didn't require lights—everyone could hear each other perfectly well in the dark.

John married Eliza Grill, a slender woman who was even quieter and more reserved than he was and who rarely left the house. She claimed she couldn't go to church, even though her husband was one of the elders, because she had gas. Though she thought cigarettes were sinful, she regularly smoked a pipe, often while rocking in a chair in the corner of the living room. She wore ankle-length gray dresses, and her hair was hidden by a blue bonnet, similar to those worn by the Amish women in the area. Eliza rarely spoke English, preferring Pennsylvania Dutch. None of which made visiting the grandparents much fun for Dickie and his siblings. Although they could play in the fields or along the creek in the daylight, when the sun went down, they had to come inside and sit in darkness listening to their father and grandparents conversing in the strange dialect they couldn't understand.[8]

Milt Steffy was the second of John and Eliza's four children, born on October 5, 1891. He grew up on the family homestead, walking about a mile to elementary school. His personality was, in many ways, the opposite of his parents. John was a stern father who believed the old maxim that sparing the rod spoils the child. One winter, when Milt was about eight, he defied his parents and went ice skating. He fell on the ice and broke his nose. Fearing his parent's reaction, he cleaned himself up, straightened his nose enough to avoid suspicion, and never told his parents. His nose remained bent slightly to the side for the rest of his life.

Living in the country, Milt grew up believing that he wasn't as good as people who lived in town, and when he walked there, he used the alleys rather than the streets. He was shy and quiet, but shared his father's appreciation for hard work and a humble lifestyle. He quit school after the sixth grade and helped his father with stone work.[9]

Although the family remained well off during most of Milt's childhood, John Steffy, or "Pappy" as he became known to the family, also served as a director of a prominent local financial institution, Sinking Spring Bank, which unfortunately lived up to its namesake. In 1929, the stock market crashed and the bank failed, wiping out its investors, including John. He accepted his misfortune and carried on with his same quiet, unassuming manner.

By then, Milt was grown and had long since returned from his tour of duty aboard the *Princess Matoika*. Soon after he returned from the war, he took a correspondence course and learned to paint. He had a natural artistic talent, but his parents and friends discouraged him from developing it, saying it wasn't a respectable way to make a living. Instead, Milt got a job as a postal carrier in the neighboring town of Ephrata, where his dashing reddish-brown hair and sparkling blue eyes caught the fancy of Zoe Fry, whose family's house was on his route.

Zoe was the second of nine children, a lively and gregarious bunch. She contracted rheumatic fever when she was in the fourth grade and never returned to school, though it's not clear if the decision was entirely health related, as she bore no signs of complications from the illness later in life. Her sister would later say that she beat her health problems with sheer determination. She spent most of her school-age years helping to raise her siblings, and her younger brother Richard was one of her favorites. Richard died at age five, probably from typhoid caused by impurities in the water. Zoe's lack of schooling didn't dampen her love of knowledge. As a young woman she traveled to the western United States, and attended theater productions and lectures to make up for her lack of schooling. She was a voracious reader and also had a love of writing. She wrote a number of poems, only one of which was ever published.

As an adult, Zoe—whose name, with the Pennsylvania Dutch accent, was pronounced "so,"—worked briefly in a knitting mill before she married Milt in 1923. By then, Milt had left the postal service to start an electrical contracting business, and the couple moved to an apartment on Main Street in Denver. Residential electricity was still in its infancy in small, rural towns, and Milt's new business thrived under the growing trend. For a time, he was the only electrician in town, and he saw his business as a community service. With his easy-going manner, he lacked the hard-nosed acumen for business, and he had no aspirations of building the enterprise beyond its small-town base. During the Depression, when many of his customers were struggling, Milt often forgave unpaid bills or took barter as payment.

Denver, Pennsylvania, had about one thousand residents in those days, a small borough nestled among the Amish farms and some of the most fertile farmland on earth. It was one of those idyllic places that seem both quaint and impossible in hindsight. Time advanced more slowly there. Even in the early 1970s, doctors still made house calls, a bakery truck made weekly door-to-door stops and a "green grocer" drove around town, selling fresh produce from the back of his car. My father and his siblings attended the same school building where my brother and I would later go to elementary school. Main Street, where Milt and Zoe lived for fifty years, doesn't look much different than it did when young Dickie was building his fleet of flour-paste boats.

Dickie, officially John Richard, was the oldest of Milt and Zoe's three children, born on May 1, 1924, ten months after his parents married. He was named after Milt's father and Zoe's brother who died in childhood. Zoe, though, insisted that her son use his middle name with a first initial, and Richard was quickly given the nickname Dickie, or "Diggy," as it's pronounced with a Pennsylvania Dutch accent. A daughter, Muriel, came next, followed by another son, Milt Junior.

Milt and Zoe built a warm home for their children, and later in life Richard would describe them as "ideal" parents.[10] Milt decreed that the children shouldn't be spanked, even though that was common practice then, because he so disliked the strict discipline with which he'd been raised. He didn't spoil his own children, but he spared them the rod— and even harsh words. He rarely got angry and was as affable as his own father was stern. Though a sturdy man with calloused hands from years of manual labor, his personality was warm and gentle, with a child-like sense of humor that he never outgrew. One of his favorite antics later in his life, repeated over and over, was to take his grandchildren to the local coffee shop at the bottom of the Main Street hill and line them up on the stools at the counter. Then he'd order a "mashed potato sandwich and a dish of fish" and listen to them cackle.

Milt and Zoe were practical people who believed in hard work and didn't like to waste things. But they both had an artistic side that, although never cultivated, was passed on to their three children. Muriel became a writer and Milt Jr., who worked in the electrical business alongside his father and brother, developed an interest in arts and crafts. Richard seemed to synthesize mechanical skills and an artistic nature. In later years, he became known both for his eloquent writing on technical subjects and his understanding of engineering and mathematics.

It didn't start out that way, though. Young Dickie was thin and tow-headed, his hair in early pictures much lighter than the jet black it would turn later in life. He had an easy smile and loved to play practical jokes. As the oldest, he often encouraged one of his siblings to gang up with him against the other, and although allegiances may have shifted among the younger two, Dickie never seemed to be on the receiving end of the jokes, preferring the role of a young provocateur.

In one of his more elaborate schemes, he enlisted his brother to help him place a vacuum under Muriel's bed, knowing she was afraid of the dark. They turned on the switch and ran the cord out her window, across a balcony, and into another room. After she fell asleep that night, they plugged it in. The resulting roar left a terrified Muriel screaming and yelling until her mother came running. Only after she calmed down did she hear her brothers laughing in their own room nearby.

Dickie started elementary school in 1930, at age six. The Denver school had eight classrooms to house grades one through twelve, with first and second grades sharing a room on the first floor. Although Dickie was spry and healthy, he showed little interest in sports and never demonstrated much athletic ability. Instead, his interest was dominated by maps and ships. He was a good student, nurtured by his mother, who passed on her love of books and reading in spite of a busy schedule. Milt worked six days a week, as did Zoe, who ran an electrical supply store out of the house. His parents' dedication instilled a work ethic in young Dickie that would become his trademark as an electrician and later as a ship reconstructor.

In those days, though, the ships he built were the paper ones, designed largely by imagination. His parents tried to encourage his interest, driving to the Chesapeake Bay, where he could watch sailboats. Sometimes, the family would eat at a restaurant in Philadelphia, and he would stare at a kit model of a sailing ship on display there while waiting for his parents to finish eating.[11] Living so far from the sea, though, they knew little about ships beyond what Milt had learned from his stint in the Navy. Zoe made sure her son had a supply of flour paste and praised his work, but he got little guidance beyond their general encouragement.

His interest, though, got a boost from an unlikely source—school overcrowding.

As Dickie started the second grade, the incoming first-grade class was the largest in Denver's history. Records of exact number of students are long gone, but the size of the class at graduation years later gives an indication of the jump: Dickie's class had nine students; the one after his had twenty-one. Because the two classes shared a room, the school didn't have enough desks for all the students. Dickie and two classmates who had the highest marks were promoted to the third grade.

His first-grade teacher had been a strict disciplinarian, but the teacher for his new third-grade class, Helen Crouse, was warm and friendly. Neither Denver nor the surrounding towns had libraries then, yet she somehow found books that kindled Dickie's interest in ships, and after class she would listen to him tell stories of seas he could only imagine. He scoured the books his teacher provided, studying the details of the ships they described. His paper models grew more detailed as he added decks, superstructures, masts, rudders and smokestacks.

Mrs. Crouse urged him to enter his paper boats in the school art exhibit, which until then had only been a forum for drawings and paintings from art class. Dickie submitted at least six, and possibly eight, models including an ocean liner, a tugboat and a barge—all made from lined notebook paper. The ocean liner won first place, though in reflecting on the contest in adulthood, he often wondered if Mrs. Crouse had influenced the results. Unlike other winners, he was the one she asked to lecture other classes about ships and seafaring. Later in life, he would credit Mrs. Crouse as a key influence, providing the spark that ignited his dreams.[12] It seems the admiration may have been mutual. Dickie's third-grade report card—the only one he kept from his grade-school years—shows all A's and included a note from Mrs. Crouse saying he was "very bright."

Dickie continued to make good grades through elementary and junior high school. He abandoned his childhood nickname for the more mature "Dick," though his friends called him "Pepsi" because he loved the soft drink. He also began playing the clarinet, which he would continue through his senior year. He was on the varsity basketball team his sophomore and junior years, but his lack of athletic talent and his age—his early promotion to third grade meant he was a year younger than most of his teammates—left him on the bench for many of the games. The rejection only fed his growing dislike for school.

Denver was a blue-collar town, and many of his classmates had no intention of graduating, planning instead to start working when they turned sixteen. By the beginning of his junior year, he took a part-time job at the local bakery and spent his spare time hanging out at the one restaurant in town that had a jukebox, which played big band music. His high school paper described him as a "tall and lanky fellow" who as a senior frequently gave classmates a ride in his truck, nicknamed "Willie." "Girls don't seem to bother him too much, yet he's continually bothering them. Always ready with a new joke, he is a constant source of entertainment to his friends."

As he moved through high school, his academic performance began to founder, and math became a particular problem. As Dick headed into his senior year, his teacher was another strict disciplinarian who was also the principal. He gave lots of homework and graded harshly. "He never provided the necessary commentary that should accompany higher math," Dick would write years later. "He did a poor job of explaining basic reasoning and practical scientific applications of mathematics, and refused to answer any questions he thought were not in line with that day's assignments."[13]

Nevertheless, he was well regarded in town, and he was a good friend of Milt's. Just weeks before graduation, he gave Milt and Zoe the bad news: Dick had flunked second-year algebra and wouldn't graduate. It may have been the closest thing to a scandal that the family had experienced. In a small town, word spreads fast, and Dick's failure quickly became a public embarrassment.

"That was a hard time in our lives, because Dick was the oldest one, and we all wanted to attend his graduation," Muriel said. "Mother was furious."

Zoe appealed to the school board. She admitted she hadn't been monitoring her son's studies as closely as she should have. She had the store to run—most of the board members were her customers—and she was taking care of her dying father, who'd moved in with them. Still, nothing had been said about Dick's problems until after the graduation invitations had been ordered, and that simply wasn't right.

Dick, meanwhile, had had enough. He wanted to quit school, but Milt was adamant that he finish. Eventually, everyone agreed that the best solution was for Dick to repeat his senior year, but the principal added a stipulation. He told Milt and Zoe that their son should avoid jobs involving mathematics because he would never be able to understand anything beyond simple arithmetic. It would be more than thirty years before the irony of that statement became evident, but the struggling math student would go on to develop his own geometric and trigonometric methods for determining the shapes of ancient ships.

At the time, though, Dick wasn't thinking of a career in ships, but he was determined to get on one. The Japanese bombed Pearl Harbor in December of his second senior year. Dick again wanted to quit school and enlist, but Milt held firm in his determination that all his children would gain the diploma he never did. Dick turned eighteen in May, graduated a month later, and enlisted in the Navy just days after that. He reported for boot camp in August in Newport, Rhode Island, then spent sixteen weeks in electrical school in Morehead, Kentucky. He completed his training in January 1943 and was assigned as an electrician's mate aboard the USS *Wyffels,* DE6, one of the new *Evarts*-class destroyer escorts the Navy was adding to its Atlantic fleet. After a brief shakedown cruise off Bermuda, the *Wyffels,* with a crew of 198, was assigned to the Sixth Fleet in the North Atlantic.[14]

By the time he entered the Navy, Dick had grown into a lithe young man with rakish good looks. His hair had turned black as he grew older, and his eyes were a twinkling shade of hazel. His service pictures show him with a steely gaze, his narrow jaw set firmly, his right hand holding a lit cigarette. He picked up the habit soon after enlisting, and he'd continue it, to his own detriment, for almost fifty years. Despite the handsomeness exuded in those pictures, though, he wasn't a ladies' man. He had inherited Milt's shyness, and although in letters home he would talk of the confidence that came with putting on a uniform, it didn't help him overcome his awkwardness around girls. Unlike the legendary sailors who claimed to have a girl in every port, he apparently had no girls in any port. In a letter to his sister in the fall of 1945, he complained of how long he had gone without a date.

"I'm one of the guys who believes you can get anything if you try hard enough," he wrote. "That includes everything from an education to women. But I can't enjoy myself like I should. Somehow, the girl always does or says something that makes me wish I was down at the power plant talking electricity with the night engineer."[15]

For much of his time in the service, he corresponded with a girl named Betty, but he never dated her, and although she apparently raised the prospect of marriage, she eventually gave up because of his lack of interest. He later told his sister he wasn't ready to get married. He still planned on four years of college after he was discharged, and he didn't want to ask any girl to wait that long. "An education," he wrote later, "means more than anyone to me."[16]

In all, the *Wyffels* made eleven crossings of the Atlantic, escorting convoys carrying food, supplies, and troops to Europe and Africa, and leading damaged ships or transports carrying wounded or dead service men and prisoners of war on the return journey. In between, she patrolled the coasts of Europe and Africa until the war ended. The *Wyffels* came under attack now and then, but most of the time Dick felt more bored than threatened. In May 1944, the ship faced its biggest battle, which was really more of a skirmish. The *Wyffels* was escorting a convoy of fifty-six merchant ships bound for Bizerte in Tunisia. Just after sunset, her radar picked up approaching planes, which veered away from the fighting ships as they approached the convoy and headed for the merchant vessels. The military ships moved to engage, and Dick's closest call of the war came when a plane appeared out of the smoke of the battle and dropped a torpedo in the *Wyffels*'s direction. Fortunately, it was poorly aimed and missed. Later, a Junkers JU 88 came up on the ship's starboard bow at about 100 feet, but under fire from the *Wyffels*'s guns and other ships in the convoy, the plane banked right. It poured smoke and rapidly lost altitude, disappearing in a burst of black. Soon after, the raiding party fled without scoring a single hit on the convoy or its escort. Dick received an engagement star for the battle.[17]

During his time in the service, Dick was never injured, and the *Wyffels* never took serious damage from enemy fire, something for which he always felt fortunate. He knew others had far more traumatic experiences, and he rarely spoke of his Navy years. As a child, my father's silence about his wartime service was puzzling. Other children would boast of their fathers' military exploits, but when they'd ask me, I didn't know what to say. I knew my father was in the Navy, I knew he'd helped my brother build a plastic model of one of the *Wyffels*'s sister ships, but what he had done in the war was a blank. Later, as an adult, he told me he didn't find war something to be proud of, that it was the only time in his life when he felt as if he were doing something destructive rather than productive. Yet he retained a strong sense of patriotism and believed his service mattered. During his final months in the Navy, he complained to his sister about striking workers who would lie across streetcar tracks, blocking service. "If I were driving one of those streetcars up there and someone laid on the tracks in front of me, I'd plow right over him," he wrote. "And believe me, I'd run over them just as heartlessly as I shot at those JU 88's in the Med a year ago. Strikers are no more American than those Nazi pilots were. It certainly isn't what I was fighting for."[18] During the 1960s, he had a similar reaction to draft dodgers. He found their unwillingness to serve appalling, even though he didn't believe the U.S. should be fighting in Vietnam.

The small taste of combat he received aboard the *Wyffels* led him to agree with John Steinbeck's assessment that "all war is a symptom of man's failure as a thinking animal."[19] Years later, Zoe would urge him to take his Navy uniforms and his service rifle from the upstairs storage room where she'd kept them after he returned home. He refused. When she died in 1981, they were still there, shunned by the thinking animal who found no pleasure in reliving his exposure to man's failure.

Returning from the Atlantic in 1945, the *Wyffels*'s crew expected they'd be sent to the Pacific to support the invasion of Japan. In August, though, the U.S. dropped atom bombs on Hiroshima and Nagasaki, and the war ended. By then, Dick was an electrician's mate first class, with more than three years' experience. That qualified him for an immediate discharge, but he gave his points to his married shipmates, some of whom had never seen their children. The *Wyffels* put into Miami in May 1945, where she began service as training ship for crews learning basic gunnery and antisubmarine warfare. Dick was in charge of twenty-one electricians who later in the summer were assigned to overhaul all the electrical systems on the ship, from 1500-horsepower motors to switchboards and lights. The Navy gradually reassigned subordinates until his crew was only a dozen men, working eighteen-hour days tearing down hundreds of pieces of equipment. Much of the work was below deck and in the engine room, where temperatures soared to 120 degrees. Two of the men passed out from heat exhaustion. Dick was following orders, but he didn't feel comfortable driving his men that hard, and he ordered some rest. All the equipment passed inspection, but he acknowledged that it was his biggest test of responsibility and he "smoked cigarettes like mad" waiting for the test results.[20]

The reason for the overhaul became clear on August 28, 1945, when the *Wyffels* was decommissioned and leased to the Republic of China as part of the Free Chinese Navy, a Taiwanese fleet being formed at the end of the war. She was renamed the *T'ai Kang,* or "smooth waters,"[21] and the remaining members of the American crew spent the next few months teaching Chinese sailors how to handle a destroyer escort.[22] In a bit of irony, the vessel formerly known as the *Wyffels* was sold for scrap in 1972, the same year that one of her former electrician's mates was beginning his reconstruction of the Kyrenia Ship.[23]

Dick's Navy service gave him firsthand knowledge of ships and how they operated, but he wasn't planning on turning his interest in seafaring into a career. The Navy had trained him as an electrician, which was, after all, the family business. He was interested in electrical engineering, and he began making plans for college. Worried that his high school math struggles would make it difficult for him to pass the entry exams, he signed up for a correspondence course in geometry in the summer of 1945. He completed it with a grade of 99.

During his final months in the Navy, Dick took classes at the University of Miami, studying composition, public speaking, and salesmanship, reasoning that an engineer had to be well spoken to sell and explain his plans to the people who controlled research budgets. Ironically, he dismissed studying literature, history, "and that crap."

"Shakespeare never wound a motor and General Custer couldn't tell Boulder Dam from a sand bar," he wrote to Muriel. Young and ambitious, his plans seemed to grow bigger by the week. At one point, he finagled his way into a seminar on electrical engineering at Harvard University while on leave in Boston by claiming to be the sales manager for "Steffy Electric Corporation."[24]

"I've got big ideas," he told his sister. "First to study basic engineering, then become a research man in some lab. I want to some day study in Cambridge, England, the mecca of all scientists. Projects like the Yangtze Savage Dam or the Amazon River Project fascinate me and I would someday like to be in on them."[25]

He would never work on those projects, nor would he study at Cambridge, but he would indeed become a "research man in some lab." Little did he know it would be his own ship lab.

3 : SHORT CIRCUITS

fter his discharge in early December 1945, Dick returned home to Denver and began settling into civilian life. Despite his big dreams of studying at Cambridge, "the mecca of all scientists," his studies began much more humbly. He enrolled in night courses to make up for the math that had bedeviled him in high school. Now that he was more mature, the subject came more easily to him. Aptitude tests administered by the Veterans Administration showed he had "superior intelligence" and a special talent for engineering. The test's administrators urged him to consider going to engineering school.[1]

He put the Navy's electrical training to use working for his father, earning money as he prepared to begin taking classes. Milt needed the extra help. His business was doing well, but his only employee had been his brother-in-law, who'd recently quit and headed west to work for the railroad. Dick tried to enroll in Penn State University, but the school was overburdened with returning servicemen. He waited until the fall of 1946 and began classes at the newly formed Lancaster Area College that met on the campus of Franklin & Marshall, a private liberal arts school. By then, he was twenty-two years old and felt out of place on a college campus. He wasn't interested in the routines of college life and decided he'd rather attend a smaller, more practical school. He transferred to the Milwaukee School of Engineering in the fall of 1947, taking a part-time job as an auto parts salesman to earn money. His grades were good, but rarely exceptional, and one of his weakest subjects was drafting.[2] A year later, he completed his associate's degree in electrotechnology and planned to continue for a bachelor's in electrical engineering.

Then, he changed his mind. He decided he had learned everything he needed for the work he intended to do, and he returned to Denver and resumed doing electrical work for his father. "That may sound strange now, but a lot of us did that sort of thing back then, when degrees weren't as important to get ahead," he wrote years later.[3]

What happened to working on the Boulder Dam and the Amazon River Project? What caused him to abandon the dream of becoming an engineer and getting his hands dirty on some of the world's biggest technical endeavors? It may have been pressure from home. As adamant as Milt was about his children getting high school diplomas, Muriel recalls her parents really didn't put much value in college degrees. What's more, Milt had always wanted to call his business M.G. Steffy *and Sons,* and Dick may have felt obligated to honor his father's wishes.

Whatever the reason, Dick left Milwaukee in 1949 without a higher degree and returned to the family business. In his spare time, he found himself drawn to maritime museums, often taking entire weekends to study or volunteer at places such as Mystic Seaport in Connecticut; the Mariner's Museum in Newport News, Virginia; and the Philadelphia Maritime Museum—all of which were within a few hours drive of Denver. He also began to frequent the U.S. Naval Academy in Annapolis, studying a collection of British Admiralty models with the same attention to detail that he had applied to the books about ships in the third grade.

One weekend in November 1950, the weather turned cold and the road conditions were too bad to travel to the coast, so Dick and a friend decided to try their luck finding dates by going to a dance studio in Lancaster. They took separate cars for the 20-mile trip. The studio taught patrons to dance to swing music and showed them popular moves like the jitterbug. His friend soon disappeared, and after dancing with several young women, Dick asked a brunette named Lucille Koch for a turn. Lucille, who was his age, wore glasses and had a broad smile. She'd recently moved to Lancaster from her hometown of Royersford on the banks of the Schuylkill River about 30 miles outside Philadelphia. Lucille didn't drive, and at the end of the night Dick offered to save her bus fare by giving her a ride home. Relentlessly frugal, Lucille agreed. On the way, he asked her for another date the following weekend, and a romance bloomed. By Christmas, he knew he was falling for her. She took him home to meet her parents, and he took her to see something equally important to him—sailboats in Annapolis harbor.[4]

Lucille Koch, whose last name was pronounced "coke," was the fifth of six children. Her father had lost his business in the Depression, then became ill and was unable to work. The family struggled until he could get back on his feet, which may have explained her frugality. Her childhood was plagued by illness. An autobiography written in the tenth grade reads more like a medical history than a life's story: whooping cough at age three, chicken pox in the first grade, measles in the fourth, and the first case of rheumatic fever in the fifth. Several years after that, she was knocked unconscious in a bicycle accident involving her brother. In eighth grade, she contracted rheumatic fever again, combined with an infection of the blood stream. She spent sixteen weeks in a Philadelphia hospital and received eleven blood transfusions. By the time she had her tonsils removed in high school, she knew many of the doctors and nurses by name, and talked about "renewing friendships" with them.[5]

Lucille made good grades in most subjects except math and art, but her report cards reveal persistent absences because of her health. With so much missed time, she graduated a year late, in 1943, when she was named the "best mannered girl in the senior class." The yearbook described her as "thorough, yet unassuming," and autographs signed by teachers and friends used words like "brave" in reference to her perseverance.[6]

The health battles would continue throughout her life, and they gave the woman who would become my mother an inner strength. It's difficult to overstate the impact she had on Dick's career. She was not only devoted to him, but had unwavering confidence in his abilities. When it came time to make some of the riskier decisions of his career, it was usually Lucille who encouraged him, who told him to set aside more practical concerns and take a chance. Without her support, it's likely Dick's life would not have been the grand adventure it became.

After graduating high school, Lucille went to work for a small pharmaceutical company that was a division of Wyeth Corporation, and eventually worked her way up to the company's headquarters in Marietta, Pennsylvania. She moved to Lancaster, staying for a time at the YWCA downtown, which housed dozens of single women like her, including a young reporter named Muriel Steffy. They were friends years before they became sisters-in-law. It wasn't the only crossing of paths between Steffys and Kochs. After he recovered from his illness, Lucille's father became a traveling salesman for Prizer-Painter Company, a stove manufacturer. His route frequently took him through Denver, where he tried to land a contract to supply stoves to Milt and Zoe's store. Unfortunately for him, he was selling mostly gas appliances and the Steffys were electrical people. Lucille's managers at Wyeth praised her efficiency and organization, and she was promoted to executive secretary for the division's director, Dr. B. Scott Fritz, who worked with Jonas Salk in developing a vaccine for polio.

Dick and Lucille married in October of 1951 and honeymooned in New England. When they returned to Lancaster, they settled into a routine of married life. Lucille continued to work on the Salk vaccine program at Wyeth, and Dick commuted six days a week to Denver. He was mostly wiring farms and houses and doing simple industrial installations. The work offered few challenges, and he didn't really enjoy it, but it provided stability for the young couple. After two years of commuting, they decided to move out of their Lancaster apartment and rent a house in Denver. Their next-door neighbor was Helen Crouse, the third-grade teacher who had encouraged Dick's ship model building.

Moving to Denver enabled Dick to step up his electrical work. The town had a substantial amount of industry for its size—factories that made shoes, hats, pretzels, copper wire, textiles, and graphite materials. Dick formed a partnership with his father and brother—the M.G. Steffy and Sons that Milt had long dreamed of—and they captured a lot of the industrial business. Dick began not only to service and install the equipment, but also to design it. He worked on an array of automated machinery and production lines, and many of his designs were still in use long after he left the business. The Steffys loved the work, but they weren't businessmen. None had the desire to expand the business or hire additional employees—Dick's aversion to being a boss may have stemmed from the lingering guilt of pushing his men to the point of exhaustion during the overhaul of the *Wyffels*—and M.G. Steffy and Sons remained a successful if somewhat stagnant enterprise.

"All my enjoyment was centered on the drafting board or strapping on a tool belt and installing big cables or fine-tuning automated machinery," Dick wrote. "I was not a good businessman and disliked handling employees. In fact, that also went for my partners so that, while we had a good reputation and made substantial incomes, none of us was ever going to pilot a dynasty."[7]

In the early days, M.G. Steffy & Sons followed a traditional billing model of time and materials—cost plus 10 percent was the usual charge. "We were just happy to keep our heads above water," Dick's brother, Milty, recalled.

The electrical business was changing rapidly in the 1950s and 1960s, with new products coming to market and increasing demands in households and factories for electrical equipment and service. The Steffys sold electrical appliances from the storefront that Zoe ran, and the men would install them. But by 1961, large stores in nearby cities began offering electrical appliances at discounts that a small family business couldn't match, so the Steffys shifted their focus. They were now strictly residential, commercial, and industrial electricians, and the store would sell parts to support that, as well as simple retail needs such as light bulbs and batteries.

Dick was the one who saw these changes coming and led the business toward its new focus. As competition increased, the Steffys abandoned the time and materials model and began using bids and estimates, a skill that Dick helped teach his father and brother.[8] By the late 1960s, the business had shifted its focus to its industrial operations, which were more profitable than residential work. My father's income from the electrical business more than doubled between 1965 and 1969.[9] Industrial work, though, brought with it demands that residential repairs didn't. Many of the factories operated around the clock, and when machinery broke down, Dick would get a call, sometimes in the middle of the night. He developed a lifelong hatred of telephones. Officially, he worked six days a week, but the "trouble calls" added hours to the workweek, so that sixty- or even eighty-hour weeks weren't uncommon.

The work was physically demanding too and could be dangerous. A compressor explosion left him battered and bloody, with damage to one eye and shrapnel under his skin, some of which was found by a doctor decades later as his hair began to thin. Had he been standing a few feet in a different direction, the blast could have been fatal. In another instance, he fell down an open manhole, injuring his knee. He was stuck there for hours because his walkie-talkie couldn't get a signal. Though he recovered, the knee bothered him for the rest of his life.

The work kept him thin and muscular and probably helped offset the effects of his smoking habit, but it could be dirty—especially in the graphite plant. He was exposed on a regular basis to industrial hazards, including asbestos, which was used to protect electrical circuits from the heat of machinery such as pretzel ovens. Nevertheless, Dick maintained his trademark sense of humor. The factory managers knew he was a top-notch electrician, but Dick used a label maker to punch out a red sign for the front of his hard hat designating himself "fourth assistant's helper."

As M.G. Steffy & Sons took on more of the factory work, Dick thought the business should shed its partnership structure and incorporate, but his father didn't like the idea. Milt was in his seventies by then, still working six days a week, and a corporation would have had to insure him. It would have been expensive to find a policy for man his age who was still climbing ladders every day.

By today's standards, M.G. Steffy & Sons would be considered an anachronism, the sort of family operation that gets gobbled up by a larger competitor eager to expand. But its small-town roots and its reputation enabled it to maintain a loyal customer base in the wake of mounting competition. In essence, by being top-notch electricians, the Steffys didn't have to worry about being good businessmen. That enabled Dick to focus on what he liked most about the job: the challenge of figuring out how to design a better system, the satisfaction of wiring a circuit cleanly. From the time of those early paper boats, he had a patience that seemed to keep frustration at bay and incredible powers of concentration.[10]

The same meticulous attention to detail that would become evident in his ship reconstructions also was reflected in his electrical work. Dick always was more interested in the design, in the problem solving, than in the completed picture. He helped my brother and me set up a model railroad in our basement. The layout was perpetually expanding—we added track, mapped out new routes, and ultimately spanned half the basement—but we never added any scenery or made it *look* like an actual railroad. My father and brother, who became an engineer, were too interested in designing a loop that would encircle the water heater or solving some wiring challenge.

As a father, Dick shared his broad sense of curiosity. He would take the family on frequent weekend trips to see big engineering projects, such as the atomic power plant at Peach Bottom, one of the first in the nation, and later the Three Mile Island nuclear power plant.[11] Sometimes, he would drive my brother and me to the railroad yard in Reading, and we'd spend hours watching the trains move in and out. We went to Wallops Island to feed my brother's interest in rockets, and we toured historical sites such as Gettysburg, Valley Forge, Yorktown, and Jamestown. We'd go to the Philadelphia airport, climb to the observation deck on the roof of the terminal, and watch planes take off and land. And always, there were the boats—weekend runs to the Chesapeake Bay, the Jersey Shore, Mystic Seaport, Newport News—just about any place where tidewater kissed the shoreline. At the time, I didn't think this was unusual. I didn't notice that other kids' fathers were taking them to baseball games or fishing, and I never missed it.

Decades later, after Dick became a grandfather, that curiosity was still as strong as ever. He came to visit when my youngest son was born and offered to take our older child from our home in Arlington, Texas, to the zoo in Fort Worth. They never made it. Distracted by road construction along the way, my father pulled to the shoulder so he could show my son the huge earthmovers and cranes the road crews were using to construct a new overpass. Well into his seventies, he couldn't pass up a display of engineering and a chance to ignite that same fascination in a child. "You never rode anywhere in the car with Dad that he didn't have something to point out," my brother, David, said.

The 1950s and 1960s were good times for Dick and Lucille. They were well-known in the small town, and they were active in the community. Dick served on the local water board and the volunteer fire department, was active in the Lion's Club, and taught Sunday school at the church that was the successor to the one his grandfather helped found. Lucille was an officer in the Women's Club. They desperately wanted to have children, to complete the perfect picture that went with the red brick house on the corner that they'd bought, which had cherry trees in the yard and an open space that cried out for a swing set and a sandbox. But Lucille's health, always a concern in the background of an otherwise picturesque life, again became an issue. She had two miscarriages in the first few years after she and Dick married, and doctors told her she had little chance of having a child. They set up appointments with adoption agencies.

In March 1958, Denver was socked in by a terrible blizzard. Roads were impassable and much of the town was without electricity for days. People had to walk everywhere, and while she and Dick trudged through the snow one afternoon, Lucille developed terrible stomach pains. They were close to the family doctor, and the pain was severe enough that Dick thought Lucille should be seen. The doctor told them she was two months pregnant.[12]

Their first son, David, was born in the September of that year (the doctor, it seems, misjudged the pregnancy by a month) and from then on, much of the family life centered on child activities and remodeling the house on Pine Street. They wanted another child, but again health issues got in the way. Lucille had another miscarriage before finally getting pregnant again in 1965. That too raised additional health questions. She was forty-one years old by then, and the damage to her heart from her childhood illnesses was taking a toll. Doctors already had raised the prospect that she might not live to see David, who was then seven, graduate from high school. She suffered from atrial fibrillation, a heart murmur caused by a valve weakened from disease. She was hospitalized several times for dizziness and a rapid pulse, and was on regular medication to stabilize her heartbeat.[13] The slightest physical exertion, even walking up a single flight of stairs, left her out of breath. The rigors of childbirth posed a risk not only to the baby but also to her. Fortunately, my parents decided it was worth the risk, and I was born later that year.

With two children, the yard had its sandbox and swing set—Dick built them both, the sandbox from sturdy wood with custom seats and a metal bottom, and the swing set anchored in concrete, with a tin slide. The family enjoyed an idyllic life. Dick was making a decent income, and Lucille worked most of the time too, because as a small business owner, Dick didn't have health insurance. She held various secretarial jobs, mostly for the health coverage, bringing in a modest supplement. In 1965, the year I was born, they earned a combined income of just under $7,800, equal to about $53,000 today.[14] It was a solid middle-class existence.

It had its drawbacks, though. The family electrical business wasn't expanding, and although the shift to industrial work was a profitable move, Dick's income leveled out after that, much as it had before. It was at a higher financial plateau, but it was still a plateau. Competition continued to mount, and none of the partners of M.G. Steffy & Sons had the benefits that come with working for a larger company—no retirement plan or insurance. Then too, Dick was getting older, and though he was in excellent health, he worried how long he could keep up with the physical demands of factory work and whether the electrical business would provide for the growing family.[15]

But there was something more, something that gnawed at him, something that hearkened to his earlier decision to leave Milwaukee before he'd gotten his bachelor's degree. Others saw it too. One of his closest relationships was with Kalas Manufacturing, which made copper wire from a small factory at the bottom of Main Street. Its supervisor, Walt Cubberly, saw in this affable electrician skills that were being under-used in the factories around Denver. "Dick," he would tell him, "you're wasting your time here. You could do much bigger things with a mind like yours."[16]

Deep down, Dick knew that too. He never expressed regret over not going to college, but he had turned away from his dreams of attending the "mecca of all scientists." He wasn't one to bemoan the past, but he also believed that people should rise to their potential. Several guest sermons given in the 1960s and 1970s at his church urged the congregation to pursue their hidden talents. Too often, he said, we're willing to take the line of least resistance rather than challenge ourselves to find our true purpose. Some, he noted, may not find their talent until they retire, yet they still contribute to the world. Others may simply hide behind excuses and deny themselves opportunities because they aren't willing to seek achievement.[17]

As he spoke those words, he may have been talking as much to himself as the congregation. For whatever reason, he had sold himself short. He had traded his dreams of world travel and big feats of engineering for the comfort of small-town life and a steady business. He had no complaints, just a lingering disquiet. In one of his sermons, he likened the flow of human ambition to the flow of electricity, and he knew his own ambitions had short circuited.

"The underlying factor that most disturbed me, perhaps without my realizing it at first, was that I knew I could do better," he wrote years later. "I could be more creative, I could use more of my ability, and most of all, I could set a better example for my sons. There was a big, wonderful world beyond little Denver, and maybe the boys deserved to at least get a taste of life outside of our quiet, conservative little town."[18]

We would get more than a taste. He would give us an educational feast.

T he words from the magazine reached across the years, rekindling a dream that had been simmering in Dick's subconscious since he'd built those paper boats in childhood. It was 1963, and he had just tucked his son David into bed. As he came downstairs, Lucille suggested he read an article in *National Geographic*. They'd been taking the magazine for a decade by then, since the early days of their marriage, when they still lived in the apartment in Lancaster.[1] This story, though, was different. *Geographic* may have brought the world to the nation's coffee tables, but that night it would bring a world of change to Dick's life.

The article was written by George F. Bass, a doctoral student at the University of Pennsylvania, who was adapting land archaeology techniques to study ancient shipwrecks. Bass had attended the American School of Classical Studies in Athens from 1955 to 1957, where he worked on land excavations in Greece and Turkey. In 1960, he led the first underwater excavation, a late Bronze Age shipwreck in 100 feet of water off Cape Gelidonya in Turkey.[2] The dig would cement Bass's reputation as the father of underwater archaeology.

The *National Geographic* article focused on Bass's second major project, a Byzantine wreck from the seventh century A.D. found near Yassi Ada—which means "flat island"—an uninhabited rock off the southwestern coast of Turkey. Bass's article focused on the artifacts that divers had recovered, as well as the logistics of running an underwater dig. Only briefly did it mention the hull, which divers had just begun to uncover at the time the article was written. Those scant descriptions, though, caught Dick's attention. He knew immediately he wanted to build a model that would recreate the wreck Bass had discovered.

Dick's childhood passion for ships hadn't subsided, though he didn't have as much time for it now that he was married and had a child. Years earlier, he'd owned an interest in a boat with a couple of friends, but he'd sold his stake to pay for Lucille's engagement ring. Nevertheless, he remained captivated by ships, and his fascination still took him to almost every maritime museum and library on the East Coast. The more he studied shipbuilding techniques, the more he wanted to test them by building models, which he found both challenging and relaxing.

After a long day of wiring or repairs in one of the factories, he would take to the basement and build models based on historical ship designs he read about or studied in one of the museums he frequented. Like the flour-paste boats of his childhood, these models grew more intricate. He scoured history books, naval journals, and articles in magazines such as the *National Geographic,* compiling research about the ships' dimensions and construction. He would visit harbors in New England or the Chesapeake Bay and photograph ships' rigging. At first, his models were basic—a Flemish collier, which was similar to the *Santa Maria,* and a Viking skuta, or small warship—but just like the models themselves, his subjects grew more complex the more he read and experimented with techniques.[3]

During the 1950s, he collected half a dozen books about modeling and ship design, which influenced his skills. Two of these books were by Charles G. Davis, whose modeling collection was on display at the Museum of America and the Sea at Mystic Seaport in Connecticut, one of Dick's favorite weekend getaways.

Like Dick, Davis had a lifelong fascination with ships and seafaring. He was the son of a clerk for Admiral David Farragut, the Union naval commander during the Civil War. Born in Poughkeepsie, New York, in 1870, Davis and his brother built boats at an early age, and Davis purportedly sailed around Cape Horn in a square-rigger when he was thirteen. He alternated between journeys at sea and work as a draftsman for boat builders in New York and Canada. After he retired in 1935, Davis began building ship models and wrote extensively on the subject.[4]

One book in particular seemed to capture Dick's fascination: *The Built-Up Ship Model.* Davis wrote it in 1933, and Dick began reading in August 1956. It's a step-by-step instruction of model building, using as an example the USS *Lexington,* a Revolutionary War–era brig. In the built-up model, the hull is constructed piece by piece, rather than being carved from a solid block of wood. The book also included "plates," or pull-out plans, of the *Lexington,* on which Dick scribbled notes and mathematical calculations. In the preface of the book, Davis describes his approach to modeling, which seems to herald Dick's own approach decades later: "I have always had better luck in building my miniature ships just as the real ships were put together. . . ."[5]

For all the discussion of modeling techniques, though, neither Davis nor the authors of the other model building books in Dick's library offered any detailed models or even discussions of ancient ships. Most of their subjects were American vessels.

Dick's modeling and his study of ship construction grew into an encyclopedic knowledge. Like his mother, he was a voracious reader, although almost always on the same subject—ships. When he spotted an inconsistency or inaccuracy, he would sometimes write the editor of a journal to point out the problem. His criticisms, however, were gentle enough that in several cases the authors wrote back, expressing gratitude for his catching the error.[6]

When Dick completed a model, he would take it to Lancaster and display it in the annual hobby show, which was held in a National Guard armory. Rows of tables were divided into display areas for stamp collections or balls of string or hatching chicks brought from around the county. Some of my earliest memories are of following my brother through the maze of displays. Nothing else seemed as interesting or as intricate as our father's ship models, and he wasn't beyond a little showing off. To the extent that anyone displayed ship models at the show, they were the ship-in-a-bottle variety. One year, Dick decided to take the cliché one step further. Rather than use a bottle, he built a model in a hollowed out flashlight bulb.

"He built all the parts, and the tools to assemble them inside the flashlight bulb," David Steffy recalled. "I think he just wanted to prove he could do it. It was so small that he set it up at the show with a magnifying glass so you could see the thing."

Although I remember seeing that model around my parents' house for many years, it has since disappeared. Neither my brother nor I can remember the exact ship design, but we did recall one of the more amazing details: It had actual rigging. Dick used strands of Lucille's hair for the forerigging, and her sister Jeanne's, which was darker, for the aft.

Mostly, though, Dick's models grew larger and more detailed, and they became a study not just in seafaring but in ship construction itself. His meticulous research culminated in a 4-foot model of a ship from the eighteenth Egyptian dynasty, about 1400 B.C. The model took him four hundred hours of work over the better part of a decade, and when it won best of show in the Lancaster Hobby Show in 1963, it still wasn't finished. By then, Dick didn't build models to complete them. They had become a three-dimensional experiment, a way of studying and testing new designs. As he learned new details about Egyptian construction, he revised the model. Like all his designs, it was an outgrowth of his curiosity about marine architecture, an interest that started in his childhood home with his father's stories of the *Princess Matoika* and the trips to the Chesapeake Bay as a youngster, where he would stand by the canal for hours, watching boats come and go.

"The models are just the result of things I come across," he told a local newspaper after winning the hobby show. "Sometimes I carve just half a hull or just a portion of the frame of a ship to understand better how things were done."[7]

Dick's interest in Egyptian seafaring dated to a trip with his parents, when he was nine years old, to the University Museum at Penn. He overheard a couple of men talking about the museum's work in Egyptology and the relics that were being brought out of the pyramids. As he grew older, he researched Egyptian shipbuilding through books but found most of the information limited. The Egyptians lacked many of the fundamental building techniques that would become common on later vessels, such as frames and keels. But he learned that shipbuilding wasn't purely a technological pursuit; it reflected the societies in which the ships were built. He began to study the people, the customs, the tools they used, and the materials they had available. He discovered that Egyptians didn't have large trees, so they built ships from short pieces of wood, most of them no longer than 3 feet in length.

All of this helped Dick understand how the Egyptian naval architects thought, and how they approached the job, and the more he studied them, the more he began to recognize the design. He'd had just enough engineering classes in Milwaukee to see that the hull design was similar to an arch or a suspension bridge. The stem and sternposts were connected by a rope truss, which was tightened to the proper pressure that allowed the rest of the hull to be put in place.

He scrapped several early attempts because he found he couldn't replicate the graceful curves depicted in photographs he'd studied of Egyptian tomb drawings. Only when he hit upon the mathematical explanation of the suspension bridge was he able to replicate the design, both through blueprints and in his actual model. That also made modeling more difficult because mimicking the building techniques of the original shipwrights required a tedious pace. He installed about six pieces an hour, and the model had more than one thousand pieces.

He began the process by testing different types of wood before settling on a brittle pine that he felt best represented the acanthus used by the Egyptians. He cut the wood into planks about 1½ inches long, true to the half-inch scale in which he was working. Because the Egyptians didn't use keels, he fastened the short pieces together to form a strake, or plank, which was laid down much as a keel would be on later vessels. Then he fashioned the gunwales, where the topsides of the hull and deck meet. This was the one area where he varied his modeling technique from those of the original shipwright, using a single piece where the Egyptians would have joined several shorter ones.

He clamped the strake and the gunwales together at each end and ran the truss between the ends, using a spacer in the middle to hold the shape. Then, he tightened the truss until the skeleton took the shape dictated by his calculations. Once he had the proper curvature, he began gluing the rest of the planking in place, starting at the center and working outward toward the bow and stern. As he worked, he realized the vertical and horizontal pressure on the bow and stern was 8 pounds, and to achieve that pressure, the truss had to be tightened to 15 pounds. The Egyptians smoothed off the hull with an adze, an ancient tool similar to an ax with the head turned sideways, once construction was completed. The technique left a rough finish that Dick replicated in his model, although that touch of authenticity took some explaining to the hobby show judges, who thought he hadn't polished the model. Even after winning Best of Show, he still wasn't convinced the model was finished. He didn't think he had the rigging or the steering oars right, and he planned to keep researching future revisions, estimating it would take another two years to complete. "I'm in no hurry," he said. "I'm more interested in perfection than in seeing it finished."[8]

The model was far from perfection, or even from the precision of his later research models, but it did reflect some of the techniques he would use on later models. Given the lack of information about Egyptian ships at the time, Dick's hull lines and details were "amazingly accurate based on what we now know," said Cheryl Ward, a nautical archaeologist and one of Dick's former students, who's studied ancient Egyptian ships. In 2008, she supervised construction of a full-scale replica of *Min of the Desert,* to which Dick's model, built forty-five years earlier, bore some stunning similarities.[9]

Dick was proud of his hobby show victory, though he didn't believe the ship had value beyond his own satisfaction. Then he read Bass's article in *National Geographic*. Suddenly, he realized the modeling techniques he'd been developing could be adapted to a scholarly pursuit. At the time of the article, Bass's crew had just started to uncover the sunken Byzantine hull, and the article offered few details of the wood. Dick saw a chance to take the study further than Bass seemed to be planning, to actually use the fragments to recreate the hull's original shape.

"He described some hull details that I disagreed with and figured I could disprove with a model and a lines drawing," Dick wrote later. "More importantly, he seemed to be bemoaning the fact that there was no way to see accurately beyond the surviving timbers."[10]

The conventional thinking was that wood fragments could lead to detailed plans of the original hull, but nothing more. Dick, however, believed he could take the reconstruction effort beyond the paper state, using his modeling techniques to actually recreate the original hull in three dimensions. He also believed his models could project the missing parts of the hull and, by mimicking the original construction methods, unlock new discoveries about ancient shipbuilding.[11]

Even at that early stage, Dick was beginning to realize that models could reveal more about a ship's construction than could be learned from two-dimensional lines drawings by themselves.

"When you build models, you are actually repeating the boat-building process," he would explain years later. "You are forced to perform certain tasks that the original builder had to do, and therefore you learn his methods from doing certain things. Also, by doing a three-dimensional construction on a model you are able to project beyond the area of the hull that existed, so that some of the parts that have disappeared become quite evident when you work on the model."[12]

In 1963, though, Dick had little more than some vague ideas of how models could be used to study ancient ship construction. Although he wanted to test his ideas on Bass's find in Turkey, Dick waited months before working up the courage to contact him. After all, Dick was nothing more than an amateur model builder, a hobbyist with no training in shipbuilding, history, or archaeology. He was a small-town electrician with little formal education. Like most Denver residents, he worked a blue-collar job. College professors—Bass was just months away from completing his doctorate and joining the faculty, and was already on staff at the University Museum—had an air of mystique that Dick must have found intimidating. "For a guy who fixes machinery for a living to just sort of barge in on a professor was rather forward," David said.

Dick finally got around to writing Bass on April 1, 1964—April Fool's Day. He explained that he was an amateur researcher and that he'd spent the past decade compiling data and building the 4-foot Egyptian model. "Basically, this research is used to build a model as nearly accurate as the information will permit. These models must, for research and experimental purposes, be quite large—one-half inch to the foot or larger. While not decorative, the models are complete down to the last plank and treenail."[13]

Bass's find, he said, could be useful in testing his modeling research theories, adding that he believed he could extrapolate a complete model of the hull. Dick asked whether he could get more hull details from which he would build a model that he would donate to the University Museum at Penn. He noted that completing the model would take several years, "as the work is painstakingly slow and many parts must be done over and over again."[14] Left unsaid was that he had a job that could interrupt his model building without warning and that he had a young family that was taking what few spare hours remained. Modeling came from time that would normally be spent sleeping.

Bass wrote back five days later:

"I would be more than happy to see a model made of one of our shipwrecks, and had hoped that I might eventually find someone interested in making such a model," he said. Bass noted that detailed hull drawings of the wreck found at Yassi Ada were already being made from the recovered timbers. Those drawings would show every "nail hole and tenon exactly; we even have lines scratched across the strakes by the ancient shipwright to indicate where he planned to put the ribs."[15]

Bass proposed they stay in touch and suggested they meet the next time Dick came to Philadelphia. Dick responded three days later, and the excitement almost leaps from the letter. He could get to Philadelphia the following week. Bass, however, was busy preparing for the upcoming summer digs and suggested they meet the following month. In mid-May, Dick eased the 4-foot Egyptian model into the backseat of his Ford sedan and drove it to Philadelphia for Bass to see. Bass was eight years younger than Dick, with reddish-brown hair, and he spoke with traces of a South Carolina drawl. He wasn't sure what to make of the model. "I didn't know anything about Egyptian models or ships at that time," he said. "I was just starting out in this too." Dick's enthusiasm and his gentle perseverance impressed Bass, who could tell that this hobbyist, this part-time modeler, had some ideas that fit well with his own.

It's the sort of chance encounter that happens when a field is young, when the pioneers are charting a course by the seat of their pants. Why would Bass, already a distinguished scholar, bother to respond to a letter from an electrician who happened to like building ship models? Nautical archaeology was still in its infancy, having started less than four years earlier at Cape Gelidonya. For years to come, Bass would attend conferences and feel defensive because many of his fellow scholars dismissed underwater archaeology as a trifle, something that wasn't serious study. "It was an uphill battle for all of us, even after we got to the university," Bass said. If scholars were not yet taking the idea of underwater archaeology seriously, certainly no one was building ship models for scientific research. Quite simply, Dick was the first person Bass had heard from who had suggested building a model from one of his digs. "By all measures, it was marvelous stretch for George to take a meeting with him, and something for which I know Dad was always grateful," David said.

The two men would forge a friendship and a working relationship that lasted for more than four decades, and within a few years of that first meeting, Bass, by then a professor at Penn, was inviting Dick to lecture to his class on ancient seafaring. Once a year, Dick would drive 63 miles down the Pennsylvania Turnpike, walk into the lecture hall of the Ivy League school and give a talk about ship construction to a classroom of students, each of whom already had more formal education than he did.

After exchanging a few more letters, Bass suggested Dick talk to Fred van Doorninck, a graduate student who was working on the Yassi Ada hull remains. Van Doorninck had made extensive drawings of the Byzantine wreck and had developed the architectural plans for the ship. Dick suggested using his models to take the paper reconstruction into the third dimension. Van Doorninck sent Dick the three years' worth of work that he had done on the hull, detailing the construction techniques, the types of wood used, and a drawing showing where each fragment was found on the sea floor.[16]

Van Doorninck had graduated from Princeton and was working on his doctorate at Penn. Like Dick, he was soft-spoken and chose his words carefully. He was also a meticulous researcher who had learned enough from studying classical Greek excavations to appreciate the importance of gathering measurements on every detail. As a result, he'd extensively documented the fragments of the Byzantine ship and used that evidence as the basis for reconstructing the hull on paper. Just as Bass had welcomed Dick's offer to become involved in the project, van Doorninck too never questioned Dick's abilities or his lack of credentials. "I was very happy about it," van Doorninck recalled. "I understood what he intended to do. He had complete respect for what I had done."

Van Doorninck knew his paper reconstruction was lacking. The ship had sunk with her bow exposed, and much of her hull from amidships forward had long since rotted away. The stern, however, was well preserved. Van Doorninck simply projected the forward section of the hull as a mirror image of the aft. Peter Throckmorton, an American journalist who had first brought the wreck to Bass's attention, told van Doorninck that if the ship had been built to the specifications of his reconstruction, it would have sunk before it left the harbor.

"I was a person who knew nothing about naval architecture," van Doorninck said. "I was aware that from a hydrostatic point of view, there was something wrong with my reconstruction—gravely wrong."

A more thorough reconstruction was needed, and if Bass said Dick was the man to do it, van Doorninck was willing to accept that. He could tell immediately that Dick shared his sense of precision and meticulous approach to research. "I could see he was being very methodical, and that was good enough for me," van Doorninck said.

The process was delayed by, among other things, my birth in 1965, but by 1968, Dick was ready to begin the model. He wouldn't build just one, though. It would take several. Just as with his Egyptian model, Dick found that while recreating the boat-building process in model form, problems arose, which sometimes caused him to scrap his design and begin again. His original prediction to Bass that the model would take several years to complete proved optimistic. The final product wouldn't be finished for more than a decade.

Dick's first step in the process was a mold-and-batten model, an unaesthetic rendering that used Masonite and thin strips of pine to replicate the ship's lines. Dick developed the idea from the half models known as a hawk's nest, or bracket, used by eighteenth- and nineteenth-century ship builders, in which lines drawings were essentially transformed from paper to three dimensions. He cut the molds to the shape of the hull, based on the curvature of the frames, spaced about 6 inches apart. Then he attached the battens lengthwise, spanning the hull from stem to stern. He clamped the battens in place so he could move them as the calculations changed. Later, he would cover the space between the battens with card stock, then glue individual drawings of each fragment to it, placing the pieces in their original positions.[17]

As the modeling of the Byzantine wreck began in earnest, Dick cleared his workbench in the basement to make room for the project. Using van Doorninck's calculations, he cut the Masonite molds to the hull's shape, then, working well past midnight one evening, he began adding the battens. He struggled with getting the last one in place; it just didn't seem to want to fit. He rechecked his measurements, and they matched the numbers van Doorninck had given him. Tired, frustrated, and anxious to finish the model, he applied a little more pressure, forced the batten into position, and went to bed. Several hours later, Lucille, who was a light sleeper, woke with a start. She shook Dick. She'd heard something downstairs. It sounded like someone was in the house. In those days, Denver was such a small and crime-free town that many people didn't lock their doors. We did, so the likelihood of a burglary was remote. A serious robber, finding our door locked, could have just gone on down the street. Nevertheless, Dick dutifully donned his robe and worked his way downstairs. Finding nothing, he moved on to the basement.

As he descended the creaky wooden steps, he saw the troublesome batten lying on the floor. It had popped from the molds just hours after he'd forced it into place. The rebellious batten was one of Dick's first conversations with an ancient shipwright, the first time a ship spoke to him. "The model was 'telling' me that I had not built it right," he later explained.[18]

He'd adhered to van Doorninck's empirical data, but now the ship was saying some of that data couldn't possibly be right. Van Doorninck rechecked his own research and discovered that in reducing his drawings from full scale to one-tenth size, he'd neglected to transfer a notation about the curvature of one of the outer frames. Once corrected, the drawings and Dick's model lined up perfectly. "That convinced the two of us that his reconstructions were reliable in so far as we claimed them to be accurate," van Doorninck said.

Dick hadn't yet thought of using his new techniques to actually reassemble the original hull fragments, but in time he realized that although models produced a deeper understanding of ship construction than lines drawings, they were no replacement for actually putting an ancient ship back together. Laboratory reconstructions, whether on paper or with models, could never duplicate every break and angle precisely. Only the original ship could tell him that.[19]

The snapped batten in the basement was just the first whisper from the past, and he didn't yet comprehend its full significance. He would only begin to realize that a few years later, on a bitter cold night, after battling through a blizzard and finding the open door to his dream.

My brother and I were supposed to be going to our grand-parents. Then we weren't. Then we were. My mother and father couldn't decide. The weather was terrible, but a chapter of the Archaeological Institute of America was hosting a talk in Lancaster by Michael Katzev, a former student of Bass's who was teaching at Oberlin College in Ohio. Dick had met Kat-zev once when Dick lectured to Bass's class at Penn, and he had seen another *National Geographic* article, this one about an underwater ex-cavation Katzev was directing on the Mediterranean island nation of Cyprus. Katzev's team had uncovered an ancient Greek merchantman—centuries older than the Byzantine wreck at Yassi Ada—and Dick desper-ately wanted to learn more about it.[1]

It was 1971, seven years after Dick had first written to George Bass. The Byzantine model was well under way, and Dick was enjoying his newfound friends in underwater archaeology. But it was still a hobby and probably always would be. He had no intention of leaving the secu-rity of his small-town home and the family business. He had a wife with heart problems and two young sons, and besides, Dick wasn't a gambler. He was the kind of guy who bought full insurance coverage when he rented a car. On Sunday afternoon drives, he'd tell Lucille that maybe, someday, after he retired, they would get a little place in Connecticut and he'd volunteer in the maritime museum at Mystic Seaport. That was the extent of the dream then, before that night in January 1971.

Dick didn't think they should go to Katzev's talk. The temperature had dropped below freezing, turning the rain earlier that day into ice. The road was almost impassable, and Lancaster was 20 miles away. It was too risky, he decided. They'd just stay home. Lucille hated driving on ice, or even in rain for that matter. In addition to her heart problems, she had poor eyesight, didn't see well at night, and never liked driving much herself. "But Lucille, for reasons I am still not certain I comprehend, insisted that we go," Dick wrote years later. "Perhaps she could foresee the opportunity."

So they dropped my brother and me at Milt and Zoe's house. We lived in the same town and saw them several times a week, but my father's parents doted on their grandchildren, and we never missed a chance to visit. As the evening wore on, though, my grandmother grew increasingly concerned. Well past the time my parents should have been back, the phone rang. When my grandmother hung up, she told us we'd be sleeping there that night. My parents wouldn't be home until quite late.[2]

Katzev's lecture was on the campus of Franklin & Marshall, where Dick had attended classes for the Lancaster Area College after the war. It was an arduous drive, but once he arrived at the lecture, Dick quickly forgot about the weather. Katzev described a wreck that at the time was the oldest classical ship ever discovered. A Greek merchantman, she sailed in the third century B.C., during the time of Alexander the Great, and sank off the northern coast of Cyprus, near the town of Kyrenia. She carried a cargo of almonds, millstones, and wine in amphoras. And then, the part that captivated Dick: the wood was well preserved. Covered like a baby in a blanket by the silt and sand, with only a crown of amphoras nestled amid seaweed to indicate her resting place.

As Katzev's team removed the cargo, the Kyrenia Ship, as she was by then known, revealed her greatest secret—wood. Lots of wood. More wood, in fact, than had been found on any ancient wreck. By the time it was all recovered, Katzev's team had found more than 70 percent of the original hull, the twenty-three-centuries-old timbers soggy, worm-eaten, and the consistency of wet cardboard, yet still there, pressed against the floor of the Mediterranean.[3]

As Katzev slowly revealed the details of the find, flashing slide after slide on the screen, Dick was mesmerized. His mind raced at the possibilities. After the lecture, he waited until the room began to clear, then cornered Katzev, and they began talking about the hull remains that had been recovered. Lucille waited patiently, making small talk with Katzev's wife, Susan. The two women were opposites in almost every way. Lucille had dark curly hair; Susan's was short, straight, and blond. Lucille was secretary who'd never been to college. Susan was a Swarthmore-educated artist with skills that would, in later years, range from photography to welding. She had already spent several summers on Bass's digs in Turkey, whereas Lucille had spent little time outside of Pennsylvania. Nonetheless, Lucille was well versed in the social graces, and the two women quickly settled into an easy conversation.

Meanwhile, Dick launched into an engrossing discussion with Katzev, asking questions about the Kyrenia hull and sharing his theories of what could be learned from it. Michael was about fifteen years younger than Dick, with a worldly, polished air about him. A meticulous researcher, he already had developed a broad knowledge of ancient Mediterranean culture. He was shorter than Dick, and his brown hair was already beginning to recede slightly. Before either of them knew it, they were the only people left in the room. After more than an hour, a janitor told them he wanted to lock up the lecture hall. Dick and Lucille said their goodbyes and got in their car. The weather had begun to clear and the roads seemed passable, but Dick barely noticed. He couldn't stop thinking about those sodden fragments of wood resting below 90 feet of water halfway around the world. He kept telling Lucille how impressed he was with both Katzev's lecture and the ship's construction. He wanted to know more. He wished they'd had more time to talk. He had so many questions he hadn't gotten to ask.

Then, Lucille suggested, why didn't they call the Katzevs at their hotel and see whether they wanted to have a drink? Dick hesitated. It was already midnight. He had a long day ahead at the factory. The Katzevs were probably tired. He didn't want to bother them any more than he already had. They should get home, he said. Again, Lucille insisted. Susan had mentioned where they were staying. Why not call them?

They found a pay phone. First, Dick called his parents and told them everything was fine. "Put the kids to bed and don't wait up for us," he said. "We have a key, and we'll collect the boys when we get back to Denver." Then they called the Katzevs. They'd been thinking about a drink themselves, and Michael had already decided he would call Dick the next day. Why wait?

They met in a nightclub on the ground floor of the hotel, and Dick and Michael spent hours talking about ship construction and making crude lines drawings on cocktail napkins. Before they knew it, the club was closing and they were once again being kicked out. By the time Dick and Lucille got back to Denver, it was 4:00 in the morning. I vaguely remember my father carrying me down the stairs of my grandparents' house and putting me in the car. It was a two-minute drive to our house. My father was still talking about the ship.

Michael Katzev called him the next day anyway. He wanted Dick to come to Cyprus to help record the timbers. Dick told him that was impossible. As excited as he was about getting a chance to work on the Kyrenia wreck, he had a family to support and a business to run. He couldn't just drop everything and fly off to the Mediterranean to look at an old shipwreck. He'd be happy to help study the construction, but it would have to be done by mail, the same way he and van Doorninck had handled the Byzantine wreck.

But Katzev had other ideas. They'd found so much wood, he wanted to actually rebuild the hull, to put the ship back together in the castle. Nothing like that had been tried before. The only wreck that came close was the *Vasa,* a seventeenth-century Swedish warship recovered in the Baltic Sea. The *Vasa,* though, had been raised in one piece, and the frigid waters and low salinity in the Baltic had protected her from shipworms.[4] The *Vasa,* almost two thousand years younger than the Kyrenia wreck, was an entirely different project. No one knew if what Katzev envisioned—reassembling a crushed and fractured ancient hull back to its original shape—was even possible.

Nonetheless, Katzev was determined. He'd returned to his hotel room in Lancaster with a wad of cocktail napkins bearing lines projections and with the certainty that Dick Steffy, this basement ship modeler who showed up in the audience in the middle of Pennsylvania farm country, was the man to rebuild the oldest Greek ship ever found. In handwritten notes he made on a page torn from a yellow legal pad, Katzev referred to "this craggy-faced gentleman" who was "so enthusiastic and knowledgeable that Susan and I left that night very elated."[5]

The phone call ended with Dick still insisting he couldn't leave his business and go to Cyprus, but Katzev was relentless. A few days later, he mailed Dick several articles that had been published on the Kyrenia wreck in hopes that he would "become more enticed with the possibility of involving yourself with the paper restoration of the ship, its actual reconstruction, and the building of a model."[6]

Katzev had reasons for being so insistent, but in their discussions he didn't let on the full extent of his concerns. The more cargo the excavation team removed, the more hull they uncovered. Something had to be done. They couldn't leave the wood uncovered on the bottom for long, and they felt, as archaeologists, they had a sacred duty to preserve it. They had raised the wood, and they intended to rebuild the ship, but they had no idea how to do it. It was sitting in freshwater tanks in Kyrenia's

Crusader castle, waiting for somebody to put it together. Whatever Katzev did next would be little more than guesswork, and what if he guessed wrong? Suddenly, he'd found someone who was genuinely excited by the promise of an ancient wooden hull. More important, Dick seemed to understand the ship's structure when no one else on the project did. The Katzevs had sailed before, but like Bass, they knew little about ship construction.

"We were beginning to uncover a hull and we were worried," Susan Katzev said. "We were scared to death. How could we ever put "Humpty Dumpty" back together again? Here was a man who'd thought about this for much of his life, and he was willing to give it a try."

One of the publications Katzev sent Dick was a report he wrote in 1970 to the University Museum at Penn, which was helping to fund the project. The report included photographs that showed dozens of large pieces of timber. The Kyrenia Ship was not only amazingly well preserved, but much of her had been preserved intact. The keel, for example, was cracked into sixteen pieces, yet the pieces remained together, as if it were still one timber.

Dick believed the larger pieces could be modeled first, becoming an aid that, when used in conjunction with measurements and data gathered on the sea floor, would make a reconstruction on paper possible. A model could be assembled and disassembled repeatedly to gain a better understanding and limit damage to the timber during the physical reconstruction of the preserved wood.[7]

In its soggy state, the hull couldn't be lifted in one piece, even though many of the timbers were still joined together. The Katzevs considered building an underwater cradle and hoisting the entire hull to the surface, then flying it to the castle with a helicopter. They gave up on the idea when they couldn't find a chopper, even among the British military that maintained two bases on Cyprus, with enough lifting power. Instead, they attempted to cut the hull in pieces, but quickly abandoned that process as well. It was difficult to remove sand and silt from the sections after they were cut, and the process made it almost impossible to record the timbers. What's more, while they attempted to maintain the curvature of the wood on the seabed, no one knew whether that was the hull's original shape or whether the wood had lost its curvature from its centuries on the bottom. Eventually, they decided the only way to raise the hull was piece by piece, disassembling any fragments that were still joined.

Divers photographed and cataloged each piece before bringing it to the surface on metal trays lifted by balloons that they inflated with air from spare oxygen tanks. Once on the surface, the wood was moved to a large room in the castle to soak in freshwater tanks, the biggest of which was the size of a shallow swimming pool. The wood had to be kept wet. If it had dried, it would have shrunk to a fraction of its original size, like a sponge drying in the sun. After soaking in fresh water for months to remove the salt, the wood was placed in heated tanks filled with a wax-like chemical known as polyethylene glycol, or PEG. After two years soaking in the tanks of PEG, all the sodden wood absorbed the wax, and the fragments were removed. They hardened into a dark, almost plastic-like substance that was sturdy enough to handle.[8]

By April, Dick's role in the project was still unsettled. Michael Katzev was wrestling with grant applications through the United Nations Educational, Scientific and Cultural Organization and proposed hiring Dick as a "technical expert" to the Kyrenia Ship project, but nothing was definite other than that he hoped Dick would begin work on the models they'd talked about.[9]

Dick was frustrated by the uncertainty. The more he learned about the ship, the more he wanted to be involved in rebuilding it. Perhaps this ship was an opportunity even beyond the work he'd already done with Bass and van Doorninck. He would, of course, build models of her. That really hadn't been in question since the napkin drawing in Lancaster. He could do those at home, in his basement, in the wee hours, on a schedule over which he had control. The models posed no disruption to his electrical work, and yet, how could he ignore the allure of actually going to Cyprus and seeing firsthand the wreck Katzev had described? Without the funding, it simply wouldn't be possible. Dick and Lucille lived frugally, and they made a decent income, but they couldn't afford an extended overseas stay. In fact, even with the funding, Dick was uneasy about leaving his business and disrupting his family for the year or more that Katzev was proposing.

Then Katzev called with another idea: If he could get Oberlin to pay the airfare and his living expenses, would Dick be willing to go to Cyprus for six weeks and teach the expedition's permanent staff shipbuilding fundamentals and terminology? Maybe he could even help record a few of the timbers and give an overview of how they might reassemble them once the preservation process was complete. Dick talked it over with Lucille, and later with his father and brother. They could cover the obligations of the electrical business, but Dick decided he could only spare three weeks, and Katzev would have to wait until late July, because the week of July Fourth was the busiest for local industries served by M.G. Steffy & Sons.[10]

The months leading up to the trip were a flurry of activity. Photographs of the wreck on the sea floor arrived in big parcels, and drawings of them in large tubes. Letters went back and forth to and from places like Cyprus and Tehran, where Laina Swiny, the expedition's architect, lived at the time. The local mailman, who'd known Dick since childhood, wondered what was going on. Word began to get around that Dick was leaving town, going to "Greece," or some such place. Some wondered whether he was having a midlife crisis.

For my brother and me, though, it seemed perfectly normal. Our father was busy, but then, when wasn't he? He never spent much time watching television, never bowled or went to the movies or played golf. The fact that he was now building an elaborate model of the world's oldest shipwreck in our basement just didn't seem all that odd. After all, he still went to work, and when he got home, while my mother was fixing dinner, he'd throw the baseball with me in the yard, a routine that almost always devolved into antics, with each of us seeing who could make the other one miss a catch.

But at night, after everyone else was asleep, work on the models continued at a furious pace. Dick was still finishing the Byzantine project, and now he was moving ahead with the Kyrenia wreck too. The basement was almost entirely a model shop, and the dining room table had long ago been pressed into service as a drafting table. My mother tolerated the loss of her dining room, but she insisted that an open archway with the living room be enclosed so the piles of ship plans weren't visible when visitors came to the door.

Dick spent hours hunched over the dining room table, figuring out the proper curvature of the lines and setting splines in place to match it, using the thin strips of wood as a template for drawing the curvature on a scale that would span the table. Still, all of it remained just a hobby, and rather than spend money on expensive drafting equipment, Dick made do with things around the house. Campbell's Soup cans, for example, worked perfectly well as weights to hold the splines in place. There was no need to buy the expensive spline weights used by professional draftsmen. Unfortunately, not everyone understood the significance of his work.

Our cleaning lady, trying to be helpful, gathered up all the cans and put them back in the cupboard, losing the curvature that Dick had spent hours calculating. When my friends came to play, the dining room was now off limits, and the basement bore serious restrictions on where we could go and what we could touch. By the time the July trip to Cyprus rolled around, model building, ship terms, and ancient history had become part of the family vernacular.

The pursuit of the dream began in earnest with a turboprop commuter plane lifting slowly off the runway at the tiny airport in Reading. My father often took us to the airport in Lancaster on Sunday afternoons, and we'd watched planes like that one take off dozens of times, but I'd never known anyone who'd actually gotten on one. Now, he was waving from the window as the propellers revved and the plane began to taxi. I looked up at my mother. Her cheeks were streaked with tears. They'd never been separated for more than a few days. Three weeks seemed like forever.

For Dick, however, the time was a blaze. Cyprus was hot and humid, with two soaring mountain ranges and arid plains dotted with olive groves. For centuries, the island had been a way station for travel between Europe and the Middle East, and antiquities seem to spring from the ground like dandelions. The population was mostly descended from Greeks and Turks, although Cyprus had spent much of the twentieth century as a British territory. It had gained independence in 1960, and although it seemed a quiet and stable place by the time Dick arrived in the middle of 1971, latent ethnic strife simmered beneath the island's sun-drenched calm.

His plane landed in the capital of Nicosia, and he was met by several members of the Kyrenia Ship expedition, most of whom were twenty years his junior. They arrived in a green VW microbus, affectionately dubbed "the Tank," to collect him for the thirty-minute trip over the mountains and into Kyrenia. The van was about fifteen years old and had all but the front seats removed so it could haul diving equipment. In honor of Dick's arrival, Robin Piercy, the project's assistant director, put an upholstered chair in the back.

The Tank broke down three times in the Turkish Cypriot sector about 10 miles from the airport. The Turkish sector was about a mile wide and ran south from Nicosia to the Kyrenia Mountains. Turkish Cypriots made up about 20 percent of the island's population, and the United Nations set up the area in the 1960s to help ease ethnic strife. Turkish Cypriots could live anywhere they wanted on the island, but Greek Cypriots weren't permitted in the Turkish Sector without a U.N. escort. Twice a day, U.N. troops led convoys of Greek Cypriots back and forth from Kyrenia to the capital.

Each time the van broke down, passers-by stopped to help get the old microbus running again. The last time, a nicely dressed young man stopped to help and wound up covered in grease and dirt before he got the engine started again. He accepted only thanks and insisted on following the group to the top of the Kyrenia Mountains. Perhaps he knew his repairs were temporary. The Tank conked out again at the top of the mountains, but from there Piercy was able to get it rolling down the other side and into town.[11]

Kyrenia had about four thousand five hundred residents at the time, about twice the size of Dick's hometown of Denver. By the time Dick arrived, much of the ship expedition had been working together for a couple of years, and the arrival of a new guy with no formal training in archaeology might have been awkward, but the team cared little about credentials. After all, nautical archaeology itself was only a decade old, and the Kyrenia ship project was pioneering new ground on a regular basis. The team had developed its own method for raising the wood and conserving it, and they welcomed the idea that someone was willing to tackle the daunting challenge of reconstructing it. Nevertheless, Dick marveled at how willing the team, and Michael Katzev in particular, was in supporting his "hare-brained ideas" and untested methods.[12]

"It was clear that Mike and Susie had talked to him at great length and that they felt that his joining the team could only be a good thing," Piercy said. "This opened up a whole new field for all of us in a way. It was wonderful to work with him because, apart from having a lot of fun and ribbing the shit out of each other, it was a great experience."

Piercy, tall and strong, with curly shocks of sun-bleached hair, was a jack-of-all-trades around the expedition. An expert diver, he also could build seemingly any equipment the team needed, from scaffolding to fiberglass molds. He and Dick shared a mischievous sense of humor, and some of their jokes would carry on between them for years. Piercy had done some restoration work on a gunboat in the St. Lawrence River, but that wreck, unlike the Kyrenia Ship, was basically intact. Despite his mechanical and technical skills, he didn't have the naval architecture background to rebuild the ship. Likewise, Laina Swiny, the expedition's

American architect, had recorded the hull on the sea floor, but she had no idea how to begin putting the wood back together.

In fact, the number of ship projects worldwide that were remotely similar could be counted on one hand, including five Viking ships excavated in 1962 and rebuilt in Roskilde, Denmark, and the Lake Nemi barges of the Roman Emperor Caligula, recovered in 1932 and restored in a museum before being destroyed during World War II.[13]

Dick reviewed each drawing of each fragment of the Kyrenia Ship, then began studying as much of the wood as he could. He filled notebooks with his thoughts and observations about each piece. "He scrutinized every drawing and every single piece of wood," Swiny said. "He couldn't rely on anything that we had done. He needed to check this all out for himself. He would obviously see it in a different way than we had seen it because he saw it in a three-dimensional way of putting it back together again."

Within just a few days of studying the wood, however, Dick came to a disturbing conclusion. He determined that the ship's frames had sagged during their centuries on the seabed, which meant all the projections he'd done during the previous six months and the model that he'd begun back in Pennsylvania were wrong. The more he studied the wood, the more clear it became that the entire hull had splayed on the seabed, compressed and distorted by the weight of the cargo. The trick would be to find the original shape.

"How we would have put the vessel together without Dick, I don't know," Piercy said. "The thing that we lacked was probably a more scientific approach that Dick had already developed by himself. He was coming at it from a different plane." By then, most of the wood was either "cooking" in heated tanks of polyethylene glycol or soaking in the freshwater "pool" in a great hall of the Crusader castle. Until he arrived in Kyrenia, Dick had only seen drawings and pictures of the wood. Now, he could actually touch it.

Wood that has spent two millennia on the seabed doesn't resemble wood at all. It's more the consistency of rain-soaked newspaper, soggy and pliable, barely able to hold its shape. The purpose of the PEG was to saturate the wood so that as the chemical later dried, it would harden the wood yet retain the original shape. Once completed, the wood could be handled and worked with, and, everyone hoped, reassembled. Fortunately, the worm-eaten wood of Kyrenia was well suited for this process, soaking up the PEG like a sponge. The process had been developed by the project's conservator, Frances Talbot, who along with the Katzevs had studied preserved ships across Europe. They considered a wide range of ideas, including freeze-drying or spraying the timbers with PEG, before agreeing that the best method for ensuring long-lasting conservation was total saturation.

It would still be more than two years before all the conservation was complete, but Dick could see the task that awaited him as he stood on the edge of the freshwater tank. Trays of fragments spread out before him like pieces of a bicycle before a frustrated father on Christmas Eve. The puzzle was much bigger than he'd imagined, and the expectations of his new colleagues and even the people of Kyrenia—this collection of American and British archaeologists working in the castle had become local celebrities in the small town—were far greater than he anticipated. His doubts, his uncertainties, he kept to himself.

"It is much more of a mystery than I expected it to be," he confided in a letter to Lucille. "However, I love the challenge and everyone seems to think I am doing wonders. Every day, someone stops me on the street and asks if I figured it out yet."[14]

The task that lay ahead wasn't just putting the fragments—some 6,000 in all—back together. First, he had to design a system of *how* to reassemble them. Just like the frames, some of the other planks had distorted, either from the impact of the hull hitting the bottom or from their centuries under the sea. Those distortions had to be accounted for and corrected, each piece had to be fit to the others from which it was torn or broken, and then the whole thing had to be restored to its original shape, a feat that required basically undoing the effects of two thousand years of rot and gravity.

Electrician's Mate First Class Richard Steffy had dreamed of traveling the world and being apart of big engineering projects. Now, a quarter century later, he was facing an engineering challenge unlike any he could have imagined aboard the USS *Wyffels,* indeed unlike anything anyone had confronted before.

6 : "YOU'RE CRAZY—YOU'LL STARVE TO DEATH"

Dick returned from the Mediterranean a changed man. He still had the same easy-going demeanor, but if he'd loved ships before, he was now obsessed. He couldn't stop thinking about the hull of the Kyrenia Ship, its fragments arrayed in the big freshwater tank. "What a mystery I had just witnessed; and what a multitude of questions were bouncing through my head," he recalled later. "By the time I headed back to the States it became clear that I would not rest well until I returned to Cyprus to study that ship more thoroughly, even if it meant getting out of my business and abandoning a comfortable lifestyle."[1]

The hull was incredible. Even in its fractured, disassembled state, it was a thing of beauty, a wonder. And all that wood—far more than Dick had imagined. He'd studied the photos and drawings intimately, of course, but knowing the number of pieces wasn't the same as actually seeing them. It was much like the jigsaw puzzles he worked to relax. The box tells the number, but only when the pieces are all spread out on the table does the magnitude of the task come into focus. For Dick, though, that made the challenge all the more appealing. This, he realized, was the opportunity of his lifetime. The more he thought about it, the more he wanted to be a part of it, the more he wanted to make working on ships something beyond just a hobby. "He came back and he'd been very well accepted; he really liked the people and he was amazed at the ship and began to really think about how he could put it together," David said.

In the fall of 1971, with visions of the Kyrenia fragments still occupying his mind, Dick got a call from George Bass. Despite Dick's burgeoning interest in the Kyrenia Ship, he was still working on the Byzantine wreck with Bass and Fred van Doorninck, and Bass still invited Dick to talk to his graduate classes at Penn. It had been seven years since Bass had gotten that first letter from Dick, and although he didn't yet have his Byzantine model, he had become convinced that Dick's encyclopedic knowledge of ship construction could benefit the emerging field of nautical archaeology. The shared passion for studying shipwrecks had cemented a friendship and mutual respect among Dick, Bass, and van Doorninck.

Bass was calling because he had been contacted by Susan Langston, who claimed she had found a shipwreck on New Jersey's Ludlum Beach in Sea Isle City. Langston, an amateur ship enthusiast, knew that many ships had wrecked in the area over the years, and when she walked the beach, she often watched for driftwood that might be pieces of a hull. One September morning, she spotted some 5-foot planks that included what she thought were treenails, the wooden pegs used to fasten ships' timbers. About a week later, a storm churned up more sand around the wood, revealing a 12-foot hump that Langston knew was part of a ship. She registered a salvage claim with the state and hired a company to dig the hull out of the sand. They uncovered a section that weighed about 10 tons with frames that were about 16 inches thick.

It was a ship, all right. But what kind—and from where? Langston had no idea how to identify her find. After all, she only had a piece—albeit a big one—of the hull. She called Princeton University and eventually was put in touch with Bass at Penn.[2] She mentioned the treenails in the call and raised the possibility that it could be a Viking ship or something else quite old. Bass had gotten lots of calls over the years from people claiming to have found Viking ships, and the chances of a storm uncovering one on the Jersey Shore was about as likely as finding a diamond among the grains of sand on the beach. Nevertheless, he decided to have a look and suggested that he and Dick both bring their families and make a weekend of it.

Together, they inspected the remains, and Dick quickly determined it wasn't a Viking ship or even all that old. In fact, he believed it was the remains of a downeaster, built in Maine between 1880 and 1910. Downeasters were among the best sailing ships ever constructed, as fast as clipper ships, but with more room for cargo. Langston checked newspaper archives and soon determined that the remains belonged to the *George R. Skolfield,* built in Maine in 1885 and stranded on the beach by a storm in 1920. The ship, which was 232 feet long and weighed more than 1,600 tons, took its name from a member of the Skolfield family of Brunswick, Maine, the only family that built, operated, and captained its own ships.[3]

Bass was surprised by the speed and certainty with which Dick identified the hull, but he was flabbergasted by what happened on the way home. The two families headed west, across New Jersey and toward the Delaware River, where the Basses would veer toward Philadelphia and the Steffys would continue up the Pennsylvania turnpike toward Denver. We'd already said our good-byes, but the cars remained in tandem on the highway. In the backseat, I dozed next to my brother, exhausted from a day at the beach and lulled into a semi-sleep by the sounds of my parents' voices in the front. I couldn't hear what they were saying, but suddenly, my mother's voice cut through the hypnotic hum of the engine: "If you feel that way, Dick, why don't you tell him?"

My father pulled the car to the side of the road and rolled down his window. We took a lot of road trips in those days, and we almost never pulled over on the shoulder. My father was meticulous about vehicle maintenance, and we never broke down or ran out of gas. Awakened by such an unusual development, I sat up as my father waved frantically out the window, urging Bass to pull over as well. The other car pulled to the shoulder in front of us, and I rested my chin on the blue vinyl of the front seat, watching as my father walked toward the other car.

Bass recounted the ensuing conversation:

> He walked to my car window and said, "George, I want to tell you something. I've decided to give up my business and become a professional"—I don't remember his exact words, but I remember him using the term "ancient ship reconstructor." I said, "You're crazy. You'll starve to death—there is no such thing." But he said, "Look, you only live once, and if it doesn't work, I can always go back to my electrical business. But I don't want to have died never having tried."

It was a pivotal moment in the history of nautical archaeology. Dick's decision would inspire Bass to do much the same thing a year later, but at the time, neither of them recognized the significance of the conversation. As the roadside meeting broke up, Bass still didn't think Dick was serious, and even if he were, who would hire him to do such a job? How would he provide for his family?

The idea of turning his ship research into a full-time job, something that had once seemed like the purest of fantasies, had been gnawing at the back of Dick's mind since he returned from Kyrenia that summer. He loved this new "ship business" he'd taken on—he just hadn't figured out how to generate income from it.[4] Standing on the shoulder next to

Bass's car, he still didn't have any answers. Those doubts, and Dick's cautious nature, might have kept him from ever informing Bass of his intent had Lucille not insisted he act on his impulse that day. Just as she had urged him to read Bass's *National Geographic* article years earlier; just as she had pushed him to hear Katzev's lecture in Lancaster despite the weather; and just as she had suggested they call the Katzevs at their motel after that lecture, Lucille again was pressing him, indeed daring him, to pursue the dream when it was in danger from his own pragmatism. "When push came to shove, she was the one that pushed," David said. "Dad wouldn't want to impose, and she'd say, 'Go impose.'"

Dick really had no idea how to follow through on what he told Bass. He only knew that he didn't want to let this unique opportunity slip away. The electrical business had enabled him to provide a comfortable lifestyle for his family, but it wasn't making him rich enough that he could pursue a full-time hobby. That year, 1971, my parents' combined income was just under $15,000, which translates into almost $79,000 today, accounting for inflation. The decision to steer M.G. Steffy & Sons into more industrial work was paying off, and Dick was earning more than he ever had as an electrician. Now, on the side of the highway, he had decided to walk away from it. He had two children, one of whom was entering high school and would be headed to college in a few years. Abandoning a healthy family business to chase ship dreams was the biggest gamble Dick ever took in his life. Within two years, he and Lucille would see their combined annual income drop to less than $4,000.[5]

Dick always downplayed the risk of his decision. After all, if nobody would hire him for his as-yet-nonexistent dream job, he still had prospects. His electrical skills were well-known around Denver, and he felt sure he could return to the business one way or another. Walt Cubberly, the manager at the Denver wire factory who'd told Dick years earlier that he should be doing bigger things, made a standing offer: Dick could have a job as chief electrician whenever he wanted. Slowly, a plan was beginning to fall into place. "Once he set his mind to something, you knew he was going to do it," his brother, Milt, said. "He had a Plan A, Plan B, and probably more."

Though Dick was determined to embark on this new career as an ancient ship reconstructor—a title, that, like the job, he had concocted himself—the rest of 1971 and early 1972 progressed much as the previous year had. He continued with his electrical work and spent his nights working on models and drawings, mostly for the project in Kyrenia. The modeling activity, though, grew more intense. Dick began working earnestly on a model of the Kyrenia wreck while still finishing up work on the Byzantine ship for Bass. He'd also agreed to write a chapter for a book Bass planned to publish, although Dick had never written professionally. All of it was still being done in his spare time, around his electrical work that required six days a week and being on call around the clock.

Ship work began to take up more of Dick's time, and it also began to take over his house. As he planned a 1:5 scale model of the Kyrenia Ship, he realized it would be too large—more than 5 feet long and 3 feet wide—to get through the door when it was finished. His solution: Build it in the dining room, a part of the house that, already buried in ship plans, was living up to its name less and less. It alone had a window that, once removed, would allow the completed model to pass through. "Lucille has made the supreme sacrifice," Dick wrote Michael Katzev. "She agreed to turn over the dining room for use as a Greek shipyard because it is the only room with a window large enough to remove the model."[6] Lucille didn't know it yet, but her dining room would never be the same again. For the rest of their married life, the dining room table would substitute for a drafting board, a modeling table, and even a college classroom.

For my brother and me, though, it was all part of the adventure. How many fathers were building a huge ship model in their dining rooms? Sure, our father had traveled to an exotic foreign country of which few in town had heard, but our lives changed little at first. The significance of our father's roadside proclamation in New Jersey was lost on us. But from the day he'd come back from Kyrenia, he'd been discussing with Michael Katzev the prospect of returning to rebuild the ship. Dick's life was coming to a crossroads, and perhaps it was appropriate that for my brother and me, the first major sign of change came as we sat in the family car at an intersection.

Denver, Pennsylvania, has one stoplight, where Main Street intersects Fourth at the top of a steep hill. My father grew up in a house on one corner of that intersection, and as we sat across from it, waiting for the red light to change, my brother caught a wisp of my parents' conversation. I was too young to follow what they were saying, but David was thirteen by then, and he'd collected enough bits and pieces from things my parents had said in recent weeks that he had an idea of what they were thinking. Now, he leaned forward in his seat, listening intently as my parents spoke quietly. Suddenly, he blurted out: "We're moving to Cyprus?"

It hadn't been an easy decision. My father had only spent three weeks in Kyrenia, but he knew it wasn't the sort of arrangement that was conducive to family life. Most of the expedition members were twenty years younger than he was and none of them had children. With the exception of the Katzevs, who had their own house, everyone else lived in a deteriorating mansion left over from island's days of British colonialism. The accommodations, however, were the least of the problems. My father would later describe the concerns:

> I was forty-seven years old, had three dependents, a profitable business, a comfortable lifestyle, two boys who needed to be educated, a wife who enjoyed her comfortable home and a thousand other reasons that made it seem stupid. In joining the Kyrenia staff, I would have quite a cut in income, an uncertain future, and a far less comfortable lifestyle in a community where we did not even speak the language and could not guarantee schooling for our children.[7]

Left off the list was the concern that my mother, with the chronic heart problems she'd had since she was a teenager, might be risking her life by living in a small town in a Third World country that lacked modern medical care. One by one, though, the worries had melted away. My father would work under a United Nations grant that would help ease the loss of income. My parents arranged home-schooling for my brother and me, and other members of the project knew of two retired British doctors, one a cardiologist, living in the area who could monitor my mother's condition. My parents decided to go for a year and then decide whether this could be a career or just remain a fascinating hobby.[8]

By early 1972, preparations were in full swing. Dick planned to wind down his electrical work in early May and begin focusing full-time on the Kyrenia Ship. We would arrive in Cyprus on June 29, with plans to stay for a year.[9] My father marked the calendar, supposedly for the benefit of my brother and me, counting backward from the departure date more than 140 days before we were supposed to leave.

As Dick envisioned the trip, we would carry all his modeling supplies and tools with us while shipping as many of our clothes and personal belongings ahead as we could. That way, when we arrived in Kyrenia, he could begin working immediately. He would start by building a crude batten model that would allow him to check the location of planking on the ship's hull, as well as the hull's overall strength. The strength tests would result in the model's destruction, a strategy that had now become part of Dick's technique for studying hull construction. In all, Dick would build eighteen models as part of his Kyrenia ship research. One would survive. Charles G. Davis surely never imagined such a thing when he wrote *The Built-Up Ship Model*.

As he prepared the family for the great adventure, no one was more excited than Dick himself. He could taste a career that only a few years earlier was beyond anything he dared to dream. Every thought, it seemed, was about the ship. The Katzevs visited Denver soon after the New Year, and we went to dinner at one of the nicer restaurants in the area. As we were leaving, Dick picked up a toothpick and put it in his mouth. Days later, he found it in the pocket of his sport coat and was inspired. "It is a double-ended wooden affair and at the points where its diameter is two millimeters the taper is exactly right for a Kyrenia Ship dowel," he wrote to Katzev. "Simply by cutting the thing at the right spots, we can get two dowels each. I must call [the restaurant] and find out where they buy their toothpicks."[10]

Rounded toothpicks were among the modeling supplies we carted to Cyprus in the summer of 1972. The dowels were used to represent minia-ture pegs that held the tenons in place on the model just as they had on the original ship. Once we'd settled into Kyrenia, I was given the task of cutting those toothpicks in the right spots, extracting the "two dowels each." Meanwhile, my brother produced the tenons, cut from oak veneer with a band saw and a modeling knife. Production of both the dowels and tenons began before we left for Cyprus, with my father telling Robin Piercy, "We are now turning out model dowels and tenons by the hun-dreds." He also experimented with making model amphoras, using a miniature potter's wheel, but the results looked like "wilted tulips" and the whole idea was eventually abandoned.[11]

Toothpicks weren't the only unconventional sources of inspiration for Dick's new career. It's an obvious comparison to liken the recon-struction of the Kyrenia Ship to a giant jigsaw puzzle, but my father *did* spend his time doing jigsaw puzzles. In the months leading up to the trip, he logged more than a hundred hours sitting over puzzles, devising strategies for how to reassemble the ship.[12]

Since seeing the hull fragments in the summer of 1971, Dick had begun to map out in his mind how to get them back together. Piercy took photos and measurements for him, and Laina Swiny, Susan Katzev and Piercy's wife, Netia, supplied drawings of each timber. Gradually, he was able to envision the placement of the frames and account for the distortion that had occurred from the hull sitting on the sea floor for so long. Although he and Michael Katzev had discussed different ways to reassemble the wood, Dick decided that stainless steel wire inserted through the wood would be the cheapest, strongest, and least visible method for joining ancient planks to frames.

He was making progress on the hull, but other parts of the ship's construction proved more vexing. The mast and sail hadn't survived the ages, and determining what they looked like was little more than educated guesswork at the time. The Kyrenia Ship's mast step—the place where the mast was mounted to the keel—was in the forward third of the hull, much farther forward than was typical for the square sails that were common at the time. Dick proposed that the ship may have had a lateen, or triangular sail, though the evidence was contradictory. Lead rings found in the stern indicated the possibility of brailing lines, or thin ropes used to draw the sail up or down on each side. Lateen sails didn't have brailing lines.[13] Although Dick's initial thoughts about the lateen sail would be wrong, the position of the mast step would continue to bother him for decades.

If his ship work picked up after his return from Cyprus, so too did his familiarity with his new colleagues. In correspondence with the expedition members, more of Dick's humor began to come out, and perhaps nowhere was it more evident than in his discussions of one of the ship's minor mysteries—the yo-yos. Divers had found about two dozen of the pieces that looked exactly like the child's toy, but with fatter ends. What were they for? Dick was focused on figuring out the placement of frames and hull planking, but discussion of the yo-yos became a running joke between him and Katzev, often scribbled by hand at the bottom of a typewritten letter. At first, Dick joked that the Greeks may have invented the yo-yo and brought a few along to entertain the crew. Later, he quipped that they may have been "dumbbells for very small seamen," or that they "were used to wind up kite string." So it went for months, with Katzev occasionally egging Dick on by ending his letters with lines like "the yo-yos are calling!"

Eventually, Dick determined the yo-yos were really toggles, used to quickly secure the rigging. The ends of the brailing lines could be easily slipped on and off of them. The yo-yos, then, helped determine that the ship had a square sail rather than a lateen rig. When Dick finally wrote Katzev announcing his conclusion, he declared that "hereafter, the term 'yo-yo' need only be applied to people and toys, never the Kyrenia Ship."[14]

Meanwhile, more serious plans for the reconstruction were beginning to take shape. The 1:5 ship model that was being built in the dining room in Denver was never completed, but Dick planned to start anew when he got to Kyrenia, a process he expected would take four to six weeks. He hoped the model would reveal any errors in his calculations and line drawings before they began to lay the preserved keel on its pedestal.[15]

Dick's research was already beginning to contradict the findings of other ancient ship experts, among them Lucien Basch. Basch was the former chief justice of Belgium, who had made the study of ships his hobby and was renowned in the world of underwater archaeology for his knowledge and expertise. But in early 1972, he was largely unknown to the members of the Kyrenia Ship expedition. In a letter to Dick, Laina Swiny noted that this Basch fellow had written an article on ancient ship construction that focused on shell-first versus frame-first techniques. "The good old Kyrenia Ship will give some opposition to his points and will make for some good discussion," she noted.[16] Even before he'd begun his great experiment, Dick Steffy, electrician and part-time basement ship modeler, was challenging one of the preeminent experts in the field.

As Dick continued to map out his reconstruction strategy, the rest of the family began preparations on the domestic front, many of which would go awry. My father may have always had a backup plan, but despite all the calendar countdowns and other efforts, the weather, a family crisis, and the daily chaos of family life would undermine the best of planning. By the spring of 1972, word was getting around town that Dick Steffy was preparing for some sort of crazy adventure. He was quitting the electrical business and taking his family halfway around the world. It wasn't long before newspaper reporters started calling for interviews. Dick made the front page of the Lancaster paper and later had a write up in the *Philadelphia Inquirer.* Most of the stories were similar, recounting Dick's plans for reconstructing the Kyrenia Ship and his unusual career change.[17]

Despite all the attention and his excitement about the trip, Dick still felt a responsibility to his customers that prevented him from winding down the electrical work as early as he'd planned. He'd told Michael Katzev he intended to leave the electrical business in early May 1972, giving him almost two months to devote to the Kyrenia Ship before leaving for Cyprus. Yet a month past his self-imposed deadline, he was still spending his days in the local factories, finishing up work that he'd promised or making sure the equipment was in top shape before he turned things over to his brother.

Meanwhile, Lucille's mother, who had been suffering from Parkinson's disease, took a turn for the worse and was moved to a nursing home near Reading, about 15 miles from our home. By March 1972, her condition had deteriorated significantly. In May, she fell and broke her hip and shoulder, requiring surgery, and Lucille began making 28-mile round trips to the nursing home most Sundays. The travel was made worse by a cold, snow-filled winter that lasted well into April.

In early June, Lucille quit her job as a secretary for a factory that made bathrobes and pajamas, and we began preparing the house for tenants, who would live there during our yearlong absence. The rental of the house gave urgency to a few home improvement projects Dick and Lucille had been putting off, including removing some 1950s-era wallpaper from the living room and painting most of the downstairs. By mid-June, that project too had fallen behind schedule. Lucille began painting during the days, and Dick took over at night, at least once working around the clock.

They had planned to spend most of June packing, preparing, and shipping clothes and other necessities to Cyprus in advance. Instead, only my brother and I were making any progress on moving our things to the attic, clearing our rooms and closets for the renters. When the painting was finally finished, a flurry of preparations began amid continued trips to check on Lucille's mother and a final round of newspaper interviews and pictures. Just as things seemed to be coming together, a natural disaster struck.[18]

Hurricane Agnes blew up the eastern seaboard and stalled over Pennsylvania and New York, dumping as much as 18 inches of rain over the area in three days, between June 21 and June 24, 1972—four days before our family's planned departure for Cyprus. It was a devastating storm, causing almost $3 billion in damages—equal to about $14 billion in today's dollars. It destroyed sixty-eight thousand homes and three thousand businesses and left more than two hundred and twenty thousand people homeless.[19] In Denver, most homes were spared, but almost every basement in town was flooded, including ours. Years earlier, Dick had installed a homemade sump pump, powered by a small electric motor strapped to a board, but it couldn't keep up with the influx of water. Denver had a volunteer fire department, which was overwhelmed by the crisis and was pumping out the homes that were most in danger of having the water rise to the ground floor. We had little choice but to bail by hand. For hours, Dick would scoop up buckets and hand them through a basement window to David, who would carry them into the waterlogged yard and dump them. It didn't reverse the flooding, but it slowed the rise of the water.

All the carefully planned trip preparations fell victim to the chaos. No trunks were sent ahead. The personal possessions that were left behind were rushed to the attic in the final hours before departure. All the clothes and necessities needed for the next year were crammed into five suitcases and loaded in the car in the final minutes before the hurried drive to the Philadelphia Airport.

One of the world's more unusual career changes had begun.

Within days of our arrival on Cyprus, Dick immersed himself in deciphering the Kyrenia Ship. He spent most of his days and often many of his nights in the castle, listening for the whispers of the ancient shipwright he'd nicknamed Aristides. Everything hinged on his accomplishments during the next year. He was on the cusp of a dream that had begun four decades earlier in a house on Main Street with some paper and a bowl of flour paste. No matter his enthusiasm, the task was indisputably daunting. Little research had been done on ship's hulls in the Mediterranean at that time, and no one had attempted a reconstruction of this magnitude. What *was* known was that the hull timbers had softened and bent during their centuries under the sea, and Dick's task would be to recreate the original shape using as many clues as possible.

Michael Katzev ran a meticulous excavation. Every detail was thoroughly and efficiently recorded, and yet for all his attention to detail, he didn't micromanage. "That Kyrenia crew operated like a well-oiled machine, each person concentrating on certain areas of expertise in a most productive manner," Dick recalled. "He put his faith in each of us and gave us carte blanche as long as the project benefited. It was an extremely happy, productive, and close-knit group—we were more like extended family than crew." Having made his decision to bring Dick aboard, Katzev showed "total confidence and [a] complete lack of interference in this previously untested method of reconstruction of a previously unrecorded type of ship."[1]

By the time Dick arrived, most of the core members of the Kyrenia Ship expedition had been working together since the initial excavation, bound by their shared devotion to the dismembered, water-laden ship. Michael Katzev had given up a teaching career at Oberlin College, and he and Susan had moved to Cyprus to work full time on conserving and restoring the old ship. As director, Michael not only ran the project but also helped out with various manual tasks. Susan helped with drawing and cleaning the wood, managed the expedition dark room and maintained a running photographic log of the work. Robin Piercy, as the assistant director, kept the operation in running order and demonstrated an innate engineering talent for designing and building almost anything, often from scant raw materials. He built the treatment tanks where the wood soaked in PEG; wired the Crusader castle with enough electric power to support the tanks, lighting, and power tools that the expedition required; took photographs of each wood fragment; and eventually welded the steel scaffolding that still holds the ship's hull in place. His wife, Netia, a journalist from London, drew and cleaned the wood along with Susan Katzev and Laina Swiny.

Swiny had been chosen by Michael Katzev to record the hull underwater, in case the fragile wood didn't survive its journey to the surface. Next to Dick, she was the most knowledgeable about the wood, cross-documenting it with precision and coddling each fragment as if it were her child. Frances Talbot had joined the project in its second year, fresh from graduating with a degree in conservation from the London Institute. As the remarkably preserved wood emerged from the silt, the decisions of how to conserve it fell to her. She was petite and soft-spoken, with a blond pony tail and an ever-present white lab smock that gave her an air of authority far beyond her years. As the wood came to the surface, Frances ran experimental treatments on waterlogged scraps, eventually developing the conservation plan that would enable the ancient ship to survive for decades to come.

Rounding out the team was Robert "Chip" Vincent, who gave up a comfortable law career in a lifelong pursuit of understanding the past. In a matter of months, he would be helping Dick build the flexible wooden scaffolding that would become the ship's first cradle in the castle. He would later go on to do photography for the Smithsonian Institute, take a position in archaeological photography at the American School's Agora excavations in Athens, and eventually become president of the Institute of Nautical Archaeology that George Bass would found. The Kyrenia expedition was a ragtag but well-skilled group, short on academic pedigree but long on enthusiasm, and what they needed most was a "white knight," someone who could actually put those thousands of pieces of ancient wood back together.

As Dick studied the remains of the ship, more details came into focus. She had been made from four hundred and twenty-five pieces of wood.

The hull's shape was derived from the planks, rather than dictated by the frames as on a modern ship. Once the proper curvature was achieved, held in place by mortise-and-tenon joints every 12 centimeters, the ancient ship builders used an adze to smooth the 14-meter hull and render it in the proper shape, more like sculptors than craftsmen. The process wasted as much as 70 percent of the original wood, but timber, labor, and time were all plentiful in Alexander's Greece. Even after that process, the wood weighed about 8 tons. Only when the hull was almost complete did the shipwright add the frames, carving them to fit the sides of the hull and affixing them with three thousand long copper spikes driven from the outside of the hull, through the frame, and then clenched, like a staple.

The ship had a small foredeck, with a small cuddy space underneath, and a larger deck at the stern by the dual steering oars. From there, the crew also controlled the large square sail that served as the ship's only source of power. Underneath the stern deck was a larger cabin for storage. The open space in the middle was for the cargo—which on her final voyage included the more than four hundred amphoras of wine and other foodstuffs such as almonds.

Dick began to decipher the many repairs too. The bow planks, which had become riddled by sea worms, got a veneer of fresh wood. A crack in the keel was repaired, and the entire hull was coated in pitch and then sheathed in lead, an attempt to protect the aging ship from further ravishing by worms.

Dick and Laina Swiny had been studying the hull for a year. When they began, most of the planking remained in the big fresh water pool that had been built in "the ship room" of the castle. Once the wood was moved into the PEG tanks, the pool would be knocked down and the pedestal for the reconstruction put in its place. The room itself had a high, vaulted limestone ceiling, and the front wall had fallen away and recently been replaced by a wood facade with large windows. Even in those early days, with the timbers on trays in their freshwater bath, a balcony ran around the upper level of the room so tourists could look down on the project as it progressed. Dick studied the wood that was still in freshwater, once again checking the pieces against the full-size drawings that had been done for about half the fragments at that point. He also reviewed the photography and site recording data from the seabed. He wanted to collect as much information as possible on each of the six thousand pieces before he began the reconstruction process. He also needed to know how many mystery pieces—which he referred to as "UMs," for "unknown members"—he still needed to decipher.

The drawings and photographs provided the basis for the first lines drawings, which were the foundation for the reconstruction process. Dick reasoned that he could use the drawings to approximate the principal dimensions of the hull, which would give him a starting point for the reassembly. Any problems in projecting the hull's lines would point out gaps in the research or errors in his calculations. Many of these early drawings were based on the curvatures of the frames, which he later realized were distorted. As a result, his first drawings were wrong in many places, especially the bow and the stern, which held many secrets they had yet to reveal.[2]

As he worked on the lines, Dick began to envision how the ship would be displayed in her reconstructed form, rising on a concrete pedestal under the keel that would loft the hull about a meter off the floor. This would enable scholars to study the underside of the hull as well as the interior. Dick would complete three sets of lines drawings, each one updating the other. Projecting the curvature with lines, though, was just the first step. The wood, after all, had rotted and been devoured by worms for centuries. To rebuild this puzzle, Dick would have to work with pieces that were broken, eroded, and in some cases missing altogether.

Determining the proper curvature of a timber or the placement of a plank could take twenty or thirty hours, often nonstop. Dick frequently stayed in the castle late into the evening, ignoring the sound of rats that would scamper in the dimly lit shadows of the medieval rooms. He would study not the just the shape of the wood but also distinguishing features such as tool marks and nail holes, looking for any signs of how the pieces might align and what techniques the shipwright used in the building them. That is, if he could find the tool marks. Aristides, Dick was finding, was an expert shipwright. "Hardly ever was I able to learn much from his tool marks," Dick wrote. "He kept his blades so sharp and struck them so evenly that they seldom showed. Where he smoothed planks with an adze, it was as if a modern plane were run over the surface."[3]

Dick could tell the difference, though, between the craftsmanship of the shipwright himself and his apprentice—he identified the workmanship of only one other person. The apprentice's marks were clumsier and easier to see. Sometimes, he could spot where Aristides had stepped in, perhaps correcting a mistake or demonstrating the proper technique.

Mostly, though, the shipwright worked on the starboard side of the hull, leaving his apprentice to handle the port. After so many hours, Dick began to feel a sense of familiarity that bordered on friendship, and it was after one such night that he began referring to the shipwright in his own mind by the name Aristides. His ancient counterpart became both a confidante in moments of discovery and a foil in times of frustration, but always he was an object of admiration. Only a few weeks removed from the electrical business, Dick still thought more like a tradesman than a scholar, and he appreciated the care he saw in the ancient builder's techniques. "Aristides would have driven modern businessmen and labor leaders to distraction. 'Good enough' wasn't in his vocabulary. Nothing was too much trouble, nothing too perfect."[4]

In studying the ship's fragments, Dick found a tiny part of an inner plank edge that had separated. Given the location and the nature of the imperfection, he could tell the separation had happened during the original construction. It didn't affect the ship's seaworthiness, and it could have simply been tacked back into place or even ignored. But Aristides wouldn't stand for such shoddiness. He fashioned a tiny piece with chamfered edges that fit into a pair of grooved recesses on the side of the plank. Then, no sooner had he completed this expert piece of joinery than it was immediately covered up by the frames and the ceiling planking in the next phase of construction. Aristides had to have assumed no one would ever see it, yet he wasn't about to allow the broken plank edge, though hidden and harmless, go undressed. It was only by chance that this ancient act of perfectionism would be revealed more than two millennia later.[5]

Throughout the reconstruction process, Dick looked at the hull through Aristides' eyes. Sometimes, when he made a particularly exciting discovery, he might tell one of the other expedition members to "come look at this; I found out what he did here," leaving his colleagues to wonder who "he" was, Piercy recalled. Dick never discussed the extent of the kinship he felt with the original builder. He never told other expedition members that he'd named the ancient shipwright. In fact, he never told anyone. The name was contained in a handwritten essay years later, which he never showed to anyone.

To determine the areas of the hull's deterioration, and to test various construction techniques such as the assembly of mortise-and-tenon joints, Dick returned to his built-up ship models. In some cases, he began models of the entire hull; in others, only specific pieces or sections that needed further study. The various models helped him understand everything from the functions of some of the unknown members to how the hull timbers dispersed on the seabed when the ship sank.[6]

He began another 1:5 scale model, with plans to display it in the castle when he was finished using it for research. Unfortunately, it too would remain unfinished. Lost for decades, it was recently discovered in a castle storeroom. The expedition team also built a full-size section of the hull, which is still on display in the castle, and Piercy built a 1:5 fiberglass replica, which was designed to test the seaworthiness of Dick's hull projection. Dick had intended to make another, larger model for formal hydrostatic and hydrodynamic tests, but it wasn't possible to do that in Cyprus at the time. Instead, the tiny handmade fiberglass model, about the size of a bathtub, was the only feasible way to study how the original ship handled in open water. My brother and I were the only ones light enough to fully crew the replica—David was 126 pounds at the time, and I was 65.[7] My brother knew enough about sailing to pilot the craft, whereas my job was primarily to serve as ballast.

Gradually, though, all the models and testing gave way to the actual reconstruction itself. The first challenge was determining the best way to display the ship. At the time, the Kyrenia vessel was the oldest ship's hull ever recovered, and it remains one of the best preserved. So little was known about ships of that age, that the expedition decided visitors should be able to view both the inner and outer hull surfaces. That meant developing a support system that would allow a clean view of all parts of the hull. For the interior, Dick decided that only a small portion of the ceiling planking—or floor boards—would be installed, allowing visitors from the balcony a better view of the structure underneath. The exterior, though, was trickier. The more he studied the hull, the more models he built and the more lines he drew, the more it became clear to Dick that even the reconstruction itself would involve much trial and error. The ship was proving more complex than he'd ever imagined, and he quickly began to see that he would never get each piece placed properly on the first try. It was one thing to set the keel on top of a rigid concrete display, but what about the rest of the hull? How could it be supported safely and still account for the prospect of errors? He decided on a temporary scaffolding, a flexible wooden web that would support the hull fragments yet be easily moved as necessary when the ship told him he'd gotten something wrong.[8] "It was up to Dick, really, saying how he thought it should be put together," Piercy said. "He had an idea in his mind, a way he wanted to try. He said, 'What we need to do is make a cradle.'"

However, before reassembly could begin, Dick had to figure out how to join the smaller fragments together. The old mortise-and-tenon joints would no longer hold. After testing various ideas with Michael Katzev and Piercy, the three decided to use wooden dowels made of birch or oak, drilled into the wood. The dowels were placed in the PEG tanks, but Dick wound up using few of them. Long before they could be used, he began to rethink the whole idea because of a conversation with a stranger.

"While having lunch in a nearby restaurant, I met a visiting geologist and quite by chance the conversation drifted to the geological fault running through the eastern Mediterranean," Dick wrote. "He said that while the fault was more troublesome in eastern Turkey and Iraq, it had caused some minor quakes from time to time in Cyprus. The conversation kept nagging me because perhaps our planned fasteners would be too rigid in the event of earth tremors. After discussing the matter with several other geologists and consulting geological records for the island, I began to consider a more flexible fastening system."[9]

A power failure drove home the concern. Power outages were almost routine in Cyprus in the early seventies, and Dick realized the lack of air conditioning would subject the wood to changes in humidity, causing a shifting of the timbers. Working with the rest of the team, he returned to his earlier idea of using stainless steel rods, like bicycle spokes, drilled through the fragments to hold them in place.

As the plans for physical reconstruction came into place, the last batches of wood were moved from the huge freshwater "pool" into the PEG tanks. After years of work, the last of the wood had finally moved into the second phase of conservation, which called for a celebration. What's more, the big freshwater holding pool had to be removed to make room for the reconstructed hull.

"At that point we didn't need the tank anymore, so we filled it right up to the brim with water," Piercy said. "It was an incredible waste, now that I think about it. But you can imagine, we'd sat and looked at it for, like, two and a half or three years, full of this turbid-looking water with large pieces of wood in it. Finally there was nothing left in it, so we filled it up with water and went for a swim in it. It was a moment of grand partying."

After the party, the tank was drained and the expedition members took sledge hammers to the sides, knocking down the concrete walls.

Then the concrete pedestal for the reconstructed keel was poured in the center of the room.

As the last of the wood was going into the PEG, other pieces were coming out, completing their two-year immersion cycle. In some cases, it was Dick's first chance to see the actual fragments, because they'd been hidden under the murky brown goo from the time he'd arrived. Nevertheless, he seemed to know each piece, thanks to his work with the lines drawings and photographs. "When it was time for the wood to come out of course, he was very excited to see it," Piercy said. "He'd be watching and seeing us clean it, and he'd be, 'Oh! That's just as I thought that would be, that piece.'"

As in the original construction, the keel of the ship was laid first. In modern ships, the frames connect to the keel to form a skeleton, with the keel itself serving as a backbone. At the time the Kyrenia ship was built, though, frames were added after the hull planking, and they didn't extend to the keel. After the ship sank, her keel broke free from the sides completely and wound up underneath the starboard bow section. As a result, Dick had few reference points. There were no fasteners or other markings that would indicate the location of the frames or whether the keel was properly positioned. In the end, he made what amounted to his best guess, realizing that at least until the frames were installed, it would be possible to move pieces around.

Dick and the rest of the team began to lay the pieces of the keel in the fall of 1972. The sixteen pieces were heated in a warming box, making the PEG on their ends soft enough to work as a mild adhesive that would hold them in place temporarily. Once all the pieces were laid and Dick was satisfied with their position, steel rods were drilled through them to secure them permanently.[10]

After the pieces of the keel were assembled, the reconstruction halted for months as the scaffold was developed and the battens that would hold the wood in place were bent to the exact curvature of the original hull, based on Dick's projections. That meant more months of model work, new measurements, research, drawings, and in some cases backtracking and correcting earlier calculations. Only about half the time he would spend on the project in the ensuing fourteen months would be devoted to physically placing the ancient timbers.[11] Along the way, he made new discoveries, including six frames he hadn't known about before, and he gained a better grasp of the amount of hull sides that had been lost to history.[12]

The reconstruction, though, was made more difficult by the absence of garboard strakes, the first planks attaching to the keel. Much of this wood had rotted away, so Dick would have to start the hull reconstruction at the turn of the bilge, rather than building up from the keel itself.[13] Throughout the process, worries about the distortion of the hull dogged him. Despite all his lines drawings and modeling, despite the rapport he felt with Aristides, the ship was a reluctant conversationalist. It proved difficult "to get fragmented hull members to tell us what their shapes were originally," Dick noted.[14] His lines drawings had to match the curvature of the actual frames, and when they didn't, he had to determine whether the discrepancy meant an error in his calculations or distortion of the wood. Many of the frames in particular had lost their original shape, and to correct the problem, they were heated in a warming box and bent back to the proper curvature.

Because he had no guidelines to work from in rebuilding the ship, Dick decided the ship itself would show him the best approach. The manner in which the hull survived seemed to be pointing the way. Although almost three-fourths of the wood was intact, much of the missing quarter was from the starboard side near the bow. The frames on the port side were in better shape than their starboard counterparts, but the reverse was true for the planking. "Portside planks were much more fragmentary, eroded, and worm eaten; starboard planks, although less extensive, were stable and contained far more original surface," Dick wrote.[15]

Once the keel was laid, Dick decided to begin rebuilding the hull in the same fashion as the original shipwright—planks first, then frames. Piercy and Vincent erected the scaffolding for the port side as Dick had envisioned it, but it soon became clear that following the ancient ways wouldn't be practical in every phase of the reconstruction. Many of the planks were too fragmented to be supported by the flexible wooden scaffolding, so Dick decided on a different tactic. He set the frames first on the port side, where they were in the best condition, and then attached the planks from underneath. It wasn't how the ancients had done it, but it was the best way of assuring an accurate reassembly.

Putting six thousand pieces back in their original places, though, isn't something that happens quickly or easily. The entire reconstruction process was a massive exercise of trial and error, a seemingly never-ending process of tinkering. Piercy and Vincent might hold a piece in place, only to have Dick see that something didn't fit, and they'd remove it again.

"He'd spend the next two days moving frames up and down or doing something, and then we'd come back and we'd try it again and it would fit much better," Piercy said.

It was the beginning of a process that Dick would refine over the years, and one that he would later pass on to students such as Sheila Matthews, who would work on a later reconstruction in Turkey. You have to let the wood tell you what it wants to do, Dick stressed to her. Even though the timbers might be cracked or warped, they still would show how they wanted to fit together. The reconstruction process, then, was about finding all those discrete signs. "That's why you put it up, take it down, put it up, take it down, in little increments all the time and adjusting until you have the basic layout," Matthews said.

The more he worked on the Kyrenia hull, the more Dick realized that no amount of lines drawings or models could account for all the intricacies of the real thing. With each small change in the placement of the timbers, he would return to his lines drawings and calculate how the change affected the overall curvature. Because much of the bow and the stern were missing, he hoped that the more accurate information would provide a more complete picture of those areas.

"Every time there was a major movement—sometimes it was a matter of millimeters in one place and by the time that change was followed through to the end of the bow or stern, it would be centimeters and that would alter his estimated length—he'd come running back down from his drawing board in the house," Piercy recalled. Gradually, the frames lined up, and the first phase of the reconstruction, with the ancient frames arcing upward from the keel, began to resemble what Piercy referred to as a beached whale carcass.

Just when things seemed to be moving along smoothly, another problem developed. Because of the way Dick was placing the frames—installing them before the planking, in the reverse order of the original construction—he realized he wasn't sure the port side would align properly with the starboard. In solving the problem of how to attach the smaller fragments, he created a new problem—misaligning the two sides of the hull. Every frame he'd positioned—weeks worth of work—had to be removed, and he had to start over. "It was a valuable lesson that, wherever possible, ships should be reconstructed in the same sequence that they were originally built," he wrote.[16] But he'd already determined that at least in this case, a shell-first-style reconstruction wasn't practical. He opted for a compromise. The frames would be placed loosely, with the planks playing a more dominant role in the placement. Working off nail holes and marks on the keel, he could adjust planks and frames, tinkering with each until he felt the ship had "confirmed" the proper alignment. Only then did he drive the steel rods through the fragments to secure them. Although it might have seemed a setback, in time he learned to welcome such problems. He was beginning to listen to the ship, and he was finding that it was a gradual conversation; they didn't speak clearly at first. "He really wanted it to change as he went along because then he said, 'I know it's going right,'" Matthews said.

Once the frames were placed, Dick began installing the planking, which quickly became another false start. His plan was to begin with the two broadest planks on the port side, then add the pieces above and below them. The two he chose were the best preserved and most stable on that side of the hull, and he intended to install them simultaneously. He began amidships, working outward in both directions toward the bow and stern. The further along the hull that the fragments were installed, the more obvious it became that he'd made another mistake, or perhaps several mistakes.

"The ship was now telling us that it did not want to go back together that way—it was demanding that we correct our . . . work," Dick wrote.[17] By May 1973, the concern over errors grew great enough that Dick decided to halt the reconstruction and review everything that had been done to that point, backtracking over more than a year's worth of work in hopes of finding and correcting any more problems. He soon found several more mistakes he'd made.

First, the curvature of the keel was incorrect, and though it could be easily adjusted, the keel's curve would continue to bother Dick the rest of his life. When he started, he was sure the Kyrenia Ship had a rockered, or curved, keel, but the more he studied it over the years, the flatter he thought it should be. Even the final assembly that remains in the castle is probably too curved, he would later say.

The second major problem he uncovered was with the aft frames. As he studied them, he realized they should be brought inward, which narrowed the breadth of the hull. That problem, like the keel curvature, could be solved with more tinkering and adjustments to the scaffolding. Dick's vision of a flexible cradle was proving to be one of the most important tools in the reconstruction process.

He also discovered a "stupid mistake" he made in some of his early lines drawings. He'd recorded the distance between two buttock lines—

which run along the underbelly of the hull—as 2.3 centimeters when it should have been 3.2 centimeters. That meant all the alignments in the stern were off by 4.5 centimeters. He caught the error by "listening to the ship"—when he tried to install a strake and realized the mortise and tenon joints didn't line up on either side. "This should not appreciably affect the schedule, although I lost two days finding the error and only completed half of what I expected this week," he told Katzev.[18]

Finally, Dick also determined that many of the timbers and planks had shrunk slightly during the conservation process. Francis Talbot had warned him it might happen. The Kyrenia Ship's timbers were riddled with tiny tunnels from teredo worms. Teredos, also called shipworms, are actually a type of clam that burrows into submerged wood. These elongated bivalves are the bane of shipwrecks in the Mediterranean, and while their tunnels helped the Kyrenia Ship's timbers soak up the PEG more thoroughly, it was inevitable that all those holes through the wood would cause it to contract. Dick couldn't do much about the problem other than try to compensate for it in his calculations. It meant that sometimes nail holes didn't line up perfectly, although in most cases the shrinkage wasn't pronounced enough to distort the all-important mortise-and-tenon alignments.

After reviewing, correcting or adjusting his earlier calculations, the reconstruction was back on track. Dick then moved on to what was perhaps the trickiest part of the entire process. He began working with the shattered pieces of the strakes where the grain mills, the heavy grinding stones the ship was carrying, broke through the hull after it sank. Katzev had told Dick if he could piece those areas together, he could rebuild anything, and by mid-July, Dick had completed those sections.[19]

By the late summer of 1973, the port side was almost finished, and Dick was especially proud of the stern, where the planks curved gracefully into the flat of the stempost. But once again, he discovered it wasn't right. Two of the strakes wouldn't fit where he thought they should go, and he sat in a chair for the better part of a day, staring at the wood and trying to figure out what he'd done wrong. About nine o'clock at night, he finally realized his mistake, and the next day he removed two frames and moved them about one-quarter of an inch to correct the discrepancy.[20]

As the port side neared completion, Dick yet again changed his mind on how the reconstruction should proceed. Originally, he'd planned to reassemble the port side along its entire length, then move to the starboard. As he worked toward the port-side bow, though, he found assembling the bow in its entirety more practical because of the pattern of how the frames came together. As he worked to fit the larger pieces, Frances Talbot worked to assemble smaller fragments into larger ones. One piece in the shattered bow, for example, was made up of about two hundred smaller bits, which Talbot assembled separately and then Dick placed as one large piece.[21] It took weeks to complete the bow section because of the tiny pieces. "The bow was a real challenge but I've successfully picked the brains of a guy who walked the earth twenty-two centuries ago and I'm feeling rather cocky about it tonight," Dick wrote to Lucille, who had returned to the States by then.[22]

The pace of the work varied greatly. Some days, Dick would install only a few pieces. Others, he might get in more than twenty.[23] Every now and then, he allowed himself a few moments to look over his handiwork. "That port side is really gorgeous. Today I just stood and admired her several times. She's old and rotten but you can't deny her graceful lines and the workmanship of her builders."[24]

With the port side and the bow complete, Dick began to work on the starboard. He still had more than 450 pieces remaining, but by then was confident that his method was working and that the biggest mistakes had been corrected. He'd already learned from what he'd done wrong on the port side, and the starboard planking was in better shape than its port-side counterparts. That allowed for more of a plank-first reconstruction and helped the reassembly go more smoothly.

With the starboard side going in, it became difficult to reach the hull's interior. Although some major interior pieces, such as the mast step—the thick plank where the mast joined the keel—had been installed before work on the starboard side began, he still had to place some smaller interior pieces and other finishing details. So Piercy designed a rolling cradle on tracks that spanned the hull, allowing Dick to lie suspended above the ship and work on the interior. True to Dick's original plan, only a minimum of ceiling planking was installed over the interior. The ship's framing structure, with its timbers that stopped short of the keel, was the only one of its kind that had been found at the time, and everyone agreed they should leave part of the frames exposed so that visitors could see the complex system of frames and scarfs.[25]

The final pieces were set on November 9, 1973. Finished, though, was a relative term. Dick declared the reconstruction complete from a naval architect's standpoint. All the lines and lofting had been fulfilled, but as many as a thousand smaller fragments still were left, in addition to the ceiling planking.[26] In all, Dick had spent almost two thousand five hundred hours building the ship, less than the three thousand hours he'd originally estimated, and slightly more than half of the more than four thousand he'd devoted to the entire project since arriving in Kyrenia at the end of June 1972.[27] He'd installed almost every piece, well over 5 tons of wood, and joined it with some seven thousand stainless steel wires, burning up two electric drills in the process.[28]

As the interior details were completed, Robin Piercy and Chip Vincent gradually replaced the wooden scaffolding with a permanent iron one. Frances Talbot had determined that the ship needed to rest on the iron stanchions for at least six months, allowing the wood to settle, before the final cosmetic work could be completed. After letting the hull settle, Dick would check each stainless steel fastening, tightening them as necessary.

Once again, he checked the entire hull for more miscalculations, and working from the States in early 1974, he found another error, this time with the bow. "There is an error of a little over 1 centimeter in the placing of the wood sheathing, which affects quite a bit of the bow reconstruction," he wrote to Katzev. "Now that the error has been discovered, those pieces which were presenting problems will fit perfectly."[29]

He was able to make the adjustments when he returned to Kyrenia in late April of that year. Such fine-tuning, though, would continue for years. The Kyrenia Ship had been built without lines drawings. The original shipwright had "eyeballed" the hull to determine its symmetry. As a result, she was lopsided—the keel wasn't dead center—and the starboard side had one less strake than the port side. That meant that the starboard side had as much as 5 percent less wood surface touching the water. Dick realized he'd been drawing the ship wrong for years, using frame-first engineering techniques to define a shell-first construction. That wouldn't do. He developed a new system that allowed him to devise more accurate lines for each half of the hull individually.[30]

By June 1974, he'd finished about 95 percent of the reconstruction. He still had a number of minor things to finish, and even this far along in the process, pieces he still couldn't identify that he hoped to place. Then there was the keel. He was still tinkering with his calculations, wondering whether the curvature was right.

It would be several more years, and the experience of several more shipwrecks, before I would finally figure out where the keel really belonged. The Kyrenia ship's reassembly was by no means precisely identical to its original assembly, even within the areas of survival. In addition to the questionable keel rocker and its distance from the rest of the hull, there were many other areas of imperfection. This was, after all, a very old ship that leaked, rotted, and required several repairs and overhauls before requiring a complete covering of lead sheathing. Then, in its waning years, it sank in 30 meters of water, where it flattened out and partially dispersed before being silted over. It then spent nearly twenty-three centuries on that seabed before being excavated, disassembled, transported to the castle, recorded, cleaned, preserved, and finally, assembled once more. That was a lot of handling and abuse for a coarse-grained softwood hull. Considering this was the first Mediterranean vessel to be so conserved and reassembled, it is a tribute to the excavation, recording, and conservation crews that it survived as well as it did.[31]

Despite the condition of the wood and the ordeals through which it survived, Dick felt his reassembly was an accurate likeness of the original design. To the extent that pieces were misaligned, the variances were less than a centimeter. If Aristides walked into the castle and gazed down upon the reconstructed hull, Dick was sure the old shipwright would recognize his own handiwork.

Dick could now call himself, as he often later did jokingly, "the Reconstructor." A few years earlier, on the side of a New Jersey highway, George Bass had told him there was no such profession. Now, there was.

8 : A DREAM IN JEOPARDY

For my father, Cyprus in the early 1970s was the place where he would either prove his theories or retreat in failure back to the quiet small-town life he'd left behind. For me, as a six-year-old boy, it was a fantastic playground of Crusader castles, beaches kissed by crystal-blue water and an endless array of adventures.

Cyprus, just 40 miles south of Turkey and about 600 miles east of the Greek mainland, was a sun-drenched island nation that had gained its independence from Britain in 1960. Its land area is about the size of Connecticut, and at the time it had about six hundred thousand people. Greek descendants made up about 80 percent of the population, with Cypriots of Turkish descent comprising another 18 percent and British expatriates and others making up the final 2 percent.[1]

Cyprus was brimming with antiquities and had been a way station for the Crusades. Crusader castles dotted the peaks of the Kyrenia range, including St. Hilarion, near Kyrenia, whose mountaintop perch inspired Walt Disney's design of the castle in *Snow White and the Seven Dwarfs.* My favorite castle on the island, not surprisingly, was the one where my father was rebuilding the ship, and the one where I spent part of almost every day.

Kyrenia Castle rises from the edge of the town's scenic harbor, on the site of fortifications built by the Byzantines in about the seventh century to defend against Arab raids. Richard the Lionheart overran Cyprus in 1191, en route to the Holy Land on the Third Crusade, and his forces expanded on the Byzantine structures. Richard later convinced his friend, Guy of Lusignan, to swap his claims to the kingship of Jerusalem for Cyprus.[2] The Lusignans retained control of the island for about three hundred years, until the Venetians conquered it in 1491. The Venetians altered the castle and gave it most of its current shape, adding outer walls and extending them around the Byzantine chapel. They surrendered it to the Ottomans in 1570, and it remained under Ottoman control until after the First World War, when Cyprus became a British territory. Under the British, the castle was used as a prison and a police school. After Cypriot independence, most of the castle was opened to tourists, though a portion was retained as a base for the Cypriot navy.[3]

Dick reconstructed the Kyrenia Ship in one of several rooms on the eastern side of the castle that had been guards quarters during the Lusignan period. During my time in Kyrenia, I wandered every corridor, every passage, and steeped myself in the lore of the Crusaders. Visiting Kyrenia thirty-five years later, the castle's passages all came back as if my feet were still six years old. My favorite corner remained the Crusader Tower, with its views of the Mediterranean through the arrow slits.

If my father's "office" was an adventure, our living quarters were almost as exciting. The ship expedition was housed in Manifold Mansion, a somewhat dilapidated yet still grand stone colonial house that sat atop a hill overlooking the town. Its distinctive orange-tile roof is visible in most postcards of the harbor. The house was built by Sir Courtney Manifold, who had been a doctor in the Indian Army and retired to Cyprus before he died in 1957.[4] The place had at least twenty rooms, all with 15-foot ceilings. The expedition used much of the top floor for living quarters, while the bottom level housed a drafting room, a conservation lab, a dark room, a workshop, and rooms full of wood in treatment.

The living arrangements were less than ideal for a family. We had two rooms off the main hall where we slept. The kitchen and bathroom were shared, and the faucets on the kitchen sink didn't work, so dishes had to be washed in water fetched from the bathroom nearby. Most of the other occupants were in their twenties, and though some were married, none had children. With the exception of the Katzevs, who had a house in the nearby mountain village of Bellapais, everyone lived in the rooms of Manifold. Often we would gather for dinners on the large veranda overlooking Kyrenia harbor. It was a hospitable, if rather communal existence, and while everyone welcomed us and seemed enthusiastic about my father's plans for reconstructing the ship, the lifestyle was jarring for my mother, who was used to her own house.

"I think camping with what were essentially a bunch of hippies, which is what that was, was not exactly your mom's idea of family life," Robin Piercy recalled. "I can see now that it must have seemed like a very, very strange set up with all these young people living in this enormous great house—on one rung above the bread line."

While my father was moving through the phases of the reconstruction, our family was adjusting to life in Kyrenia. By the end of September, four months after we arrived, we moved to a rented house around the corner.[5] Manifold, with its abandoned rooms and overgrown gardens, continued to be a favorite playground for my brother and me. We cleared out the crumbling gardener's cottage, which had two rooms and a small basement, and claimed it as our workshop. The cottage and many of the unused rooms of Manifold were filled with all sort of glorious junk, which we collected with grand plans to reuse. With little on television and books in English hard to come by, we spent much of our time designing grand projects, such as a pinball machine, which was never completed, and a three-hole miniature golf course, which was. Being home schooled, we completed most of our assignments by lunchtime and spent the afternoons working in the castle, making tenons and dowels for my father's 1:5 model, snorkeling in our favorite cove, or simply exploring anything and everything that Kyrenia had to offer.

Our education included working with different members of the expedition on various aspects of the Kyrenia Ship. My brother learned photography from Susan Katzev, and I fell under the patient tutelage of Frances Talbot, who allowed me to help with the conservation of the 2,300-year-old almonds that had been found amid the amphoras at the wreck site.

In the hasty packing in Pennsylvania, my toys and books were overlooked. The library in Nicosia had few children's stories, and I was still young enough to enjoy a bedtime story. No matter how busy my father was working on the ship, he almost always came home for dinner and spent a few hours with my brother and me before returning to work. About the time I was getting ready for bed, the power often went out, and in the winter, that meant we were in the dark. Between the lack of literature and the lack of lights, my father and I began a routine. I would cuddle up next to him on the couch, and he would tell me bedtime stories, usually from great moments in history. I learned about the Battle of Thermopoylae, the conquests of Alexander the Great, and, of course, Richard the Lionheart and the Third Crusade—and the role that the castles of Cyprus played in it—all in our darkened living room. When he ran out of history lessons to share, he made up his own, sitting down one night with some typewritten pages to read me the story called *Crooked Aleppo,* the tale of the zigzagging pine tree that became the keel of a very special ship. My father intended to publish it, but the political upheaval that swept over Cyprus soon after we left changed his mind.

While my brother and I adapted to our new environment, our parents were adapting to a new social standing. Because my father's salary was being paid by a UNESCO grant for the first three and a half months, he was listed as a technical expert in one hundred and sixty-five countries. Within a week of our arrival on the island, my parents were invited by the U.S. ambassador to a formal reception with diplomats, government officials, and other prominent citizens. The only transportation my parents had was the expedition's shared van, the Tank, which they parked far down the street, away from the line of black diplomatic cars.[6]

Even more daunting, the Kyrenia project had a higher profile on the island than my parents anticipated. Within months of our arrival, my mother was among a group of American women, mostly diplomats' wives, invited to meet the Cypriot president, Archbishop Makarios III. Makarios was the leader of the Greek Orthodox church on the island, who was elected Cyprus's first president when it gained independence from Great Britain in 1960.

My mother quickly learned to juggle these new diplomatic duties with more fundamental domestic ones. She had to navigate the local shops without speaking the language. Fortunately for us, Cyprus had spent much of the first half of the century as British territory, and many retired Britons still lived there, so most shopkeepers spoke at least some English. But it still was an adjustment. She learned to buy meat in open-air markets; our hectic departure from Pennsylvania meant we had arrived with far fewer clothes and household items than we'd planned, so she bought clothes for us in sizes that weren't familiar to her.

By the fall, we'd settled into a comfortable routine. My brother and I studied at the kitchen table in the mornings, with my mother teaching me, and my brother mostly teaching himself. Our progress was monitored by Michael Katzev, who basically agreed to vouch for our education with the school district in Denver. On the weekends, we frequently traveled to other parts of the island and saw many of the abundant antiquities that dot hillsides and plains all over it. We toured the ancient Roman theater at Soli and the Greek city of Salamis. My father might have been in the castle conversing with Aristides until three in the morning, but he still managed to take us to air shows, parades, and other events. In April, we took an actual vacation—though the whole year already seemed like one—and spent several days in Israel, touring sites in Jerusalem and Bethlehem.

As exciting as the entire year was, it also had its share of difficulty.

Lucille's mother died in March 1973. Her condition had continued to deteriorate during the time we'd been away, and we got the news by telegram from Lucille's sister. Lucille considered returning to the states for the funeral. By the time she got the news, though, it was unlikely she could make it back in time, and with four siblings to handle the other affairs, she decided to stay in Kyrenia.

Emotional struggles aside, the bigger problem my parents faced was money, a worry that would stretch throughout our year of living on Cyprus and through the end of 1973. They had made the decision to move to Cyprus in part because the UNESCO grant was paying Dick more than he'd made as an electrician. In addition, it came with an expense account that enabled him to buy tools and equipment for the reconstruction.

Less than two weeks before we left the States, though, five men were arrested in Washington for breaking into the headquarters of the Democratic National Committee in the Watergate office building. As one of the greatest political scandals in American history began to unfold back home, it was having severe consequences abroad. President Nixon a year earlier had pulled the United States out of the Bretton Woods system of international monetary exchange and devalued the dollar, part of his efforts to combat inflation from domestic spending and the Vietnam War. The change in policy and the uncertainty of Watergate pushed the dollar to an all-time low internationally.

UNESCO paid its specialists in now-sinking dollars, but the Cyprus pound was tied to the British pound. That meant the money Dick made was suddenly buying far less than expected. "I'm sure Mom had calculated to the penny what we were going to spend on Cyprus. All of a sudden we had 10 percent less in our wallets," David recalled. What's more, the falling dollar created a funding crisis within UNESCO, and the agency began cutting specialists, starting with the newest ones. What was supposed to be a year of increased income was, after just a few months, shaping up to be a year with no income at all.

Dick—who had just begun laying the keel, the earliest phase of the reconstruction—went to Katzev and told him the grand adventure was over. Dick would have to return to the States. Dream or no dream, he had a family to support and he simply couldn't remain in Cyprus until the following summer without an income. Perhaps Bass had been right. Dick had chased his crazy notion of becoming a professional ship reconstructor, he'd made the most of the opportunity, but he could feel his dream slipping from his grasp before he'd had a chance to assemble the first timbers and test his theories.

Katzev wasn't about to let that to happen. "Michael somehow scraped some funding together to keep me on; I have always suspected it was his own money," Dick wrote. "Financially, we did not do so well after that but in all other aspects, we liked what we were experiencing."[7] For the next few years, financially not doing so well would become a theme in the burgeoning field of nautical archaeology. While Dick was wrestling with the price of chasing his dreams in Kyrenia, his bold adventure had given encouragement to an old friend back in the States.

On September 15, 1972, George Bass submitted his resignation as an associate professor of classical archaeology at the University of Pennsylvania. He then fired off a letter to Dick in Cyprus that began: "I have, today, pulled a J. Richard Steffy!" Bass vowed to "try my damnedest to make a living out of underwater archaeology."[8] Fred van Doorninck, who had continued working with Bass on the Yassi Ada wreck while Dick was in Kyrenia, had also been thinking of leaving his professorship at the University of California at Davis. Together, they wanted to create an institute that would provide a graduate course in underwater archaeology. In the letter, Bass breathlessly outlined his plans, with follow-up thoughts scribbled in pencil around the margins. Although it wasn't clear where the money would come from, Bass was envisioning a staff that included himself, Dick, van Doorninck, and Katzev, with a base in Turkey, Greece, or Cyprus, and a focus on shipwrecks in the eastern Mediterranean.

A week later, Bass wrote Katzev to explain his decision, saying he was determined to devote himself to the prospect of creating a center for underwater archaeology. "At this point, I don't have any idea how I will support my family next year, but I *must* have the freedom to travel around, both here and abroad, in order to find the best location for such a center."[9] Bass desperately wanted to bring Dick on board, but expressed frustration that he needed to find the money to hire him.

Katzev was enthusiastic, but also adamant that the new institute needed to hire Dick.

> You asked how Steffy is working out. . . . From my point of view, he is simply GREAT, IRREPLACEABLE, and an absolute must on any future project. He brings an awareness and knowledge of all things ships that has been lacking from past expeditions with which I have

been associated. He also brings an enthusiasm and excitement in work which is a constant reinforcement to myself and all of us associated with the Kyrenia Ship. His dedication is unparalleled. I think you could search the entire world and not find his peer."[10]

By early 1973, Bass had raised enough money to hire a basic academic staff, and van Doorninck had agreed to resign his professorship and join the center.

Our year in Kyrenia came to an end in early June 1973. My father had hoped to have the reconstruction finished by then, although that timetable was largely self-imposed and dictated more by the one-year commitment he'd made to himself to decide whether he wanted to return to the electrical business. By the time of our departure, though, such a decision was moot. Bass was forming his institute, and although it still wasn't clear whether he would have the money to hire Dick, Dick's work, taking shape in the great Crusader hall of Kyrenia Castle, was a dramatic testament to his theories of reconstruction. There simply wasn't anything like it in the world.

Bass had formed the American Institute of Nautical Archaeology (AINA) after resigning from Penn, though it began more modestly than he'd hoped. By mid-1973, he'd managed to raise only about one-third of his planned budget—enough money for himself, Katzev and one other staff member. He had to delay plans to hire Dick, van Doorninck, Susan Katzev, and Lucille, to whom he'd hoped to offer a part-time secretarial position.[11]

As we prepared to leave Cyprus in June, 1973, my father was still finishing the port side of the ship reconstruction, barely halfway through the entire process. After taking a couple of weeks to tour Europe, he put us on a plane to Philadelphia from London. He spent several days meeting with various experts at the British Museum and the Society of Royal Naval Architects. From there, he went to Denmark to study the Viking ship reconstructions on display at Roskilde before returning to Cyprus to complete the Kyrenia Ship.

The ensuing six months proved among the most difficult in Dick and Lucille's otherwise stable marriage. In returning to Denver, Lucille found herself back in the comfortable life she'd always known, but she wasn't used to dealing by herself with many of the decisions that awaited her. Soon after we returned, the basement flooded again and the sump pump failed, needing replacement. The old black and white television was finally losing its picture, and the family had no car. We'd sold our Galaxie 500 before we'd left.

About the same time, Bass and his family arrived in Kyrenia. He'd spent the summer surveying shipwrecks along the Turkish coast, hoping for additional finds that would enable him to raise more money for the fledgling institute. Seeing the port side of the Kyrenia Ship almost completed, he told Dick he was now convinced that reconstruction was as important as excavation.[12] Still, money issues continued to dog AINA, and the wrangling would go on for months. Katzev was so determined to get Dick hired he even proposed accepting a one-dollar salary and turning his pay over to Dick.[13]

Not only did the new institute need more money, it also needed credibility. For all the success of the Kyrenia Ship project and Bass's digs in Turkey, nautical archaeology had yet to win the respect of most scholars. Even though Dick had no doubts about his research, it came under fire from skeptics who believed the idea of ships built shell-first were fantasy. One of the most prominent doubters was Lucien Basch, whose article Laina Swiny had pointed out to Dick in 1972 would be contradicted by Dick's discoveries on the Kyrenia Ship.

Like Dick, Basch hadn't been trained in ship construction, but he was known as a thorough researcher whose reputation was far more established than anyone working in Kyrenia. "He's a big figure in ship archaeology because apart from having a legal mind that's like a Venus fly trap, there is nothing that he has not seen or photographed or looked at in the world that has to do with ships either on paintings, on mosaics, on frescoes, anywhere in the world," Robin Piercy said.

One of Basch's articles basically dismissed the idea that either the Kyrenia Ship or the Yassi Ada wreck was built using shell-first techniques. Basch's declaration angered several members of the newly created AINA, including van Doorninck and Katzev, who wrote a rebuttal letter. In the summer of 1973, Basch decided to come to Kyrenia to face his upstart critics. Van Doorninck wasn't there, and the day Basch arrived, Katzev had gone to Nicosia. That left Dick to face the intimidating figure alone.

As Dick recounted the story of that first meeting, Basch appeared in the castle "hopping mad" and "went on for an hour condemning our work." Dick didn't mind academic disagreement, but he avoided face-to-face confrontation. He allowed Basch to say his piece and then said that while he understood Basch's concerns, he wanted to show what the

Kyrenia Ship itself had to say on the matter. Basch agreed. "I showed him the whole operation, emphasizing the science and thorough documentation of the ship. He had given me three 'good' theories that 'proved' we did not have a shell. I pointed out right on the ship why his theories were faulty. I then gave him a dozen indisputable reasons for the ship being shell-first-built—reasons he could see just by looking at the evidence."

After Dick was done, Basch grew silent. "Then, he started shaking my hand and apologizing, saying he would apologize in print and called our project the most scientific work he has ever seen. I had shot down the great Basch."

"Convinced" was perhaps a better word. Dick, who'd based his whole research technique on listening to the ship, had in turn allowed ship to speak for him, to show how it was built. As a thorough researcher who appreciated such meticulous study, Basch could come to only one conclusion. The conversation in the castle gave birth to a friendship between the two men that would last more than thirty years. They went to dinner that night, and Basch spent the next few days observing the reconstruction in the castle, sharing discussions about ships with Dick as he worked. "I find him very intelligent and interesting," Dick wrote. "I must say I thoroughly enjoyed our nautical chess game."[14] Basch apparently did too. Years later, he would refer to the "happy days of July 1973" when they spent hours discussing ancient ships.[15] More important, though, Dick had won an important ally, someone who could lend credence to his theories of ship reconstruction. He may not have been making a lot of money in his quest to become a professional ship reconstructor, but he was beginning to reap the rewards of scholarship. Basch later told Dick that the success of the Kyrenia Ship would enable him to work at any of the big museums in Europe should AINA not work out.[16]

By the fall of 1973, word of the Kyrenia Ship reconstruction was getting around the archaeological community. Katzev had given a talk in London that drew a large audience, and Dick began to receive requests to work on other projects. The Canadian Department of Antiquities contacted him about identifying parts of a ship found in the St. Lawrence River.[17] Because of his success in Kyrenia, Peter Throckmorton, the journalist who had discovered the Cape Gelidonya wreck in Turkey, recommended him as a corresponding member of the prestigious Hellenic Institute of Marine Archaeology. He was accepted in May 1974.[18] The National Geographic Society, which sent film crews to Kyrenia several times during the project, embraced him as a consultant. There was even talk of an appearance on the television game show *What's My Line?* in which celebrities tried to guess a participant's occupation.[19]

All the recognition was thrilling, but it didn't solve the persistent worries about money, and those concerns only intensified during the six months that Dick and Lucille were separated in 1973—he in Cyprus and she back in Pennsylvania. UNESCO once again was supposed to be paying Dick, but the checks were slow to arrive as usual, despite his constant badgering. When the money didn't show up, Katzev stepped in again and paid him, but that had to be done in cash, which then had to be wired to the States. The delays were frustrating, and at least once a payment was lost in transit. The declining value of U.S. currency eroded about $3,000 of Dick's salary, and the difference between what he was paid by Katzev and what UNESCO paid was another $9,000.[20]

Dick had moved back into Manifold again and was eating cheaply at several favorite local restaurants and generally living a spartan existence. He spent his days in the castle, working on the ship, and his nights in the old mansion, bent over the drafting table. He even cut back on cigarettes to save money. "Right now, I feel like a nautical success and a financial failure all rolled into one," he told Lucille.[21] Lucille, meanwhile, was becoming increasingly distraught, and neither of them liked the prolonged separation. Dick began including a "box score" in each letter, detailing how many pieces remained to be installed on each section of the ship and counting down the days until he returned to the States.

With less than forty days until his return, Dick's father, Milt, had a heart attack. He had been having eye troubles, and because he could no longer drive, he allowed Lucille to use his car. He was hospitalized and although Dick considered coming home early, he worried about the financial impact. A round-trip air ticket would cost almost $1,000, and by returning then, he would lose the tax benefits for his overseas work, all of which was money he and Lucille simply didn't have to spend. He wrote his mother and explained that he planned to stay as long as his father's condition remained stable.[22] Dick also, though, was becoming increasingly worried about how the stress of the separation was affecting Lucille, who had heart problems of her own.

Bass returned from his survey in Turkey, having found enough shipwrecks to keep the fledgling AINA busy "for the rest of our lives." The finds spanned more than two thousand years, dating to as early as

1500 B.C. Dick, Bass, and Katzev convened a daylong meeting at Bass's house in Nicosia. It was the day Dick had been waiting for most of his life. He desperately wanted to be a part of AINA. He already had plans to spend the winter back in Denver doing research and writing his findings on both the Kyrenia Ship and the Byzantine wreck in Yassi Ada. Money remained the big hurdle. Bass told Dick he simply didn't have enough to hire him.

> I said "I can't insult you by offering you a job." And he said, "Well, try me." I said, "Well, the most I could possibly come up with is $8,000 — no fringe benefits, no insurance, no retirement plan." "I'll take it," he said. I said, "You've got a family, you've got kids about ready to go to college." He said he'd give it a try, so that's how he joined us.

After their roadside talk in New Jersey two years earlier, Bass had wondered who would hire Dick to rebuild ancient ships. Now he had his answer: he would.

Lucille started working again when she returned to the States, securing health insurance for the family. Bass also had two young children, and he too was working without insurance or other benefits. Raising money became a constant concern, and although Dick had a commitment from the Institute, it wouldn't make him rich. The final months of 1973, before his AINA pay kicked in, were especially difficult. He noted in a letter to Bass early the next year that he hadn't "had any form of income for three months. It wasn't our best Christmas."[23] Bass suggested that Dick should consider supplementing his AINA salary with other work. He didn't want to risk losing Dick permanently because he couldn't afford to pay him more.[24] It had been almost two years since Dick left his electrical business, and having had a taste of nautical archaeology, he had no intention of doing anything else.

"I have not been doing any moonlighting," he told Bass. "I've simply been too busy with ancient ships. To be sure, a little extra income would mean a lot but it is very important that I spend as much time as possible researching our wrecks." Dick believed that for AINA to establish itself, it needed to push forward and publish information about the finds, such as the Kyrenia Ship, that were already under way. "Lucille has been very understanding about all this and, while we do appreciate your concern for us, we're not starving yet."[25] Dick spent most of the last half of 1973 and the early part of 1974 in Cyprus, with brief trips to Turkey, and the return trips that he made to the States to be home for the holidays he paid for himself. In the thirteen months after his family returned from Cyprus, Dick was home for only about four of them.[26]

Despite the upbeat tone of his letters to Bass, he secretly was growing worried that he wouldn't be able to create the career of his dreams. Katzev recommended consultant work and lectures as a way to supplement his income, but Dick feared he would have to return to the electrical business despite his accomplishments in Kyrenia. Having made a leap of faith, having dared to chase his dream halfway around the world, he was now worried that everything might soon fall apart.

My mother's face had the frozen white look of fear. She stood on the concrete slab that served as the back porch of our house, looking at me across the yard, but her eyes focused somewhere beyond the towering pine trees at the end of our property. I froze. I had been romping in the yard, enjoying the midsummer sun. It seemed as if, for that day only, the honeybees had surrendered the clover flowers that infested our yard, allowing me to run barefoot through the grass without being stung. As I stared at her, I saw the tears welling in her eyes.

"I didn't do anything," I started to say. Not this time, anyway. My father had returned to Kyrenia almost three months earlier, in late April 1974. He had completed the reconstruction the previous December, returned to the States for a few months, and then left again for Cyprus to see how the ship had settled on its stanchions. His handiwork had held, and he planned to install some of the ceiling planking and other cosmetic touches, all of which was supposed to take him about three months. That meant he should be home in just a few more weeks.

His plans to avoid another separation hadn't worked out any better than his promises to my mother that once he began working for AINA, he would work fewer and more flexible hours. Money had remained tight throughout the winter, though my father's pay was better and more stable than it had been the two previous years. AINA was paying him a consistent salary, but it was still about half what he'd made as an electrician. What mattered more to him, though, was that his professional reputation had been growing, and he believed if he could publish his findings on the Kyrenia Ship and the Byzantine wreck at Yassi Ada, the money would follow.[1]

Still, a second separation only added to the stress, with my mother left alone again to deal with the close of the school year. We'd spent the months after our return from Cyprus getting our lives back in order.

My brother and I returned seamlessly to our old classrooms, and my mother and her siblings handled the final affairs from their mother's death. Milt Steffy's health continued to deteriorate. In the fall of 1973, when my father was still in Cyprus, Milt had laser surgery to repair a torn retina in his eye. As he was recovering, he had a heart attack. By the time Dick returned to Denver, Milt seemed to be improving. Then, in early March 1974, he had another, more severe heart attack and died about a week later.

Through the hospital visits, funeral proceedings, and well-wishing from friends and family, Dick continued to work on the Kyrenia Ship, often jotting notes in the corner of the hospital waiting room or slinking off to his study late at night to take solace in work.[2] By the time he'd left for Cyprus, our lives had returned to what by then passed for normal — my father flying halfway around the world to pore over pieces of ancient, rotted wood. We even talked about returning with him, if not that year then surely the next one. Now that he was working for AINA, we all expected that Cyprus and ancient ships would be an integral part of our lives. His worries about being forced to return to electrical work seemed to subside with each paycheck.

But we hadn't gone to Cyprus that summer, and with my father gone, my mother was on edge. Before he'd left, my father had lectured me about helping and about behaving myself, but I was eight years old, and promises were made more easily than they were kept. My mother stood on the porch, as if wanting to say something, but the words seemed to choke her. No, I quickly realized, I wasn't in trouble. The look on my mother's face wasn't anger — it was something else. It was fear.

She was just shy of her fiftieth birthday then. Still plagued by poor health as she had been most of her life, but she had learned to manage the condition so well it wasn't obvious to people who didn't know. I knew she couldn't run like some of my friends' mothers. She didn't swim, she didn't hike, and she didn't like to sit in the sun. I was supposed to help her, to carry things up the stairs for her because every trip up or down was an exertion. Her hair was jet black, as it would remain until the final months of her life. She wore it short and curled, and it was a constant source of frustration. Her hair was too fine, she complained; it wouldn't stay in place. She wore thick glasses, in part to correct a lazy eye that she'd had from birth. She was thin and stood about 5 feet, 8 inches tall, which from the slab of the back porch gave her a towering presence. She was wearing a colorful sleeveless dress, which was typical attire for her, even around the house. My mother usually had an easy, broad smile and a hearty laugh, her lips parting over large, perfectly straight white teeth that had never needed braces.

But this day there was no smile. The corners of her mouth sank, as if they were trying to retreat around the bend of her chin. Her eyes seemed dull and distant, despite the tears beginning to fill them. The more I looked at her, the more her face spoke of worry and loss and fear. Dreams that had seemed just within reach were crumbling under the weight of a few words crackling over the transistor radio inside. Before I could ask what was wrong, she began to speak in a distant tone, as if she were hypnotized. "Somebody assassinated Archbishop Makarios. There's been a coup, and they've taken over the presidential mansion."

I didn't know what a coup was, but the rest of it I understood. As my mother stared at me in her unseeing hypnosis of fear, the significance crept over me, like spiders with legs of ice. The connections clicked together gradually in my brain. Makarios, of course, was the president of Cyprus. I thought of the old man, draped in black, his thick beard jutting from under the vestments that reminded me of an upside down pillbox with a black cloth draped over it. Somewhere, we had a picture of him meeting my mother and some other American women in Cyprus. How could he be dead? And who would have killed him? Cyprus had been our home—and might be again. How could this happen?

As suddenly as my mother had emerged on the porch, she put her palm to her forehead and turned back inside. Like most of the German descendants in central Pennsylvania, she didn't like to show emotion. Grief was borne on the inside, and problems, whether medical or financial, were dealt with in private. I hurried after her, the wood frame of the white screen door banging behind me, this time without maternal reprimand. We huddled around the transistor radio on the kitchen table. She always listened to the news at noontime, and as we waited through maddening commercial breaks and other reports from closer to home that suddenly seemed insignificant and annoying, she snapped out of her reverie and explained to me what the reports meant.

A coup was like a war. It meant that some people—Greek loyalists— were trying to take over the country. I thought back to the previous year. We had been driving home from Papa George's, a restaurant on the outskirts of Kyrenia run by a Cypriot who'd spent some time in New York and knew how to make a pretty good burger. I loved much of the Greek and Turkish food in Cyprus, but I'd never pass up the chance for a cheeseburger. Papa George also made the only milkshakes on the entire island. They weren't good by U.S. standards, more milk than shake, but they contained a rare ingredient we cherished—the faint flavor of home. We passed a white stone wall that bordered one side of the road, a familiar landmark on the way home from the restaurant. This night, though, it was different. Someone had spray-painted a single word in black: *enosis.*

It was unusual to see graffiti. Cypriots were an island people, and they embraced an easy-going manner. Rebellion seemed far removed from the friendly smiles and easy conversation with which most islanders greeted strangers. The locals in Kyrenia had a saying, accompanied by a shrug, with which they would foil our American obsession with punctuality: "If you don't get there today, you get there tomorrow. Eh, no matter."

There were latent ethnic hostilities, often expressed in passing, but the island always felt safe, even to a small boy wandering its streets. A single spray-painted slogan didn't seem to change that. If my parents were concerned, they kept it to themselves. I asked my brother what it meant. *Enosis,* he explained, was the Greek word for "union." A movement was afoot to make Cyprus, whose population was mostly of Greek descent, part of Greece. My mother cautioned me not to talk about it outside the family because it might upset some people. I'd nodded and filed the comment away, a simple curiosity that meant nothing to my daily exploits of snorkeling and castle exploration. I knew of the friction between Greeks and Turks, but I couldn't really understand the depth of the ethnic conflicts simmering beneath Cyprus's sunny veneer. To me, the island was a playground, a place of wonder and adventure, where everyone was friendly and welcoming. Even as an adult, realizing that I was blind to political turmoil and that my parents tried to shield me from their own concerns, I still find it hard to reconcile. Yet during our short, magical time there, the brief, tenuous Cypriot independence was falling apart.

Cyprus gained its independence from Great Britain in 1960, and a decade later it was still a fragile thing. The United Nations set up a presence in 1964, to broker peace after changes to the constitution a year earlier prompted Turkish Cypriots to withdraw from the government and drew threats of an invasion from mainland Turkey. Throughout its history, Cyprus has faced threats from one group or another. By the early 1970s, the world was again meddling in Cypriot affairs. Greece, at the time ruled by a military junta, fueled the pro-Greek factions simmering beneath the calm facade of Cypriot society. Although those working on the Kyrenia Ship project may have caught a few murmurings of discontent, no one anticipated the uprising that ensued. The junta ordered the assassination of Makarios, the Cypriot president on July 15.[3]

The pro-*enosis* forces fired on the Presidential Palace in Nicosia, and a junta-controlled radio station declared that Makarios had been killed. In fact, he'd escaped, fleeing the palace and eventually taking refuge at one of the two British military bases on the island, before leaving the country. At the time, though, the junta's message about his death was being repeated around the world. Five days after the junta-backed coup, Turkey invaded, eventually occupying about 40 percent of the island, including Kyrenia, an occupation that continues more than three decades later.[4]

Back in Pennsylvania, in those early days after the violence erupted, we received no word—no letters, no phone calls, not even a telegram of my father's whereabouts. Decades before cable news channels, the information was scant. Cyprus was too small and too remote to grab many headlines in the United States. In the coming days, we listened for any mention of Cyprus. I remember one fleeting image from a newscast of two soldiers—I believe they were Turkish—one crouching, the other lying flat, firing rifles at an unseen enemy. I caught a glimpse of what I thought were monkey bars in the background, and I immediately knew it had to be the playground equipment of a small seaside park in Kyrenia. From the video, it appeared the soldiers had dug a foxhole into the soft sand where only months earlier I had played. Often, we would walk along the sea wall in the early evening, enjoying the cool breeze blowing off the water, and I would run ahead, trying to climb to the top of those monkey bars before my parents caught up. I could have been mistaken. I didn't ask my mother or brother, who sat next to me, stone-faced and worried, hoping that the news report would contain some mention of whether foreigners had been able to leave the island.

We assumed my father was safe. While he was putting the final, cosmetic touches on the Kyrenia Ship, he had agreed, at George Bass's request, to spend a week at Yassi Ada in Turkey, lecturing by campfire at night to about a dozen students who were working on AINA's newest excavation.[5] It was also his first time to see an excavation underway, because by the time he'd arrived in Kyrenia, most of the wreck had already been raised.

He'd planned to return to Cyprus for about a week, getting in one final burst of research on the ship, then return to the States. When he arrived in Kyrenia in April, he still had about eighteen hundred pieces that needed to be placed on the ship. Most were mere splinters, the size of thumbnails, which had been found around the wreck site and were designated as "UMs."—unknown members. Just before leaving for Turkey, he spent a week rebuilding the ship's port bow for the second time. "It just never suited me how it was but now it looks much better," he wrote. "Probably nobody will tell the difference, but since the original builder was such a perfectionist, it hurt my conscience to see anything less the second time around."[6]

By then, he'd been gone three months, and we were eagerly awaiting his return. He, Bass, and Katzev had agreed he needed some time off, and he already had plans to return to Kyrenia again late in the fall to complete the last details of the Kyrenia reconstruction. His last letter arrived on July 16, one day after the coup, but it had been written on July 10. "Two weeks from now I'll be taking off and headed your way," it began.[7] It wouldn't happen.

He was scheduled to leave Cyprus for Turkey the following day, and we could only assume that he had. There were no cell phones, of course, and international phone calls even in the best of conditions were expensive and unreliable. As the days passed, my mother became more distraught. Then, July 24, the day he was supposed to return to the States, passed without any word. Lucille contacted the State Department, but they had no information about Americans in Cyprus. Dick was supposed to be in Turkey, of course, but we'd received no word since his last letter from Cyprus a day before he was scheduled to leave. Had he made it to Turkey as planned? Or had he somehow gotten caught in the coup? It was unlike him to not communicate, especially when he knew my mother would be worried. If he were in Turkey, why hadn't he sent a telegram? Why hadn't anyone else from the Kyrenia Ship project—most of them had already been in Turkey for weeks—gotten word to us? What if he were still in Cyprus and caught in the fighting? My mother began to fear the worst, although she tried not to let on to my brother and me.

Even though the fighting was in Cyprus, the conflict threw the entire region into chaos. Although Dick was safe, he found it impossible to get out of Turkey. Soon after news of the Cyprus coup reached him on Yassi Ada, he left for the mainland, stopping in the seaside town of Bodrum to send a telegram letting us know he was all right.[8] All flights to

Cyprus had been halted and then, two days later, the Turks invaded the northern side of the island. Turkey was put under martial law, which included canceling all commercial flights.[9] By then, Dick had arrived in Izmir, the closest airport, hoping to get a flight back to the States. His air ticket, though, had been issued in Cyprus, and he wound up on a lengthy waiting list of passengers trying to get out of the region. After five days there without a flight, he took a bus to Istanbul, hoping he'd have more luck. Once again no carrier would honor his non-negotiable ticket from Cyprus, nor would they accept his credit card. While he was camped out in one of several airline offices, he drank some bad water and became ill. He spent his time alternating between airline ticket counters and doctor's offices before he finally found a sympathetic official with Sabena, the Belgium carrier, who put him on a charter flight to New York at three in the morning on July 28.[10]

About a day before his plane landed, a telegram arrived at our door. We'd learned to greet them with trepidation because they tended to bring bad news. A telegram brought the news of my grandmother's death while we were living in Kyrenia. This time, though, it was long-awaited good news—the cable my father had sent from Bodrum almost ten days earlier, which read: "All OK home soon." My mother must have read it twenty times, clutching it to her heart in between. When he finally landed in New York, my father called. He had just enough cash left to buy a bus ticket to Reading, where his brother picked him up at 1:25 in the morning.[11] He arrived back home in Denver with $1.27 in his pocket.

As harrowing as the ordeal was, other members of the Kyrenia Ship expedition were in more dire straits. Laina Swiny and her husband, Stuart, were still in Cyprus, working on a land archaeology dig in Soli. They eventually were taken in a UN-led convoy to one of the British bases, which became a haven for foreigners during the conflict.[12]

Meanwhile, the Katzevs, who were also in Yassi Ada when the coup erupted, were trying to get back to Kyrenia. In Turkey, they'd heard a frightening rumor: Turkish television showed warplanes shelling Kyrenia Castle, and they were told the ship had been destroyed in a napalm attack. After several days in Greece, they were relieved to get word through *National Geographic,* which was working on an article about the ship, that the reconstructed hull had survived intact. Eventually, they and the Piercys booked passage to Limassol, on the southern side of Cyprus, making their way to the British military base at Episkopi. From there, they moved on to Nicosia and eventually Kyrenia. They found their house in Bellapais looted and ransacked, but largely undamaged. The Piercys, whose house also had been looted, joined with the Katzevs in pressing the Turkish authorities to allow them into the castle to check on the ship. It took ten days, but they found the ship in decent shape. She sagged in places from the lack of air conditioning, but it was nothing Dick couldn't fix.[13]

While the Katzevs and Piercys began an on-again, off-again battle to restore air conditioning to the ship room, Dick, now safely back in Pennsylvania, was resuming his research. Throughout the Kyrenia Ship reconstruction, he had continued to work on the Byzantine wreck from Yassi Ada, often splitting his workdays in half and devoting equal time to each project. The contrast was staggering. "The Byzantine hull has so little evidence that it's rough going," he wrote. "The Kyrenia hull has so much evidence that things become contradictory."[14]

With two ships being researched, our house simply didn't have enough room for all the models my father needed to build. Dick needed more space, which meant my mother's long-suffering dining room would soon be used for dining again. After his father died, Dick's mother, Zoe, had intended to rent her three-car garage with an attached workshop to a local painting firm. She didn't drive, and with Milt gone, she had no need for the garage. Dick convinced her that AINA would be a more interesting, if less profitable, tenant, and the space soon became an expanded ship lab, complete with a 30-square-foot modeling area and two workbenches. Now, my father split his days between our home and his mother's, a five-minute walk away. Sometimes, for a coffee break, he would return to the diners where he used to congregate with other workmen when he was in the electrical business, taking his seat at the counter as if nothing had changed.

Meanwhile, Lucille, who was working full time for the local school district, still served as Dick's *de facto* typist, recorder, and assistant, as she had for years. After Dick returned from Cyprus, she developed a system for filing and recording hull components that Dick would use for the rest of his career, adapting it for computer files and databases, and eventually passing it on to many of his students.[15]

As my father was returning to the routine of small-town quiet he'd known most of his life, George Bass was moving from one hot spot to another. With the outbreak of the Cyprus conflict, Turkey suspended the dig permits in Yassi Ada. He considered remaining in Turkey, then moved his family briefly to Lebanon, back to Cyprus, back to Turkey again, and ultimately to Europe. Much of the trip was made in one of the Volkswagen vans that had originally been used on the Kyrenia Ship expedition. At one point, sneaking into Cyprus after curfew, he was fined $300 and nearly shot, then eventually let through the Turkish-controlled side of the island. At times, Bass, his wife, Ann, and their two children were moving as often as three or four times a week. "I decided, after numerous twelve- and fourteen-hour days in the minibus with the whole family, that life wasn't worth living under such conditions."[16] He decided to head back to the States. But where?

When Bass first conceived AINA, he envisioned an institute devoted to shipwrecks in the eastern Mediterranean, with a base in Turkey, Greece, or Cyprus. Now, with Cyprus shattered by war and work in Turkey halted, the global focal point for nautical archaeology shifted to a place far less exotic. Bass and his family arrived in the States and made their way to Denver, Pennsylvania.

Probably few people in Denver knew the small town's status as the world's hub of nautical archaeology, but for the remainder of 1974 and into 1975, Dick and George Bass hammered out plans around one dining room table or the other, figuring out how to keep AINA going despite the political turmoil that had engulfed its expedition sites in Cyprus and Turkey. Things didn't look good for the fledgling institution. After the Cyprus war, AINA's directors urged Bass to abandon the whole idea of an institute. Since it had begun in 1973, AINA had been run on a shoestring budget, and Bass and Michael Katzev continued to lament the low salary they paid Dick. Now, with Bass back in the States, it was clear that neither he nor Dick could support their families on the money AINA paid them.

Neither of them, though, was willing to give up on the dream. War might have complicated things, but the Kyrenia Ship remained an impressive achievement. Then there was the Byzantine wreck and others discovered during Bass's recent survey of the Turkish coast. Bass, after all, had predicted they had enough wrecks to occupy them for the rest of their lives. How could they abandon these ships when everything they'd worked for finally seemed so close to fruition? Clearly, though, the ambitions of AINA's leaders surpassed its funding and resources.

One of AINA's directors offered a solution: Affiliate with a university. AINA could remain separate, with its own board and staff, but share facilities and faculty with the university. It was a promising idea, and soon Bass fielded an offer from the University of North Carolina at Wilmington. He and Dick drove down from Denver to investigate. UNC already offered programs in marine biology and marine geology, and marine archaeology seemed a good fit. The school offered a building for AINA, set on pilings over the water. It had a long pier where Dick imagined himself sitting and writing. The two of them, as well as Fred van Doorninck, would have faculty positions.

The university had one requirement: As a state school, they wanted the Institute to do some work closer to home, to focus on New World ships, hopefully off the North Carolina coast, rather than just ancient wrecks half a world away. That meant they needed another archaeologist to seal the deal. Bass contacted Carl Clausen, who had recently become the state underwater archaeologist for Texas. Previously, Clausen had filled a similar role in Florida, where he had helped to explore Little Salt Spring, a sinkhole that yielded artifacts ranging from seven thousand to twelve thousand years old, some of the earliest evidence of human existence in the New World. He also had been involved in the salvage of a fleet of Spanish galleons that sank near Cape Canaveral in 1715. After moving to Texas, Clausen helped excavate Spanish ships that sank off Padre Island, on the southern Texas coast, in 1554. It was the earliest example of Spanish seafaring recovered in American waters, and it garnered widespread attention.[1]

Bass approached Clausen at a conference, and Clausen said he was interested in joining AINA at its new home in North Carolina. While Bass was still working out the details with UNC, Clausen accepted an invitation to give a lecture on the Padre Island wreck at Texas A&M University in College Station. Located about 90 miles northwest of Houston, A&M had been founded in the late 1800s as a land-grant school specializing in agriculture and engineering. It had a large military training program and had been all male until the 1960s. As it expanded, it added a college of liberal arts in 1969 and two years later hired Vaughn Bryant, a botanist who'd been teaching in Washington state, to start an anthropology program.

To differentiate A&M's program from anthropology offerings at other state schools, Bryant decided to focus on archaeology. The program was too small to offer a degree, so Bryant brought in interesting guest speakers, hoping the lectures would promote anthropology to potential students. Clausen, with his tales of sunken Spanish treasure, fit the bill. His speech attracted several hundred attendees, and afterward, he and Bryant discussed plans for the A&M program over dinner. The best way to build a unique program, Clausen suggested, was to focus not just on archaeology, but *underwater* archaeology, which would be unique not just among schools in Texas, but in the world. The way to do that, Clausen said, was to hire George Bass.[2]

Clausen called Bass to tell him that he thought A&M would make a counteroffer for AINA, but he didn't think it was serious.[3] If nothing else, however, the pitch might force UNC to increase its own bid. Three A&M officials called Bass a few days later, but Bass was coy. He implied that AINA was considering a number of universities. But as the discussions intensified, it became clear that A&M was indeed serious. Ultimately, it topped UNC's offer by agreeing to hire four faculty members, requiring them to teach only one semester a year and providing them with facilities for their research. Then came the discussion of who those faculty members should be. Bass, of course, was at the top of the list, as was van Doorninck, who had earned his doctorate. But what about Dick? He didn't have a recognized degree. How could he teach graduate students? Bass was adamant, explaining that no one else could teach what Dick did. A&M relented.

"I don't think any other university in the world would have hired somebody for a graduate faculty who didn't have a PhD, much less nothing [sic] except maybe a certificate from a technical school," Bass said. By April 1975, the deal was taking shape. A&M had agreed to pump as much as $140,000 into AINA, which would cover teaching salaries for four faculty positions. But the agreement offered far more than that. The Institute would at last have a permanent home and, perhaps most importantly, the jobs would come with health and life insurance benefits. Finally, it seemed, after years of a whimsical existence, AINA would be on solid footing.[4]

While the details were being discussed in Texas, Dick had plenty of research to keep him busy. During his months in Kyrenia before the war, van Doorninck had joined him, and they had spent many nights working as late as three in the morning on the Yassi Ada hull. The model that Dick had discussed with Bass back in 1964 still hadn't been finished, but several research models had expanded on van Doorninck's paper reconstruction. Even so, Dick wasn't satisfied. He couldn't understand why the shipwright had tapered the strakes of the hull, and during those months in Kyrenia he essentially revisited all his previous work. "That was a question that he was for a long time unsure about," van Doorninck said. "He just methodically did it all over again. Once he understood that to his satisfaction, then he was satisfied with the reconstruction."

He still had the final model to build, and he still had work to do on the Kyrenia Ship. He finally returned to Cyprus in the spring of 1975 to finish the final touches on the ship that he'd had to abandon the previous year. Politics made getting into the occupied northern side of the island almost impossible, but Katzev eventually was able to get clearance. Most of the remaining work involved attaching tiny outside hull pieces, re-placing the rest of the scaffolding with iron stanchions and tightening all the earlier connections of wood. Although it was a short trip—just six weeks—Kyrenia was a different place. All our favorite restaurants were gone, and Manifold House was occupied by the Turkish military. Only the ship remained, as majestic in her castle home as when Dick last saw her.

Since the invasion, the ship room had been plagued by a lack of air conditioning, and the sweltering Cypriot heat had caused the hull to sag and shift in some places. Dick again examined the ever-troubling bow section and didn't like some of the planking fits on the port side, so he began removing pieces and refitting them, ultimately finding places for a few extra fragments that he referred to as "floaters" because he hadn't been sure where they belonged. Where sections of the shattered bow were simply too unstable to endure his tinkering—and Frances Talbot told him it simply couldn't be moved—he noted the misalignment of a few centimeters and decided to address the issue in the final publication of his study.

He filed an entire stenographer's notebook with new observations and thoughts, such as how the bow was repaired. He had known for a while that the wood sheathing along the bow had been added as part of a patch that probably involved replacing several strakes. Perhaps, the wood sheathing was added as a way of attaching the lead sheathing that covered much of the outside of the hull when the ship sank.[5]

By the time Dick returned from Cyprus in the summer of 1975, the deal with A&M was headed toward fruition. Hammering out the details would take until the early part of the following year, but it was begin-ning to seem likely that the Institute would have a permanent home and that Dick would become a college professor. Ironically, though, he continued to work from the same home he and Lucille had bought in 1952, and his ship model lab was in the garage where M.G. Steffy & Sons had parked trucks and equipment. The only difference: He had now re-built two ancient ships—Kyrenia and, on paper and with models, the seventh-century Yassi Ada wreck.

Before he knew it, he was involved in another project. The same sum-mer that he returned to Denver, AINA began an excavation of the *Defence,* a Revolutionary War privateer that had sunk near Castine, Maine, in the Battle of Penobscot Bay. The 1779 battle has been largely forgotten in the United States, perhaps because it represented the worst naval defeat in

American history before Pearl Harbor. It began as the Americans marshaled a fleet of three warships and more than a dozen private vessels—the largest American naval expedition of the war—to drive the British from the bay, where the redcoats had begun to build a fort. Brigadier General Peleg Wadsworth, grandfather of the poet Henry Wadsworth Longfellow, led the American assault on the fort, with a force of four hundred troops. Wadsworth, however, failed to capture the fort.

The British Navy arrived during the siege, chasing the Americans up the Penobscot River. Many of the American vessels were scuttled or burned along the way. In a bit of historical irony, Paul Revere, who would be immortalized in Longfellow's poem, was a key organizer of the doomed mission. Left out of Longfellow's poem: A board of inquiry into the Battle of Penobscot Bay accused Revere of insubordination and cowardice, dismissing him from the militia. He later got the charges cleared. Wadsworth, who organized a strategic retreat, wasn't charged.[6]

Despite the inglorious history, the *Defence,* with AINA's help, would become the first Revolutionary War ship to be scientifically excavated, and Dick was in charge of examining the hull. He had completed two ancient ship reconstructions; now he managed to impress his colleagues with his knowledge of New World construction as well. The murky waters limited visibility to no more than 6 feet, and the divers—most of whom were graduate students—had difficulty seeing the entire hull. Dick became their guide, of sorts, telling them what to anticipate. "He would say 'there will be another frame here' and then they'd find one," Bass said. "How did he know that, being entirely self-taught?"

It was the rudimentary beginnings of Dick's teaching career, and he soon found himself with another trapping of academia: a lab assistant. Paul Johnston, who worked on the *Defence* project, was studying for a graduate degree in classical archaeology at Penn. Johnston volunteered to make the hour-and-a-half drive to Denver in his parents' Chevrolet Suburban four to five times a week to help Dick with the modeling in Zoe's garage. He got no course credits for the arrangement, but he felt that it was worth the time. "Dick was such an engaging guy," said Johnston, who is now the curator of the National Museum of American History at the Smithsonian. "Even then it was obvious that whatever he could pass along would be worthwhile. With a couple of pieces of wood in his hands, he was Sherlock Holmes."

Like that famous detective, Dick's methods often drew disbelieving stares from the people of Denver. Though many people in town had known Dick since he was a boy, they still couldn't understand why he had given up a steady job for this ship stuff. To most residents, even in the mid-1970s, work didn't need the adjective "hard" because it went without saying. Supporting a family made your back hurt and your hands crack with calluses, and everyone saw you doing it. They saw you under the hood of a car, or fixing a toilet, or wiring a home or building a barn. What was Dick Steffy doing? Could he actually be making a living?

Now, he'd commandeered Zoe's garage, which bordered on an alley up the hill from the town's only bank. Many customers used the alley as a shortcut to the bank's drive-through window. Dick continued to tinker with his understanding of the Kyrenia Ship's hull, and in an attempt to better understand how the ship had dispersed on the seabed, he quickly built a representation of the stern out of scrap wood. On his first attempt at testing the dispersal, though, it dispersed a little too well, spilling lumber into the alley. Denver had only one police cruiser, but it just happened to have pulled down the alley on the way to the bank when a load of lumber fell out of Zoe's garage, blocking the roadway. The policeman stared in disbelief. "After all, how does one fill out a report stating an ancient ship's stern fell into a street a hundred miles from the sea?"[7]

Denver's finest didn't have to worry about falling ship timbers much longer; Dick was wrapping up his Kyrenia Ship study. In early 1976, he told Bass his research was complete. "I seem to have exhausted every avenue of study to the point where it is no longer practical to continue formal research."[8] It was a quaint notion. In fact, research on the Kyrenia hull continues more than three decades later.

What was complete, however, were the negotiations with Texas A&M. Finalized in March 1976, the university agreed to hire Bass, van Doorninck, and Dick as full-time faculty, and all three would continue to work for the Institute as well, teaching one semester and doing research the rest of the year. A&M planned to offer a master's degree and provide AINA with offices and a ship lab for Dick. He'd been thinking about it for months, planning how he would approach teaching. He envisioned a technical course in ancient ship construction, but if he'd spent the previous few years in intellectual pursuits, he remained a workman at heart. He wanted his students to actually get the "feel" of shipbuilding, using tools to build sectional replicas that would be assembled and taken apart each semester.[9]

A&M offered little guidance in terms of the courses or how they would be taught, and Bass gave Dick similar deference in developing his own approach. The challenge, of course, was that Dick, former electrician and basement ship modeler, had no real idea how to assemble a graduate course. His only exposure to grad school had been an occasional lecture to one of Bass's classes at Penn. Years earlier, he'd written to Lucille from Kyrenia when talk of a university affiliation had first come up. "Imagine me, a college professor!" he'd said.

Now, his dream was taking him beyond his own imagination.

Dick approached his move to academia much as he had the Kyrenia Ship reconstruction. He pushed ahead with quiet confidence. If he had insecurities about his ability to teach college students, he kept them buried inside. He never seemed plagued by doubt, although he must have been. After all, the university had taken a big chance hiring him, and no one knew whether he had the skills to teach at the college level. The nature of his classes themselves may have helped. The nautical archaeology program was small—the first semester it had eight students. Dick didn't have to contend with auditorium-style lecture halls, and in fact the facilities were spartan. A&M had been expanding since the late 1960s, and it couldn't build new classrooms fast enough to keep pace with the growth. The nautical program was housed in one room in the sociology building, a small, aging facility in the center of campus. The space doubled as a classroom and offices, and if one of the professors needed to talk to a student in private, everyone else had to leave. Some students later moved desks into the hallway so they could write their term papers uninterrupted.

A&M promised AINA its own building in the neighboring town of Bryan on a former military air base that the university had converted into a research annex, but the building wasn't ready when classes started. The lack of space was especially problematic for Dick's classes, because there simply wasn't room to spread out ships' plans or demonstrate modeling. Once again, he returned to the garage. He set up a couple of models in the attached garage of his home, and the students would gather around his workbench. Often, the classes would move from the "lab" to the "classroom"—the dining room table, sacrificed once again for the cause. Occasionally, because the class started in mid-afternoon, Lucille would make dinner for everyone. It was grad student heaven.

Dick started the course by defining basic ship terms and having the students read a few general texts, like Lionel Casson's *The Ancient Mariners*. His lack of academic experience didn't seem obvious to his students, who were rather overwhelmed themselves by the unusual nature of the course.

"The topic was so completely different from any other structured school course where you've got math or you've got history, and you start with Neolithic and you work your way up to the Greeks and the Romans and World War II," said Sheila Matthews, who was in the class. "There was nothing to base it on. I knew nothing about boats—absolutely nothing except they sat in the water and they sometimes sank."

Rather than spend time talking about different types of construction from different eras, Dick decided to start with the details of naval architecture itself. "We just dived right in and started working on ships lines—he showed us how they went, how you used the tools, and we all had to follow a line," Matthews said. "Then he had us draw out the body lines. He sort of showed us what to do, and he had a generic ship shape, and we had to draw on the lines. And then, he had some body lines, some cutouts, that he used to then shape together a half model. Some people had more trouble with it than others, but most everybody picked up on it pretty well. I seemed to have an aptitude for visualizing things three dimensionally, so that's why I really enjoyed it."

Dick taught the students how to take a design from a drawing to a model, and then assigned them each to do their own set of lines drawings, in one-tenth scale, based on a ship from a period in history that they researched. He was more concerned with the lines being hydrodynamic than accurate. He graded not just on the design but also on tidiness. When he discussed specific features, such as mortise-and-tenon joints, the lectures focused on the function—how they worked, the structural strength they brought to the hull, and how the spacing got wider over time—rather than how they changed from region to region or culture to culture.

"Basically, he taught us what to look for, more than anything else," Matthews said. "From there, you had to take that one step further yourself. He wasn't like a lot of professors who have all this information and then you have to repeat it. He actually taught more on an intuitive level. He just was trying to show us what was available and the kind of things to be looking for."

His teaching style favored the tactile over the cerebral. He showed the students blocks of wood on which he'd made tool marks, demonstrating how they might appear on a shipwreck. He taught them to follow the grains of the wood and let them use tools themselves to get a better feel for construction techniques. Rather than giving formal lectures, the class simply sat around the dining table talking about ships. In other words, the professor who'd never been to college himself was structuring his classes around the type of teaching he would have responded to as a student. It was the only reference point he had, and it worked.

"He was really unacademic in some ways," said Fred Hocker, who began as a master's student in 1984. "The knowledge he'd gotten he hadn't gotten out of books. What he knew he got from looking at real ships. It was something he understood in a way that a craftsman understands."

Perhaps most important, he taught his students how to record shipwrecks, how to meticulously assemble the data. "You record what you see, not what you think you see," he told them. If you're drawing a piece of wood and you think a line looks like a crack or a nail hole and you record it as such, it could turn out to be something different upon further study. "By drawing what you think you see, you're making facts," Matthews said. "You're putting down facts and statements that will just extrapolate into getting it wrong later on and you have to sort of start all over again. Three or five years later you can go back and see why it isn't what it first appeared."

By the following year, AINA's building was ready, and the Institute moved into its official headquarters. Dick got the university to build a drafting table he'd dreamed of for years, with 3-inch-square cubicles beneath for storing hull drawings. The school also provided real spline weights—no more soup cans. Dick even managed, to his delight, to get an office without a working telephone. A&M seemed thrilled to have the program and Dick found he enjoyed the scholarly environment of academia. "For me, it is Mecca. I am finally getting the shops, drafting rooms, and other facilities I've always wanted," he wrote. "This is one of the few places I have been where people seem to understand what I am doing or talking about."[1]

He continued, despite his earlier pronouncement that it was finished, to research the Kyrenia Ship hull, and the Byzantine wreck from Yassi Ada still needed a display model. But now that he was on a university faculty, and with no new wood being raised in Turkey that year, Dick decided he needed to take on a new project, something that would show any doubters on campus that he wasn't just resting on past laurels.

He agreed in 1977 to work on a New World project. The Brown's Ferry wreck was a pre-Revolutionary merchant vessel that sank in South Carolina's Black River, probably during the 1730s. She turned out to be the most significant shipwreck discovered in the United States, establishing evidence of American shipbuilding fifty years earlier than previously thought.[2] Dick's display model of the wreck would garner widespread media attention and remains one of his few models still on display.

The affiliation with A&M raised the Institute's profile, especially in North America, and each new project seemed to beget others. The workload increased, in both academic and research demands, each year. Academic life wasn't the leisurely eight-hour days that he had mentioned to Lucille years earlier, not that anyone who knew Dick thought he would embrace such a lifestyle. But he was working harder than he ever had, even at the height of the Kyrenia Ship reconstruction.

By May 1979, he declared:

> It was the busiest four months of my life. . . . Since January 15, I've lectured one hundred and eighty class hours and twelve publicly; read eight hundred pages of term papers and project reports, four theses and one dissertation; wrote two articles; did three preliminary ship reconstructions; completed the Byzantine ship model (six hundred hours this semester, one thousand one hundred twenty-six for the complete model); held thirty-five student conferences; developed a new system of bottom recording for hulls; and established permanent status in the graduate college."[3]

By then, Dick had earned a reputation as the preeminent expert in his field. The Kyrenia Ship remained his crowning achievement, and with the completion of the study of the seventh-century Yassi Ada ship and other projects such as the Brown's Ferry vessel, he had demonstrated his techniques were in fact a method that could be used to reconstruct virtually any shipwreck in the world, regardless of its age.

That didn't mean, though, that he could teach it to others. Even though he seemed at ease in the classroom, and his students adored him,[4] it wasn't clear whether he could pass his reconstruction methods, which existed mostly in his own mind, to others. The answer came in Sheila Matthews. Matthews had been in that first class in the garage, and she stood out from the beginning. Dick sensed an innate mechanical ability, and one day in the ship lab he tossed her a pair of pliers. It was a trick he'd learned from his own father. Milt Steffy had used it to test how well a potential electrician could handle tools, and Dick wanted a lab assistant with the same skills. He could tell by the way Matthews caught the pliers, by the way she naturally adjusted her grip, that she was used to working with her hands.

Like him, Matthews had a wide-ranging curiosity that would lead her to develop expertise not just in ship reconstruction but in diverse areas such as three-dimensional map-making. Dick made Matthews his first teaching assistant, an unusual move at the still-male-dominated A&M. She already held an undergraduate degree in anthropology from the University of Texas and had done field work in Texas and Florida, as well as a land dig in Mexico. In 1978, she joined Robin Piercy's team excavating a seventeenth-century Portuguese wreck in Mombasa, Kenya. Later that same year, she went to Turkey to begin diving on a wreck found in Serçe Limani, a natural harbor on the coast north of Rhodes. The wreck dated to the early eleventh century and carried shards from as many as twenty thousand glass containers of various shapes, sizes, and uses, most of it raw slag or broken pieces to be recycled. The cargo, 3 metric tons in all, is still the most extensive and significant discovery of Islamic glass ever recovered.

The ship had sailed from southern Syria, then ruled by the Muslim caliphate of the Fatimids, who had signed a peace treaty and set up trading routes with the Byzantine Empire. The raw glass and broken glassware were being transported somewhere inside Byzantine territory, which stretched from the Balkans to Asia Minor, in the interior of the empire. Glass making was still a new art, and the raw materials were scarce. Dubbed "the glass wreck," the Serçe Limani ship became famous for her beautiful, multicolored cargo. Even though it was scrap, the expedition team, under George Bass's leadership, managed to piece together much of the discarded glassware—bottles, plates, and other vessels—from the shards, though no single piece was complete.[5]

The hull itself was another matter. Although centuries newer than the Kyrenia Ship, little of the Serçe Limani hull remained. Divers recovered most of the keel, which was made of elm, and scattered pieces of the pine hull planking and frames. The fragments averaged less than a foot in length, and there were more than a thousand pieces.[6] Like the seventh-century Byzantine wreck at Yassi Ada, the Serçe Limani vessel was built using "mixed" construction—the keel was laid, then a few frames attached, followed by the hull planking and then the rest of the frames. As Dick described it, the vessel itself was a "tubby, lateen-rigged merchantman that was neither large, attractive nor particularly fast." It's arrival in port would have been "about as exciting as a new delivery truck coming to town."[7]

Matthews helped excavate the wreck and sort the millions of glass fragments. She then began to trace each piece of wood onto plastic sheets, using different colored pens to mark each nail hole, tool mark and other features. The tracings were then sent back to College Station for Dick to study and begin work on one-tenth-scale research models. Matthews completed her master's degree in 1983 and joined the Institute's full-time staff in Bodrum, Turkey. Her first job was to physically reconstruct the Serçe Limani ship in a specially designed room inside Bodrum's Crusader castle. The project took five years to complete, and it remains on display as a center piece to the castle's underwater archaeology museum. Its scant wood fragments above the turn of the bilge are suspended, as if floating in mid-air, along wire trusses that trace the original shape of the hull, giving visitors an idea of each piece's original placement.

When he'd almost completed the main portion of the Kyrenia Ship reconstruction in 1974, Dick told Lucille that he didn't think he would ever do another. Bass wanted him spending less time with the manual labor and more time researching and writing. "That's okay with me. I did the first one and set the standards and that will always be in my favor. I'd rather somebody else do the hard work next time."[8]

That somebody else was Matthews. Dick, though, was more directly involved than he might have imagined during the final days of the Kyrenia project. His hands-on involvement gave Matthews a chance to witness something few other nautical students had: watching Dick work on an actual reconstruction. They spent hours in Bodrum's castle drawing the wood fragments and studying the hull design. Matthews marveled at how he could glean so much information from such minuscule details as a tool mark or a change in wood grain. Dick had a habit of talking to himself as he studied the wood, and Matthews would sit and listen to what he was saying. When he returned to the States, he left her a checklist for completing the reconstruction. Although almost no one in Kyrenia had been privy to his methods, Dick proved adept at articulating his process to students.

For much of the Serçe Limani project, he and Matthews worked in tandem. Dick would send Matthews lines drawings from Texas, and she would tell him when a piece didn't fit, sometimes sending back drawings taken off the actual fragments to illustrate the problem. Just as in Kyrenia, he relished the setbacks, welcoming the changes that the hull was forcing him to make in his drawings. This time, he was listening to the ship through Matthews, and they were hearing it together. He'd revise his drawings, then suggest something new for her to try.

Unlike the Kyrenia Ship, the Serçe Limani wreck hadn't landed flat on the seabed. Her stern had come to rest on a rock outcropping, leaving it protruding from the bottom in mid-water. Much of the stern, left exposed, eroded over the years. The uneven resting place meant a large portion of the keel had rotted away near the stern, making it difficult to determine its curvature and, consequently, the shape of the remaining hull.

"The ship's keel had a curvature to it, and he couldn't make up his mind whether that was original curvature for the ship—what we call a rockered keel—or whether it was the sagging of the ship's keel over time from the ship's use, due to overloading and being an old ship, or whether it was deformation due to the way it was lying on the seabed," said Cemal Pulak, a student of Dick's in the early 1980s, who now teaches in the nautical program at A&M.

So Dick turned the problem over to his students, assigning them a class project to attempt to determine the shape of the stern. The class was stunned. "He'd been working on this problem for such a long time," said Pulak, who was in the class. "We're going to figure this out?"

Students each took one possibility—straight keel, rockered keel—but their results weren't any more conclusive than Dick's efforts. In fact, even when he thought he had the answer, it still wasn't right. In all, the reconstruction of the Serçe Limani vessel went through three major rebuildings before he decided the shape was correct.[9]

The last time came as Fred Hocker was working on the models back in Texas. Early on, the Serçe Limani reconstruction proved more frustrating than Kyrenia because it had far fewer fragments from which to work. Matthews had been reporting that nothing seemed to be fitting. One Monday morning, Dick came into the ship lab at A&M, his eyes red and puffy from lack of sleep but twinkling with the thrill of discovery. He'd had one of his late-night epiphanies, suddenly realizing why the planks weren't fitting the frames. The keel was indeed straight, not rockered. He had built a quick cardboard model to illustrate his point, and he showed it to Hocker. Hocker had spent two months working on his 2-meter-long model, and now Dick told him to demolish it and start over.

"It only took me a week to rebuild it, because he was right," Hocker said. "He had seen through all of the detail to the underlying truth and stayed up all night to test it with a quick-and-dirty paper model that he experimentally crushed on his dining room table."[10] With a flatter keel, all the pieces fell into place.

For Dick, the Serçe Limani reconstruction was a shared success. He got a sense of accomplishment from seeing his students succeed, and Matthews showed that his system, developed in a basement in central Pennsylvania and tested in a castle in Cyprus, could be transferred to future generations. More important, it showed the archaeological community that Dick's methods could be applied to ships from other time periods. Often, experts in a specialized field who become known for one successful project translate that to all others. But Dick understood that what worked on Kyrenia wouldn't necessarily apply to Serçe Limani. Just as the ships were different, so too were the shipwrights who built them, and in his approach to studying ships, Dick always sought the minds of the original builders. "He didn't teach you ships as things," Hocker said. "He taught you ships as the products of somebody's decision-making process."

Over the years, Dick refined his teaching methods, and lectures became more specific, his classes less free-form. But the tactile teaching style remained. Each year, he made highly detailed diorama models of the partially preserved remains of a different hull type, lying on the seabed. His students were required to excavate, map, raise and record the remains, then reconstruct the hull and determine the historical period to which it belonged.

The dioramas became more elaborate. Eventually, he split his class into two teams, neither of which could discuss the project with the other. The first team drew up plans and built a ship model, using water-soluble glue. Then they'd sink the model in a tank and watch it fall apart. Dick would make sure to break some of the pieces and scatter them to resemble a real shipwreck. Then the second team would "excavate" the pieces, record them and reconstruct the hull. They'd finish with lines drawings that would be compared with the original plans.

In later years, he adapted some of his techniques to computers, working on graphics programs for reconstructions, but he remained skeptical that computer programs alone could replace the lessons that could be learned from model building.

"While a good graphics program permits almost any form of computer modeling, much of it approaching three-dimensional aspects in quality, I still like to feel the tension of a batten as it is pushed into a sternpost or the resistance of a plank as a seam is closed, or even the smell of the wood as it is cut. The flat screen has never presented such details in as gratifying a manner."[11]

For someone who had come to academia having spent little time in the classroom, Dick proved a natural teacher. "His joy at solving the puzzles of smashed, rotten ships was infectious," Hocker said. Dick had a knack for making the details of ancient ship construction interesting even to those who had no interest in history or seafaring. He nurtured that same enthusiasm in his students. Just as he turned every family road trip into a lecture tour for my brother and me—pointing out an upcoming landmark, sharing some fact from history, or simply turning a passing freight train into learning experience—so did he share his thirst for knowledge with his students. "He was the model for what a professor ought to be," said Kevin Crisman, a former student who now teaches in the nautical program at A&M. "His whole approach to his students and his research and the way he inspired everybody to get excited about the topic—if I can convey the same sense of excitement and practical quality and common sense that he had, that would be the best thing."

Former students who are now professors still marvel at how he made time for them and how willing he was to listen to their questions. Sometimes he would come back to them weeks later with the answer to a question they'd forgotten they'd asked, yet he'd been thinking about ever since. The reward of teaching, he believed, was that his students would go on to surpass him, to make discoveries far greater than his own. Teaching brought with it an obligation to the future that Dick took as seriously as the ancient ships he so cherished.

"Students have priority over academic work or research, so feel free to interrupt me at any time for any reason," he wrote in his course description for the spring semester of 1984. "You are encouraged to look over my shoulder while research is in progress, especially during the model building and drafting sessions."[12]

A&M administrators felt that professors shouldn't serve on more than five thesis committees at a time, fearing they wouldn't be able to devote enough time to more. By 1985, Dick was serving on twenty-two, chairing nine, and managed to find time for all of them.[13]

Although he could be demanding, he also infused his classes with his deadpan sense of humor. In assigning projects for his final teaching semester in 1990, he informed students that the deadline was five o'clock on April 23. "Valid reasons for late submission (life-threatening illness, extra-terrestrial conquest, the end of life as we know it) do exist, but you should know that one student in this program was run over by a car and still turned her assignments in on time."[14]

Dick engaged his students in the struggle to unlock the minds of long-dead shipwrights, and he never made ship reconstruction look easy. If he were struggling with a project, as he did with Serçe Limani, his students could see it. He never hesitated to admit when he got something wrong. Indeed, he often argued that getting something wrong at first was the only way to ensure you'd eventually get it right. "It's not something professors talk about a lot in their work—the failure stuff," Crisman said. "That is so important for students to get too. People who are less secure in themselves don't want to be wrong and show weakness. I don't think I ever had [another] professor quite like that."

His students took the "failure stuff" to heart. Notes they made in some of his classes include descriptions of techniques that didn't work and the need to rethink their approach to the project at hand.[15] In fact, failure was a key piece of Dick's reconstruction process. Serçe Limani cemented that method by showing that Dick could adapt his techniques used on the Kyrenia Ship to other vessels, but his persistence in overcoming the problems with the Serçe Limani reconstruction also showed he wasn't fixated on one approach. Once again, he had to listen to the ship, and that ship spoke to him in quite a different voice from Aristides' whispers in Cyprus. Even when he succeeded, Dick knew a project was far from complete. His early notions of the Kyrenia Ship being finished proved folly, because he would return to that same wreck throughout his life, making new discoveries.

Eventually, the ship would teach you to ask questions you hadn't thought to ask when you first studied it, he told fellow archaeologist Shelley Wachsmann years later. "You are going to solve one question and raise five," he said. Then he fell silent for a moment and gave a little chuckle. "And that's the story of my life."[16]

12 : STUDIES IN MUD, CHARCOAL, AND BRONZE

Dick had begun to get requests from all over the world to assist in different projects. In all, he would work on twenty-two reconstruction projects during his career, consult on scores more, and travel to more than a dozen foreign countries. All of them, however, served a larger purpose. The more Dick studied ships, the more fascinated he became with how they related to other technology like measurement and geometry. By studying such a broad array of projects, from ships that sailed hundreds of years before Christ, to those that plied the waters of early America, he was tracing the evolution of ship construction across more than two millennia. Three projects begun in the 1980s highlight this undertaking.[1]

In the early years of his teaching career, the projects focused closer to home, starting with the Brown's Ferry wreck and two projects in Yorktown, Virginia, to excavate British ships scuttled at the end of the Revolutionary War. In the fall of 1981, when he wasn't teaching classes at A&M, Dick began a visiting professorship at the University of Haifa in Israel. Archaeologists there had uncovered in the Sea of Athlit, on Israel's northern coast, a bronze battering ram that had been attached to the bow of an ancient warship. Ancient warships remained a great mystery of the nautical world. Although they had been depicted in artwork and described in written texts, and although history records many naval battles dating back thousands of years, few hulls have been recovered. One theory is that without cargo to press the hull into the mud of the sea floor, they simply rotted away.

The ram found in Athlit was wood sheathed in a half-ton of beautifully decorated bronze, with a flat, three-pronged end used to batter enemy ships in battle. Dick found it a hypnotic combination of fine art and terrible destructive power.[2] It was a stunning find, but no one in Israel had experience with handling wood and metal that had soaked in salt water for two millennia. Dick suggested they contact Frances

Talbot Vassiliades, the conservator on the Kyrenia Ship a decade earlier. She had married and was still living in Cyprus, and after hearing of the unique wood-and-bronze combination, recommended that the wood be removed from the ram because it would require a different type of conservation than the metal.[3]

Dick was asked to supervise the removal of the wood. Even though the ram contained just sixteen timbers, he hoped they would be enough to give some insight into the hull that was once attached to the weapon. It might be the greatest test yet for the nascent Steffy Method. A conference was assembled that included some of the most prominent names in the field, including Dick's doubter-turned-friend Lucien Basch and noted classicist Lionel Casson. The ram was immersed in a specially built freshwater tank, and it would take another year of conservation work before the wood was ready to be removed. By then, the ram had been dated to the second century B.C., about a hundred years younger than the Kyrenia Ship.

The bronze casing of the ram projected from the bow but was flat on the end. Looking at it head on, it resembled an I-beam with a third bar across the middle. The flat nature of the ram indicates it was designed to pound or shatter the enemy hull rather than pierce it. The ram was, after all, attacking other ships with edge-joined hull planking, and its unique shape was designed to split the hull timbers along their seams, loosening the mortise-and-tenon joints and causing the enemy ship to sink.[4]

With conservation completed, Dick returned to Israel to supervise the removal of wood. The process took longer than he expected because the bronze casing was weaker than he realized, which slowed the extraction process.[5] The first 200 pounds of timbers, or about one-third of the total, were removed without difficulty, but the rest proved more stubborn. Dick was concerned about cracking or damaging the bronze overlay. Several of the side timbers were encased in a concretion, a buildup of sand and other material that formed a cement-like mass. The more he worked on the ram, the more concerned Dick became that removing the wood would damage the bronze. With about half the wood removed, he suggested his colleagues make a latex mold of the ram, in case further wood extraction altered its shape or caused it to crack.[6] Eventually, Dick reluctantly agreed to cut the wood and remove it in pieces. The extraction process took four months and wasn't completed until June 1983. Never before had Dick been so fascinated by such a small amount of wood.

Although the bronze covering was impressive, the real ingenuity of the ram's design was found in the underlying timbers. It was built to absorb the force of the impact from ramming another ship, spreading the kinetic energy along the hull timbers. The ship, as Dick put it, was the weapon; the ram was the warhead. Defusing that warhead—unpacking the pieces—revealed an intricacy and an understanding of engineering that Dick found surprising. The ram's design was simply brilliant. Its blunted end ensured it would batter its enemy yet not ensnare its own vessel as a pointed, spear-like design would; its underlying wood structure, by dissipating the force of the impact along the hull, minimized the damage to the ramming ship.[7] Once again, as he studied the fragments coming out of the ram and their interlocking exactitude, Dick found himself communicating with a shipwright centuries dead, unlocking the mysteries of such masterful joinery of large timbers.

"Although most people seem fascinated by the bronze casting, I was more impressed by the timbers inside the ram," Dick wrote. "Shipwrights were necessarily good craftsmen, but this one was an artist. Seldom have I seen such perfection in the fitting of seams and surfaces or such precision in the cutting of mortises."[8]

He was also a little disturbed by what he saw. Backed by one hundred and seventy oarsmen, the ship that bore the ram was a sleek destroyer of antiquity. No expense had been spared in her construction—the warship had represented the finest in its society's materials, innovation, craftsmanship, and engineering. Yet, to Dick, it also seemed pathetically familiar. Was this ancient battleship all that different from the USS *Wyffels?* As Dick stared at the bronze, he was reminded of those years in the Navy of which he so rarely spoke. More than two thousand years separated the ram ship from his own destroyer escort, yet the theme spanned the ages. Both societies spared no expense and devoted their greatest expertise to weapons of war, yet for all the technological improvements, mankind hadn't progressed beyond Steinbeck's view of its greatest failing—its unending proclivity for war.[9]

As he was completing his initial study of the Athlit Ram in 1982, Dick got a four-page telex from the National Geographic Society. Archaeologists excavating a site near the ancient city of Herculaneum had uncovered a boat that had been trapped in a mudslide following the eruption of Mount Vesuvius in 79 A.D. Geographic wanted Dick to stop off on his way back to the States and take a look.[10] What he found was unlike any ship he'd ever studied.

Herculaneum, near present-day Naples, sat on the opposite side of the volcano from Vesuvius's more famous victim, Pompeii, but the damage was similar. Stifling ash clouds and lava flows hit Herculaneum about seven hours earlier than Pompeii, probably in the middle of the night. The boat was uncovered by archaeologists near the Suburban Thermae, a strikingly well-preserved bath house that bordered on the beach. The volcanic avalanche from the eruption of Vesuvius would push the beach more than a half-mile from the original shoreline.[11]

In the early excavations of the city, archaeologists had found few skeletons, prompting speculation that the city's residents may have fled ahead of the lava flows. Later, though, in excavating closer to the beach, they found dozens of skeletons in what may have been boat sheds or storerooms, as if the citizens ran toward the water trying to escape the clouds of molten debris and asphyxiating gases that rained down on the city from the angry mountain.

The boat that Dick had been asked to examine was found not far from those sites, and appeared to have been flipped over by the hot volcanic winds that must have roiled the sea as the eruption intensified.[12] The boat, found inverted beneath 23 meters of volcanic ash and debris, appeared to be about 30 feet long, a sweeping hull decorated with painstaking wood carving. Much of the hull had been uncovered by the time Dick arrived, and the differences with other wrecks he'd studied were immediately apparent. For one thing, the wood wasn't sodden. The boat hadn't seen the water in centuries. Instead, the overturned hull had been carbonized by the heat of the eruption, leaving her more the consistency of charcoal from an abandoned campfire. Because she was inverted, the vessel's upper hull and stern post were remarkably well preserved, unlike wrecks found on the sea bed in which those parts usually rotted away. Without saturation, the wreck had none of the problems typically associated with an underwater excavation—no shrinkage, swelling or distortion.[13]

Though she had been charred to a crisp, Dick immediately was struck by the beauty of her craftsmanship. "When I first saw the Herculaneum boat, I remember thinking what marvelous craftsmen must have built it, because there aren't any scarfs in the planks," he would say later. "The planking chosen for the boat was excellent. Each strake was constructed from a single plank. So I thought, 'Gee, this fellow is great at selecting wood.'"[14]

Even so, the boat would prove to be the most challenging study Dick had worked on. The nails fastening the frames to the hull were brittle, and the mortise-and-tenon construction created a natural breakage pattern among the charred planks. An overturned hull is extremely strong, but nevertheless one side had split away from the keel "in the same way an orange peel opens when pressed too hard in a juicer."[15]

A skeleton lay adjacent to one of end of the hull, and although the team excavating the site would later dub the skeleton "The Helmsman," it's not clear that he was. In fact, it wasn't clear the boat had spent much time in the water. Unlike every other ancient shipwreck found in the Mediterranean, the Herculaneum boat had no signs of teredo worms boring into the hull. That meant either it was newly built or it had been hauled out of the water when not in use.[16] Near the skeleton were the remains of what Dick believed was a steering oar, a find almost as significant as the boat itself because so few had been recovered from the time period.[17]

As significant as the discovery was, far more could be learned about the boat if it were turned over, revealing the frames, the inner hull construction, and details about steering techniques. "It won't take me five seconds to tell you what this boat was all about once I see its insides," Dick told a *National Geographic* reporter as they stood on the ancient beach. "I can tell you how it was built, how it was steered, how repairs were made, where the mast was, whether the sail was square, and probably what it was used for."[18]

Before it could be flipped, though, the blackened hull had to be preserved. Traditional methods such as the polyethylene glycol that Frances Talbot Vassiliades had used on the Kyrenia Ship wouldn't work because of the carbonized nature of the wood.[19] "I've never confronted a charcoal boat before," Dick told the *Geographic* reporter. "Obviously, we're going to have to invent something."[20]

He proposed an elaborate, nine-step process to treat the hull, build a polyurethane mold around it, and then lift it out. Dick knew that most of the frames and ceiling planking would remain stuck in the mound of volcanic debris under the hull, but those could be reconstructed after removal. Once reassembled, he proposed treating the entire hull with a fixative. His metal wire method of attaching frames and planks on the Kyrenia Ship would cause more vibration than the wood could tolerate, so he proposed attaching the loose fragments using various adhesives.[21]

Sadly, none of it happened. Changes in the Italian government affected the leadership of the excavation, foreign projects were halted, and

Dick was excused from Herculaneum.[22] He never would get to see the interior of the hull. At one point, concrete pylons were erected, the beginning of an elaborate plan to flip the boat over, almost as if it were a pig on a spit, but the contraption was never completed. In 1986, Dick resigned from the program, the only ship project he ever quit. He'd gone almost two years without getting an answer from the project's directors, and he'd received reports that the boat was in "pathetic condition." He didn't believe much more could be learned from it and feared that "remaining involved with the project could be hard on my reputation."[23]

The boat was finally extracted and eventually put on display in 2009, twenty-seven years after it was first found. The orange-peel split of the hull timbers from the keel is still plainly visible, a sign that the reconstruction to its original shape that Dick had envisioned never happened.

For Dick, though, Herculaneum was soon to be surpassed by another first-century boat, one that was a stunning contrast to the Herculaneum boat yet would generate far more international attention. On February 16, 1986, Dick got a call from Shelley Wachsmann,[24] an archaeologist for the Israeli Department of Antiquities and Museums. An ancient boat had been found on the shores of the Sea of Galilee, and they desperately needed Dick's help.

Wachsmann had first met Dick during the study of the Athlit Ram a few years earlier.

A drought ravished Israel in 1985, and to irrigate fields in the northern region of the country, water was pumped from the Sea of Galilee, Israel's largest supply of fresh water. Despite its name, the sea, located near the Golan Heights and fed by the Jordan River, is really a freshwater lake about 13 miles wide and 8 miles across. Also known as Lake Kinneret, the sea is famous for the biblical scene in which Jesus stepped out of a fishing boat and walked across the surface of the water.

The pumping of the lake lowered the water level significantly, turning large expanses of "seabed" into broad mud flats. Two brothers from the Kibbutz Ginosar, on the lake's northern shore, saw a tremendous opportunity. Both amateur archaeologists, they decided to spend their afternoons "boat hunting" along the receded shorelines. Professional archaeologists hadn't bothered to search the shores of the Galilee. Wooden vessels tend to decay rapidly in warm freshwater lakes like the Galilee, and Wachsmann and others had never given much thought to finding ancient ships there.

No one told the brothers any of this, though. Inspecting the shores near Migdal, the ancient home of Mary Magdalene, they found corroded bronze coins that had been unearthed after a driver had gotten stuck in the mud and spun his tires to get free. They searched the site for two weeks, finding a nail, then another and another, and eventually they noticed the outline of a boat's hull pressed into the mud. Given the depth—only the top edge of the hull was visible, as if someone had drawn the outline of a boat in the mud—they believed it must be quite old. In Israel, with its rich history spanning thousands of years, "old" is a relative term. The brothers contacted professional archaeologists, and the boat was brought to Wachsmann's attention. As he stood in the mud, studying the slow curve from the top of the hull, he was able to identify a mortise-and-tenon joint. Suddenly it hit him. They had mostly likely found an ancient boat in the Sea of Galilee.

It didn't take long for the word to leak out, and soon newspaper stories began appearing referring to the find as "the boat of Jesus." The New Testament doesn't mention Jesus owning a boat, but it didn't matter. Suddenly, Wachsmann was at the center of a media firestorm. Rumors began to swirl that the boat was full of treasure and that the archaeologists were hiding it. People began scouring the shores looking for the "Jesus boat." Wachsmann feared what might happen to the fragile hull, whose only protection was a coating of thick mud.

"A determined farmer, with a shovel-equipped tractor, was all it would have taken at this point utterly to destroy the boat in a matter of minutes." He'd heard too many archaeologist horror stories of arriving late to the scene only to find some valuable font of historical knowledge gutted and looted by treasure hunters. In this case, given all the publicity, the outcome could be far worse. He imagined the headlines: "Jews Destroy 'Boat of Jesus' Looking for Gold Coins." Most excavations take months of planning and years to complete. In hopes of saving the boat, this one would be done in a matter of weeks.

Wachsmann had pushed ahead with the project in the winter, digging out mud from around the vessel in hopes of moving the ship before looters, religious fanatics, or curiosity seekers could damage it. The excavation was cold, damp, and muddy, and continued almost around the clock under gaslights normally used by fisherman at night. Once the hull was uncovered, someone had to make a preliminary study in case it was damaged during the removal.[25]

Across the crackly long-distance connection, Dick could detect a trace of desperation in Wachsmann's voice. They needed Dick's expertise, and they needed it fast. Wachsmann would have settled for one of Dick's students, several of whom had experience in field work by that point. But Dick had developed a fondness for Israel during his work on the Athlit Ram, and he may have suspected that the glare of media attention meant that this project shouldn't be left to students. He had read a newspaper article about the boat a few days before Wachsmann called, and he was struck, even in the cursory description, by the similarities with the Herculaneum boat. "The Herculaneum boat was a beautifully crafted little vessel from the center of the Roman Empire, and here was a wonderful opportunity to see what was happening at the same time in the Roman provinces—in the boondocks," he said.[26]

Dick agreed to set aside his teaching schedule and other commitments and head to Israel, arriving two days later. He stayed eight days, which was pushing things. His son, David, was getting married, and Lucille had warned him. No ship, not even the boat of Christ Jesus Himself, had better keep him from making the wedding.[27]

Wachsmann was already enamored with Dick's work, with the depth of his knowledge of shipbuilding, his astute reasoning, and his easygoing manner. He built up the arrival of "The Reconstructor" to the staff and the volunteers excavating the boat, telling them "Dick reads wood the way you or I would read a newspaper."[28] By the time Dick arrived, having come straight to the site from the airport, everyone on the project was eager to watch this reader of ships work his magic. For Dick, it was unusual. None of his earlier first encounters with a new hull had come with such scrutiny, with so much expectation. He wasn't used to having an audience.

Wachsmann recounts what happened:

The evening was dark and moist. Dick descended into the excavation pit alone, and in the warm, glowing light of the gas fisherman's lamps, began walking slowly around the hull, stopping to examine it. The planks on the hanging platform had been removed to give him an open view of the parts of the boat that had been cleared of the mud. Every few steps he would bend over, supporting himself by putting his hands on his knees, to examine this or that detail of the boat. As opposed to the Herculaneum boat, where Dick could view only the exterior of the hull, on our boat he could see only the hull's interior.

Everyone there stood watching and wondering. What was he seeing in the timbers? What would the wood reveal to him? A palpable air of expectancy hung over the site. All eyes followed Dick as he made his rounds. Finally, satisfied, he finished, wiped some mud from his hands, and walked back to us. There was absolute silence.

"Well, what do you think?" I asked.

"Yep," he said. "It's an old boat."[29]

In fact, Dick had a pretty good idea how old the hull was, but he was reluctant to say anything based on his first impressions. He was well aware of the publicity, indeed the fanaticism, developing around the boat, and he recognized some of the construction techniques right away. The alternating frame design was similar to the Kyrenia Ship. The mortise-and-tenon joinery—especially with the planks that adjoined the keel, known as garboards—resembled what he'd seen among the charred planks of the Herculaneum boat. The age of that boat was known because the date of Vesuvius's eruption had been recorded. Seeing the Galilee boat firsthand only reinforced his notion of the similarities with the Herculaneum vessel. Dick went to bed that night feeling pretty certain Wachsmann had found a first-century boat on the Sea of Galilee.

He needed a more thorough investigation to be sure, of course. After all, this boat had been built to travel on a big lake. Construction might have been different for a vessel that didn't have to navigate the Mediterranean. The frames looked crooked and crude, and the method of fitting the planks together wasn't familiar to him.[30] Besides, a sudden pronouncement that it was a first-century boat would only stoke the media frenzy already building around the boat's discovery. Dick had never worked in this bright a spotlight. The Kyrenia and Serçe Limani wrecks were done in relative obscurity, and he could make his mistakes and fix them, revealing his findings when the project was completed. With the Sea of Galilee boat, he had no room for error. If he declared it a first-century design, it would be impossible to reconsider.

The morning after his "old boat" comment, Dick got his first look at the hull in daylight and made a more enlightened assessment. Wachsmann now got to see firsthand Dick's stunning ability to identify hulls, much as Dick had impressed George Bass on the New Jersey shore years earlier. Dick made Wachsmann a rough drawing of what he thought the boat had looked like. It had a recurving stern, two steering oars on either side of the hull, and a pointed bow with a cutwater. Dick wasn't sure if the boat had had a sail. He thought it likely, given the size of the Kinneret and the regular winds that blew across its surface, but he'd found no evidence of a mast step. A few days later, Wachsmann was speaking with two Franciscan archaeologists who were visiting the site. They'd recently excavated an ancient house in Migdal that contained a mosaic depiction of a boat. Wachsmann pulled out his tattered field notebook and asked one of them to draw the boat in the mosaic. "Looking at the drawing was like being hit by a lightning bolt. It depicted a boat with a cutwater bow and a stern that was high and curved. Except for the addition of a mast, a yard, and a furled sail, it could have been a carbon copy of the drawing that Dick had just shown me."[31]

The dig attracted Christian pilgrims on a daily basis, and they peppered the staff with questions. The favorite seemed to be whether the boat was big enough to hold Jesus and the Twelve Apostles. The mounting public scrutiny created a pressure-cooker atmosphere rarely found in archaeological excavations, a situation Wachsmann described as "hellish." Dick, though, managed to inject some levity.

"Dick came to one of our evening meetings looking very serious. 'I have calculated,' he said, 'the exact number of people who could get into the boat.' Silence fell over our little group. Dick was quiet for a while, seemingly lost in thought. 'Dick . . . how many?' I finally asked. He looked up from his notepad and said, 'Well, I figure twelve could have gotten in the boat, the thirteenth would have had to walk alongside.'"[32]

The biblical overtones were never far from the project. From the time Dick had first begun working on the Kyrenia Ship, people who knew little of his work would ask if he were involved in the search for Noah's Ark, which several adventurers had undertaken in the 1970s. He would politely say no but offer little explanation. Around our dinner table, though, he offered more details. Noah's Ark, he said, wouldn't be found, and those who looked for it missed the point. For Dick, the Bible was a lesson told in symbols more so than literal truth. Noah's Ark was a tale told to illustrate God's promise to mankind, not necessarily an account of historical fact.

He viewed the Sea of Galilee boat in much the same way. This was a vessel, a time capsule of ancient technology, completely divorced from the biblical tale of Christ walking on the water. The chances of this boat being the *same one* mentioned in the Bible were too remote to contemplate. Wachsmann, knowing Dick was a Christian and active in his church, asked him how he felt about being involved in the project.

"It went through my mind that this boat might be the type mentioned in the Bible," Dick told him. "But you see, to me the Bible is sending a message so that the stories of Galilee don't have to do with the boats or the fishing or anything else. It's the message behind that presentation that's important to the Christian. The boat may let us imagine more vividly what went on in that period. I don't look at it as do some of those people around here, as a symbol of worship. To me it's just another piece of ancient technology. I don't connect the two. I consider it a contribution to biblical history, not a holy icon."[33]

In fact, Dick initially didn't see anything remotely divine about the boat. The workmanship appeared shoddy, a far cry from the delicate craftsmanship of the Herculaneum boat. Some of the planks were narrower than others, some frames were nailed to the keel, and others weren't. Some of the frames still had bark on them. Others didn't fit flush with the hull, leaving gaps. Unlike Aristides and the other ancient shipwrights he'd come to know through their work, the builder of the Sea of Galilee boat didn't impress Dick. The boat builder didn't seem to know what he was doing.

A few days later, though, he told Wachsmann he'd been wrong. He'd judged the builder too harshly. He knew exactly what he was doing. Wachsmann was confused. He hadn't yet gotten used to the vacillations of discovery that comprised the Steffy Method. Getting inside the mind of a boatwright who died centuries ago would undoubtedly start with a few misunderstandings. No, Dick told Wachsmann, the boat builder was talented and resourceful. The problem was that he had only inferior materials available. The Galilee area lacked the trees needed for good boat building. Those skinny planks were recycled timbers from other vessels. The frames, although apparently newly cut for that boat, were nonetheless made from limited selections of available wood. The scarcity of boat building materials on the outer reaches of the empire meant the boatwright had to rely on whatever he could scrounge. "If the Herculaneum boat is a Ferrari, this boat is a pickup truck," Dick said.[34]

Extracting the ancient "pickup truck" from its muddy parking space took eight days, and packing it for its journey to a conservation tank took three more. Because the hull remained intact in the mud, no reconstruction was necessary. Fiberglass frames and trusses were built to reinforce the soggy timbers, and the entire boat was encased in polyurethane foam. Then the site was flooded and, after two thousand years in its muddy tomb, the ancient boat took to the water once again, floating up the Sea of Galilee. She was escorted by excavation staffers—though not twelve of them, despite Dick's tongue-in-cheek suggestion.[35] Once the boat arrived at the Yigal Allon Museum at Ginosar, the polyurethane cocoon was removed and the boat immersed in freshwater to keep it from drying out and deteriorating. It then entered a polyethylene glycol bath, just as the Kyrenia and Serçe Limani ships had. It remains on display in the museum.

The whirlwind excavation had been a success. The "Jesus Boat" had been saved, and Dick still made it home in time for his son's wedding. The wild rumors surrounding the boat, however, never seemed to subside. Years later, a supermarket tabloid ran an article declaring that Noah's Ark had been found atop Mount Ararat in Turkey. Its "world exclusive photo" of the find was actually a shot of the Sea of Galilee boat in conservation, its haphazard frames and un-ark-like hull curvature clearly evident.

As significant as each of these projects was, none surpassed the reconstruction of the Kyrenia Ship. Although INA—it had dropped the "American" from its name soon after the move to A&M—was recognized worldwide for its work on the study of ships, the uphill battle that George Bass had been fighting since 1960 to establish nautical archaeology as a recognized scientific discipline continued. Little by little, the perceptions were changing, but for Dick, the even more specialized study of ancient ship construction still wasn't regarded as a serious field of scholarship. He intended to change that. In 1982, he began working on the definitive report of the Kyrenia Ship's hull. He wanted it to be the most complete and scientific hull interpretation that had been done. After all, he was working from one of the most complete ancient hulls ever found, and he had done the first reconstruction of its kind. His goal was to get the article accepted in the *American Journal of Archaeology,* the industry bible. That would establish the study of ship construction as a bona fide discipline, "even to the pottery crowd," as Dick put it.[36]

Two years later, he submitted a twenty-two-thousand-word article, even though AJA had a ten-thousand-word limit. He had left out much of the details, especially about the model building, but he had documented the science behind his greatest achievement. Not only did the editors accept it at its original length, they selected it as the lead article in the centennial issue. The selection meant ships were now recognized as an important artifact in the study of ancient cultures.[37] Two decades after he'd first written to George Bass about building a model of the seventh-century Yassi Ada wreck, publication in the AJA was a highlight of his nautical career. Ship reconstruction had been accepted as a scientific discipline.

It seemed like his crowning achievement, but it would be superseded the following year by an even greater honor.

The phone was ringing, which was odd. No one ever called "the depot," as the expedition house in Bodrum was known. Today, Bodrum is a bustling resort town, but in the mid-1980s, it was still a quiet fishing village on Turkey's southwestern coast, far removed from the clamor of larger cities like Istanbul. The Turkish phone system, especially in Bodrum, was rudimentary, and calling internationally was both expensive and unreliable. Because the depot was full of mostly American students working summers on the Serçe Limani and other shipwrecks, the phone was little more than a decoration, sitting on a small coffee table.

Cheryl Ward, who was an A&M graduate student at the time, wasn't feeling well. Rather than being out on a dig site or in Bodrum's castle that, like Kyrenia's, doubled as an ancient shipwreck museum, she happened to be in the living area on the depot's second floor, where the students bunked. Everyone else—some summers there were as many as eighteen students living there, sharing a single bathroom—had left hours earlier. The ring cut through the silence of the room, which was lined with cheap paperbacks that students had left there over the years. Ward answered and a man asked in English to speak with Richard Steffy. Dick was at the castle, where the Serçe Limani wood was being cleaned and prepared for the reconstruction. Ward offered to take a message.

The man said he was calling from the MacArthur Foundation in Chicago, and he would try to call later when Dick was there. When she heard the name, Ward shivered, despite the sweltering heat of the Turkish summer. She'd heard of the MacArthur Foundation and its "genius" grants, even though the program had only been doling out prizes for about three years at that point. They were every scholar's dream— six-figure awards with no strings attached. They were given to people who were true pioneers, people who were literally changing human understanding of the world. When Dick returned to the castle later in the day, she gave him the message. She could see the surprise on his face, but his reaction was faint and muted as usual.[1] He quietly wondered what they could want.

That evening, he was waiting in the room when the phone rang again. Everyone cleared out to give him a chance to talk in private. When he emerged, he merely shrugged and said that these MacArthur folks had decided to give him some sort of award, which was very nice.[2] It wasn't just Dick's gift for understatement. The phone connection had been so bad, Dick really didn't understand what was involved. He wasn't familiar with the MacArthur Foundation or its fellowship program. He didn't realize that he had just been chosen to join an elite group of scholars, scientists, and artists, including paleontologist Stephen Jay Gould, economist Alice Rivlin, and writers Robert Penn Warren and Cormac McCarthy. He didn't hear that he had received $288,000, tax free, or that he could designate an organization to receive another $15,000 a year for five years. Only later, when he returned to the States and began reading the newspaper articles and sifting through the flood of congratulatory letters and phone calls that Lucille had carefully cataloged, did he begin to grasp the significance of the award.

Back home, though, word spread quickly. The foundation had first called INA looking for Dick, and then, after failing to reach him in Bodrum, called Lucille.[3] Together, both she and the foundation representatives tried for almost two days to get through to Bodrum by phone. The foundation officials even considered notifying Dick by telegram, before the call that Ward answered went through.[4]

The MacArthur Foundation had begun awarding its "genius" grants in 1981, and in just a few years they already had gained prestige. John D. MacArthur made a fortune in insurance and real estate, becoming one of the wealthiest men in America before he died in 1978. The foundation, which had assets of more than $5 billion in 2009, was set up after his death and awards grants for a range of humanitarian and educational causes. It's best known, however, for the fellows program, which gives five-year unrestricted grants to individuals in the United States who show "exceptional merit and the promise of continued creative work."[5]

The grants are designed to give innovative thinkers the financial freedom to pursue work they might not otherwise be able to do. For Dick, that meant a chance to tackle a project he'd been thinking about for almost a decade. Since he'd begun teaching, he'd wanted to write a textbook on ship construction, one that would help fill in the historical gaps and set down his unique method for rebuilding and studying wrecks. Dick's book plans may have factored into the foundation's decision. At least one of the experts the foundation contacted in considering Dick for the award mentioned his desire to write a textbook as a natural extension of his "gift for transmitting his expertise to others" and included an outline and partial manuscript in the recommendation letter.[6]

The award did more than simply give Dick time to finish the book. It brought public recognition to his work and gave his research an academic validation that his accomplishments alone never did. It bolstered nautical archaeology too, which was still fighting an uphill battle for credibility. Fourteen years earlier, Dick started his day by strapping on a tool belt. Now he was recognized among a rarefied group of thinkers who were pushing the limits of human knowledge and achievement.

This final phase of his improbable journey began in a roundabout way. Texas A&M had hired Dick as a lecturer, part of a compromise reached with George Bass in the deal to bring INA to the university. Because Dick didn't have a college degree, A&M said he would have to remain a lecturer for the rest of his teaching career, an agreement that he happily accepted because, after all, the university was already bending its rules by hiring him.

Four years after he came aboard, A&M officials changed their minds and promoted him to assistant professor, putting him on the tenure track. In much the same way he disliked unions, the idea of tenure made him a little uncomfortable. He didn't like the sense of entitlement that seemed to come with guaranteed employment. He believed in meritocracy. Tenure was "something I never cared about since I want to be thrown out if I ever stop producing," he told Bass.[7]

It was a moot point. Neither INA nor A&M were going to throw him out, and he never stopped producing. In the ensuing decade, he moved through the ranks as an associate and then a full professor. He later received an endowed chair and, after he retired, was made an emeritus professor. "The fact that he didn't have a degree didn't seem to make any difference," said Vaughn Bryant, who ran the anthropology department during most of that time. "It never stood in the way. He got tenure just like anybody else, he was promoted to associate professor, he was promoted to full professor and that question was never raised." In 1987, a committee considering his promotion to full professor noted that Dick's "lack of formal academic credentials has become an irrelevant factor."[8]

Outwardly, Dick showed little concern about his academic background. After all, he had the ship lab he'd always dreamed of, and he had an abundance of interesting projects that would probably last him the rest of his life. Rather than focus on what he didn't have, he embraced these things for which he'd worked most of his life and ignored those that he enjoyed less, such as campus politics. "He very much avoided conflict within the department," Fred van Doorninck said. "He didn't take as full a part in the workings of the department nor in the Institute of Nautical Archaeology as he might have to the benefit of both. I will admit I was certainly annoyed at him when I was left in charge of the program and George was in Turkey, because he was no help."

Dick, however, frequently avoided conflict, and he never liked the idea of managing people, as if those sailors under his command who collapsed from heat exhaustion during the overhaul of the *Wyffels* so long ago still haunted him. He hadn't been anyone's boss since. But his reluctance to play a more active role in the administration of the program ran deeper than that. He had come to the field later in life; he had taken chances, had worked for years for little or no money, and had overcome a lack of education. He had fought his way into nautical archaeology at an age when many people began to look toward retirement. He knew he had a limited time—there would only be a certain number of ships—and he didn't want to be distracted from the dream now that he was actually living it.

Yet the latent insecurity lingered. He remained uncomfortable as a non-degreed "expert" among so many scholars with doctorates. He would quietly wince when someone referred to him as "Dr. Steffy," a default academic protocol for instructors in the graduate school. Dick wasn't one for regrets, and he didn't spent a lot of time fretting over things he couldn't change, but in a university setting he was surrounded by reminders of that inexplicable decision in Milwaukee almost forty years earlier to leave school for the family business. Even after he'd been on the faculty for a decade, he described himself as an "academic nobody."[9] "I sometimes got the impression that because he didn't have a PhD, he almost felt like a secondary citizen," Bryant said. "I always tried to tell him that he was an equal to everybody else."

Bass got much the same impression. They'd known each other for almost two decades by then, and Bass, perhaps more than anyone else, could read Dick's insecurities. In 1983, Bass thought he had the solution. He'd heard from a friend that Anders Franzén, the amateur Swedish archaeologist who discovered the *Vasa* in 1956, had received an honorary doctorate. Franzén studied naval architecture but never graduated. Why not find a school that would award an honorary doctorate to Dick? Bass wrote to about five universities, including the University of Haifa, where Dick had been a visiting professor during his years working on the Athlit Ram, and Bryn Mawr College in Pennsylvania, which offered a degree in archaeology.[10]

Neither school gave honorary degrees, but Barbara Kreutz, Bryn Mawr's graduate dean of arts and sciences, knew Dick's work. Kreutz was a Medieval historian, best known in nautical circles for studying aspects of Mediterranean ships, including the use of the lateen sail. Her interest brought her to A&M for several weeks to study Dick's research on the Serçe Limani and seventh-century Yassi Ada ships. "She was really into the Byzantine period and was of course aware of what Dick had been doing," van Doorninck said.

Although she couldn't offer Dick a degree, Kreutz told Bass, "I have your letter about Dick in my briefcase and will continue to carry it around with me more or less indefinitely in the hope that I, if constantly reminded, will come up with some sort of useful idea."[11] After Dick received the MacArthur award, Bass wrote her another letter, saying he believed she had been the nominator. Her response: "Let's just say that Dick Steffy has a lot of friends."[12] The MacArthur nomination process is secret, and the foundation declined to reveal Dick's nominator even posthumously. Kreutz died in 2003.[13]

As a MacArthur recipient, Dick was invited to a lavish banquet in Chicago, where he got to mingle with other winners of the "genius grants." He and Lucille always looked forward to the meetings, and attended for many years. The first one, though, came with an added surprise. Soon after arriving at the reception, they were greeted by Dr. Jonas Salk, who by then was a Nobel laureate and a director of the foundation. While he congratulated Dick on his award, he was astounded to see Lucille, whom he remembered from her days at Wyeth when he was working on the polio vaccine.[14]

Whatever Dick's plans for the MacArthur grant, little changed in the next few years. Though he intended to work on the textbook, he had only a rough outline. The award had directed even more international attention his way, and requests to consult on ship projects flooded in, as did requests for conference appearances. The Serçe Limani reconstruction was ongoing, Herculaneum was still in the works, and the Sea of Galilee boat was proving an intriguing study. He continued to teach and advise students, and the program at A&M was drawing a bigger enrollment each year.

By 1990, Dick realized that he had yet another contribution he wanted to make — an interactive database of ship information through the ages. He had been an early adopter of computer technology and in the mid-1980s became fascinated with the possibility of using computers for both drafting and data compilation. With the Serçe Limani vessel, he began to transfer much of the fragment data to a computer. He envisioned it as the start of a comprehensive database that students and researchers could expand on and refer to for years to come.

That project, like the textbook, required more time than he could spare as long as he continued teaching. He notified A&M that he intended to retire before the start of the next school year in the fall, though he admitted that "retire" was somewhat misleading. He had no intention of divorcing himself from the program, and he continued to serve on nineteen graduate committees and chair two doctoral student committees. "What I want to change is the structured life I lead now, so that I can work without interruption when the research and writing are going well," he explained in his resignation letter. "I would appreciate if I could have a desk in a corner somewhere (without telephone, please) with the occasional use of the large drafting facilities."[15]

His reasons weren't purely academic. By then, he was sixty-six years old and Lucille would be the same age in a few months. They'd married late, had their last child in their forties, and now, with the children finally grown, their income secure and an international travel schedule of research projects and lectures, they wanted to enjoy it. Lucille began to accompany Dick on some of his trips, and he, in turn, promised her travels to some places that had no relation to seafaring. She held him to it, planning a tour of the western United States that took them to Utah, Las Vegas, and the Grand Canyon, but nowhere close to tidewater.

Their first grandchild was born in November 1990, just months after Dick's retirement, and the second came five months later. By then, Lucille's health problems returned with a vengeance. She'd had few troubles since having a heart valve replaced in 1980, but the damage to her heart from her childhood bouts with rheumatic fever had taken their toll. She had a heart attack in early April 1991, followed by open heart surgery. In recovering from the surgery, she developed pulmonary hypertension, an abnormally high blood pressure in the arteries of lungs. It's an incurable condition, which in Lucille's case stemmed from her lifelong heart problems. She spent several months shuffling between home and the hospital. During one visit, she told me when my father was out of earshot that she could tell she wasn't going to get better. She didn't. She died in July 1991.

Dick had spent weeks at her side in the hospital, and when she was moved to intensive care, he would wait hours for the fifteen-minute visits. He brought files and papers with him to the waiting room, thinking he might work on the textbook or other projects, but they sat idle at his side as he spent hours simply staring at the walls of the waiting room. Even reading was impossible. Her death, after forty years of marriage, left him devastated. He took a solitary trip to the Jersey shore, returning to one of his favorite coastlines from childhood and not far from the place where Lucille had insisted he pull over and tell Bass of his crazy intention of becoming an ancient ship reconstructor.

When he returned to Texas, he pushed himself back to work. Lucille, long the force that had urged him to take the chances that had formed the foundation for his career, would have wanted nothing less. She'd always been practical that way. He tried to be philosophical about it. Her heart valve replacement in 1980 had bought her eleven more years, and those had been some of the best of their lives. She got to see both sons graduate college, marry, launch their careers and begin their own families. She saw Dick reap the rewards for all the years she'd sacrificed. Dick was still in good health and young enough that his contributions to ship studies were far from finished. He signed a contract to publish his textbook and traveled to London to resume research on a book for the British Museum that he'd put on hold when Lucille got sick.

Somehow, though, his passion for ships had drained out of him. He no longer had a desire to remain active in nautical archaeology. Lucille had been the anchor through the entire adventure, the steadying force that kept the voyage from electrician to ship reconstructor on track. She had encouraged him, she had supported him, and she had taken the family to Cyprus and made a home there. She had endured long separations and shared in the glory of his achievements. Without her, the dream seemed hollow and meaningless.

He turned the British Museum book over to Fred Hocker, his former student who had taken over his ship reconstruction class at A&M.[16] Only one thing seemed to matter: his textbook. That weighed on him like a debt to the future, an obligation to his students and to their students who would follow. It also was a promise of sorts to Lucille. Her secretarial skills made her an excellent proofreader, and she had once again served, as she often did for Dick's writing, as the first editor for the portions of the book on which he'd already worked. Over the years, when he'd gotten discouraged and thought about scrapping the entire project, she'd encouraged him to stick with it.[17] He owed it to her to finish it. Slowly, he began to pull himself back into his work. A year and a half after Lucille's death, in November 1992, he completed the manuscript.

Finishing the book was a salve of sorts, helping to heal the wound of Lucille's death. He would never remarry, never even think about dating, but he did, in time, return to the other great love of his life—the ships. He got some encouragement from an old friend, from a familiar voice calling to him, once again, from across the ages. It was Aristides. The Kyrenia Ship had more to say.

14 : THE LAUGHTER OF ARISTIDES

The Kyrenia Ship's latest message actually grew from work Dick began more than a decade earlier, while he was juggling his other major projects during the 1980s—the Serçe Limani wreck, the Herculaneum boat, the Athlit Ram, and the Sea of Galilee boat. In the midst of those projects, he took on another one, one that made the Kyrenia project all the more special.

For some people, studying the building techniques of ancient ships is more than a curiosity; it's a consuming passion. That was true for my father, and it's also true for Harry Tzalas. Born in Egypt and living in Athens, Tzalas spent most of his career as a marine consultant, selling and chartering yachts, evaluating them, and providing other services. Tzalas's job involved him in almost every aspect of modern seafaring except boat construction.

In the 1970s, he spent several winters on the Greek island of Symi, building wooden *caïques*—about the same size as the Kyrenia Ship—to understand traditional boat building. He built four of the boats and sold them to U.S. Air Force officers stationed nearby. Tzalas wasn't doing it for the money; his passion was Greece's rich shipbuilding history, which spanned the millennia. He feared that modern building techniques were eroding the skills of Greek shipbuilders. "My intention was not to sell *caïques,* it was to revive that industry before the knowledge was lost," Tzalas explained.

That experiment in preserving lost boat-building techniques prompted him in 1980 to form the Hellenic Institute for the Preservation of Nautical Tradition, and Tzalas had the Institute's first project in mind: the Kyrenia Ship. Just as Dick had done with models in the early 1960s, Tzalas believed much could be learned about ancient techniques by building full-scale ships, replicas that actually mimicked the original design in every way possible. It would be the most accurate method for testing theories about how the Kyrenia Ship sailed, far beyond the sort of scaled-down fiberglass test model my brother and I had tested in Kyrenia.

Tzalas had first heard of the Kyrenia wreck in 1967, but by the time he sold his four boats in Symi, the politics of postwar Cyprus made it almost impossible for a Greek citizen to travel to Kyrenia, which the Turks had renamed Girne. He read everything he could about the ship, though, and the more he read, the more determined he became to build a full-scale, sailable replica in the ancient way. "I did not realize how difficult that would be," he said.

No one had ever attempted such a thing, and although Dick's reconstruction had demonstrated that the strength of shell-first construction derived from the mortise-and-tenon joints, that strength had never been tested beyond his scale research models. Although the models supported his theory, it didn't mean the system was able to withstand a voyage at sea. In fact, some researchers still argued, as Lucien Basch once had, that shell-first construction had never actually been done at all. It simply wasn't possible, they said, arguing that the ancients used some sort of mixed construction method similar to that found on the Yassi Ada and Serçe Limani wrecks. Could the construction technique that disappeared by the seventh century be recreated? "The question was, after fourteen hundred years, if that knowledge that had been completely forgotten could be revived," Tzalas recalled.

Having worked around boatyards since the early 1960s, Tzalas knew a few craftsmen in Greece who still specialized in wooden ships, and he approached one he thought could handle the job. Manolis Psaros was a third-generation boat builder whose family hailed from the island of Samos, known for its shipbuilding prowess. Psaros and his father ran a shipyard in Perama, near Athens, mostly building yachts and other pleasure craft from wood. When Tzalas first approached the younger Psaros about building a replica in the ancient way, shell-first, with mortises and tenons, Psaros thought it couldn't be done. But the more he listened to Tzalas discuss the idea, the more plausible it seemed. After all, if it was done two thousand years ago, we should be able to do it today, he reasoned.[1]

Once Tzalas got Psaros to agree to the project, he approached Michael Katzev. Displaced by the Cyprus war, the Katzevs wound up living in Athens, and Tzalas, a writer who penned articles about shipbuilding on the side, interviewed Katzev for a piece that would appear in a yachting magazine. By the questions Tzalas was asking, it was clear he was no weekend boater, but someone with a deep knowledge of wooden ship construction. Katzev had considered the idea of a full-scale replica years before. He and Dick had talked about it even as the reconstruction was underway in the early 1970s, and Dick had worked up a rough cost estimate as early as 1976—$35,000 for materials and labor at that time.[2] The Cyprus war and the expense, which would have taxed even Katzev's formidable fund-raising skills, caused them to shelve the project. Over the years, though, Katzev continued to look for wealthy Greek tycoons and others who might fund a project, and even discussed actually doing much of the labor with the original members of the excavation—Katzev, Dick, Robin Piercy, and Chip Vincent.[3] Still, when Tzalas first suggested the idea of a replica, Katzev was skeptical that he could pull it off. But Tzalas was determined. He continued to woo Katzev, taking him and Susan on an Aegean cruise out of Corfu. By the time they made port in Piraeus, Katzev realized that Tzalas wasn't some sort of amateur. He may have been an unlikely replica builder, but then, Katzev had a good record of assembling top talent from unlikely places. After all, he had once hired an electrician from Pennsylvania to reconstruct the oldest Greek ship ever found.

Before long, that former electrician was on his way to Perama to meet Tzalas and Psaros. "We needed to meet the man who really knew the ship," Tzalas said. "Michael was not a boat builder. I realized that as there were questions [about the construction], Michael would not be able to answer those questions."

Dick arrived in Perama with his usual low-key manner. For him, this was the ultimate research model. He had tried to recreate the original construction techniques on a smaller scale; now he would get to see them just as they had been done two millennia earlier. He would again be listening for the lessons of Aristides hearkening across the centuries, this time channeled through the handiwork of Manolis Psaros and his master shipwright, Michaelis Oikonomou.

The Psaros Shipyard was a startling contrast in old and new. Huge yachts were pulled ashore for maintenance, yet in one corner, Dick, Tzalas, and Psaros would revive the past. Neat stacks of wood sat beside giant band saws, and workers still used ancient tools such as an adze to shape those timbers into ships hulls. Many of the techniques used in building the original Kyrenia Ship, though, had been lost to the ages. In that corner of the shipyard, they would come back to life. Tzalas funded much of the construction costs himself. Psaros donated the materials at cost, only charging for his workers' labor. In exchange, the workers had to agree to build the ship using the old ways, by adhering to ancient techniques as strictly as possible. As his guide, Psaros would use Dick's lines drawings.

Psaros's boatyard quickly became a special place for Dick, where years of work and research were manifesting themselves before his eyes. It was agreed that Dick would oversee the construction process, offering scientific insights and weighing in with his thoughts on what techniques might have been used. He knew the ship better than anyone, but he didn't provide construction plans or dictate how Psaros should build the replica. Because Psaros's crew was working from his lines drawings, Dick knew they would uncover new lessons about his favorite ship. Just as he had encountered problems with his models and the reconstruction, he expected new ones to arise with the building of the replica. He wouldn't be disappointed. In fact, Dick's approach was to keep quiet and let those problems develop.

"He would often say 'let's hear what the boat builder has to say,'" Psaros recalled. "He wanted the opinion of people who were traditionally in the business." What developed was a back-and-forth relationship similar to the one between Dick and Sheila Matthews during the reconstruction of the Serçe Limani wreck. When Dick couldn't be there to oversee the process directly, Michael Katzev would go to the shipyard to record the progress. "For everyone involved, it was like a religious process of going back into the past," Psaros said. "The instructions we were getting from Dick Steffy were like the Bible. We believed that he knew where he was leading us."

It wasn't an easy journey, and the difficulties became apparent almost immediately. The first step, finding the wood, was among the biggest challenges. At the time, Dick and the Katzevs still believed the ship was made from aleppo pine, and that was the wood chosen for the replica as well. In ancient times, shipwrights looked for curved timbers and instructed woodsmen to fell a specific tree and haul it from the forest. Unlike pine trees common to North America, the pines of Greece grow erratically, curving and zigzagging. In Dick's imagination, the other trees may have laughed at Crooked Aleppo, but in the Greek forests of reality, the once-and-future keel would have lots of company. Psaros was determined to get only Aleppo pine from Samos, but in modern times, of course, shipwrights don't get to walk the forest and select their own wood. In fact, shipbuilders had stopped using curved timbers centuries ago. The only supplies he could find were all straight trees, yet almost all the wood on the Kyrenia Ship had been curved. He couldn't even begin until he found a curved keel, 10½ meters long. The replica's keel would be longer, thinner, and more curved than its modern counterparts, and it took three tries to find a piece that would work. Ancient shipbuilders didn't see keels as backbones of the ship, the way we do now. The strength of the hull came from the curvature of the shell, reinforced by the mortise-and-tenon joints, and the long curvature of the keel from stem to stern formed a kind of longitudinal box girder.

When Psaros finally found an acceptable piece of wood, he attempted to cut it to the proper curvature, but the process left the keel 2 centimeters—or three-quarters of an inch—too thin.[4] The cutting also changed the composition of the wood itself, narrowing the heartwood—the inner fibers that provided the greatest strength—at each end. Ancient shipbuilders didn't do it that way, and if the replica's keel were cut in such a manner, it probably wouldn't be strong enough, Dick cautioned.[5] He was still listening to the ship, to the whispers of Aristides, even if this was some new incarnation. He had an idea of how to solve the problem, but he waited to hear Psaros's solution before he said anything.

Psaros proposed wetting the wood and bending it by applying pressure from above and keeping that pressure in place until several rows of planking were installed. That, Dick replied with a sly smile, was exactly what he was thinking. Psaros was slowly learning that his family-run shipyard in Perama had become a laboratory, and he and his workers were as much a part of the experiment as the ship they were building. Dick may have drawn the plans, and he may have understood the Kyrenia Ship better than anyone, but he wasn't about to lead these modern shipwrights anywhere. He was waiting to see their mistakes and analyzing the setbacks they encountered. It was the same process he'd used in his basement ship models. Now, the basement had been replaced by the shipyard off a narrow road on the Perama waterfront.

Although Dick's lines drawings worked as a blueprint for the hull construction, it soon became clear that understanding the hull was just the beginning. Building a full-scale replica in the ancient way raised thousands of new questions, many of which had been little more than guessed at during the reconstruction in Kyrenia. As quickly as one problem seemed solved, another developed. For Dick, it was a familiar pattern: Solve one question and raise five more.

The first attempt at forging a keel failed. The second one was cut to the proper length and bent to the proper shape, but it became infested with insects, and in a matter of days the entire piece looked like Swiss cheese. The ancients would have coated the wood with red pitch to keep the bugs away, but Tzalas and Psaros opted to use a modern preservative—it would be more effective and look better—on the third attempt at setting the keel.[6]

Tzalas was adamant that all the construction be done in the open, even if it failed. He encouraged researchers to come and observe Psaros's work. He didn't want any accusations later that they had faked the techniques, and if they were going to deviate from the ancient ways, he wanted to be public about it. The entire process was an adjustment for Psaros and his chief boat builder, Oikonomou. Although they were used to building wooden vessels, the construction techniques had changed completely during the two millennia between the Kyrenia Ship's construction and the work now taking place in their shipyard. Ancient ship builders didn't work from plans, and while the modern craftsmen wanted to correct asymmetry in the hull, the shell-first construction method almost assured that the hull would not be symmetrical. Ironically, Dick had made the same mistake during his reconstruction, attempting to make the hull symmetrical before realizing the ship was, essentially, slightly lopsided. Dick's response was once again quiet patience. He understood the difficulty that Psaros and his crew were confronting in undertaking the replica. "Think how difficult it would be for modern builders to reproduce the Parthenon using only ancient tools and no modern machinery to put the pieces in place."[7]

One of the few things the modern builders shared with their ancient forebears was the ability to use an adze. In a corner of Psaros's shop, they used the ancient tool to shape frames. They cut wood by hand and hammered nails through the thick frames with sledgehammers. The copper nails, some three thousand of them, were hand-forged by a local artisan. However, none of the workers in the shipyard had ever worked with mortise-and-tenon joints. The tongues of the tenons had to line up precisely with the mortise grooves in the next piece of wood. Along a fifty-meter plank, with the tenons spaced about 12 centimeters apart, it proved an arduous task.

Rarely did Psaros ask for relief from the stricture of the experiment, but this time he did. Couldn't they use modern tools to cut the mortise grooves? Again, Dick understood the frustration. The purpose of the replica wasn't to study the cutting mortises, he said, so he gave Psaros permission to cut them with electric tools, one of the only concessions to modernity.

The closer the replica got to completion, the more questions arose. After all, although almost three-fourths of the Kyrenia hull had been recovered, that still left more than a quarter of it that was little more than an educated guess. Much of that was on the upper hull, which had rotted away on the original ship. Should the sides extend above the deck? If so, how far? The Kyrenia reconstruction in Cyprus couldn't answer those questions. What did the steering oars look like? One original oar was recovered with the upper part of the blade preserved, but it offered few clues for the handle that the captain used to steer the vessel. And what about the rigging? That would be largely hypothetical. The solutions to many of these problems were approximated, based on secondary evidence such as illustrations. Dick was excited about what he might learn from *Kyrenia II,* but saying it recreated the exact appearance of the original vessel was probably incorrect.[8]

Then there was caulking. No matter how well Psaros fit his mortise and tenon joints, the planks still had gaps between them. In some cases, sunlight shone through. The ship couldn't possibly stay afloat. Dick had insisted that he'd found no evidence of caulking, but if he knew how to solve this problem, he once again kept the answer to himself. Psaros was familiar with an ancient technique for building smaller boats that called for soaking the hull and allowing it to swell. The swelling wood would seal the gaps between the planking. No one knew if it would work, but one thing was clear: *Kyrenia II* would sink on her maiden voyage.

It wasn't the auspicious launch that Tzalas had planned. Athens had just been named the first "Cultural Capital of Europe," and its culture minister, the former film actress Melina Mercouri decided that *Kyrenia II*'s launch should coincide with the opening-day ceremonies on June 22, 1985. Tzalas was busy arranging military bands, folk dancers, priests who would provide blessings and a cadre of speech-giving dignitaries who would all be part of the festivities. Slipping the replica's hull into the water only to watch it sink like a leaky old garbage scow just wouldn't do.

Faced with the impending deadline and the need for *Kyrenia II* to quite literally make a splash while the whole country watched, Katzev and Psaros decided on a private launch to soak the hull before the public christening. Sure enough, almost as soon as they slipped her into the water, *Kyrenia II* began to leak, quickly sinking up to the bulwark. Psaros, though, noted she stayed upright and afloat, showing signs of buoyancy even as she was awash. After several days, they pumped the water from the hull and she rose proudly to the surface, her seams swelled tight. Like some nautical phoenix, the Kyrenia Ship was about to sail again.

But how would she be powered? Although the appearance of square-sailed rigging was known—it had been depicted on pottery and other artwork—no one knew from what material the sails were made. The same was true for the rope used in the rigging. "A shipwreck does not give you the sails, the rigging," Tzalas said. "A shipwreck is static. It's not made to be moved." And the whole point of *Kyrenia II* was for her to move.

Tzalas and Katzev decided not to sweat these details. Just as the purpose of the experiment wasn't to cut mortises, nor was it to determine the fabric used in sails. They had several options, including papyrus and animal skins, but they chose linen because it seemed more feasible. The trick was finding someone to make it. Linen sail makers had become as scarce as curved ships' timbers. Katzev discovered that the *Mayflower* replica in Plymouth, Massachusetts, had a linen sail that had been bought from the British Royal Navy. Katzev contacted them and managed to secure a piece of the surplus, since *Kyrenia II*'s sail would be much smaller than the one used for the Pilgrim's transport.

And so it went. Ancient texts showed the top of the mast was covered with a hyena skin, but Tzalas had no intention of slaying a hyena in the name of authenticity. Should the lead sheeting be added to the exterior of the hull? The Kyrenia Ship was sheathed in lead when she sank, but that would increase the ship's weight by 5 tons. Because the lead wasn't added to the original hull until later in its sailing life, they decided that too could be foregone.

Even the crew had to be selected with care. Tzalas was determined to find a four-man crew who would sail *Kyrenia II* in the ancient way, just as she had been built. He interviewed as many as one hundred volunteers, but just as Psaros's shipbuilders had to get used to leaving technology behind and learning the ancient ways, so did the prospective sailors. "Everyone wanted to improve the sailing capabilities of that ship," Tzalas said. "Everyone wanted to go faster." Eventually, they found a four-man crew that agreed to forget everything they knew of modern sailing and operate the ship as it had been in 300 B.C. After three years of work, the modern interpretation of the ancient ship of Kyrenia was ready to take to the water again.

On June 22, 1985—almost three years after construction began—amid fanfare that included three attempts by Greece's culture minister to christen the hull by breaking a champagne bottle over her bow, *Kyrenia II* officially resumed the voyage that her predecessor had been unable to complete twenty-three centuries earlier. Made almost entirely with hand tools and containing eight thousand mortises, four thousand hand-carved tenons, eight thousand wooden pegs and nails made of pure copper and driven by hand, *Kyrenia II* brought to life the wonders of ancient shipbuilding.[9] After undergoing sea trials, she eventually sailed the Aegean, returning to Cyprus, though not Kyrenia. She entered the port of Paphos, on the island's southern side, but because of the division of Cyprus following the war in 1974, she would never ply the waters of Kyrenia harbor.

For more than a decade, *Kyrenia II* served as a nautical goodwill ambassador, journeying throughout the Mediterranean. She participated in the procession of ships in New York Harbor to celebrate the centennial of the Statue of Liberty. She visited Australia and Japan, where another replica, *Kyrenia III,* was later produced using modern building techniques. Eventually, Harry Tzalas donated *Kyrenia II* as the centerpiece for the Thalassa Museum of the Sea in the resort town of Ayia Napa, near Larnaca in southern Cyprus.

The many voyages of the *Kyrenia II* provided Dick with more data on how the ship sailed, but his understanding of the ancient vessel was still incomplete. Despite having reconstructed the original hull and overseeing the construction and sailing of a modern replica, the Kyrenia Ship still held many mysteries, and the man who knew her best continued to work on unlocking them. After Lucille's death, as he finished his textbook, he reviewed many of the questions the *Kyrenia II* had raised that he'd been unable to answer. One of the most vexing: How much cargo was the Kyrenia Ship carrying when she sank?

Early estimates from the excavation in 1968 put the number of amphoras at more than three hundred, with possibly another two hundred that had yet to be raised. That number later shrank to a little more than four hundred in total. *Kyrenia II* was a study in shipbuilding, designed to examine the seaworthiness of the hull. Only about fifty amphoras were ever loaded aboard, and Tzalas, Katzev and Dick all knew that the replica rode higher in the water than the original ship had when she sank.

The amphora count bothered Tzalas in particular. Four hundred amphoras simply wouldn't fit in the hold of *Kyrenia II*. In fact, if the original ship's captain had taken on anywhere close to four hundred amphoras—even if some were empty—plus the millstones, almonds and iron ingots, the ship would have been so overloaded that a good wave would have capsized her. Could this have caused the sinking, rather than Katzev's theory of a pirate attack? Could pirates have even gotten to the bottom of the hull to scuttle her if she were overflowing with amphoras? Dick had always had his doubts.[10] Any evidence of it was lost in the missing section of the starboard bow, the area where pirates may have broken through the ship's hull planking to disable her.

One explanation for the lack of cargo capacity was that the hull was simply too narrow. Perhaps Dick had miscalculated; perhaps it should have been bulkier. But between the lines drawings, the models, and the physical reconstruction, Dick was certain the ship would have told him long ago if he'd made such a major error. Part of what made the Kyrenia Ship such a unique find was that she had been in service for many years, perhaps several decades, and she had been repaired. The lead sheathing was added to protect the hull from teredo worms, and the hull had been completely overhauled more than once and the mast moved forward. When *Kyrenia II* was built, Dick and Tzalas agreed to pick a period in the ship's life when she was still fairly young, before many of the repairs. Even so, Dick and Psaros debated the depth of the hull. Ultimately, they agreed that the hull should extend two planks above the existing remains in the Kyrenia Castle. They could debate the height of the sides, but the overall shape of the hull was clear from the reconstruction.

The discrepancy, then, may have been with the amphoras themselves. How they were stacked in a ship's hold was little more than speculation. Another possibility: what if they were empty? Almonds had been found in some of them, but many others were believed to have carried wine, cargo long ago released to the sea. Perhaps, instead, the Kyrenia Ship was simply hauling empty containers.

By the time these questions were being discussed, however, *Kyrenia II* had been retired to the museum in southern Cyprus. What was needed was another replica. In 2002, Glafkos Cariolou, the son of the sponge diver who originally found the ship in 1965 and who died in 1977, began building another ship. *Kerynia Liberty*—"Kerynia" being closer to the ancient spelling for the town—was constructed using modern techniques but following Dick's lines drawings, just as *Kyrenia II* had. *Kerynia Liberty* was built in Cyprus, using modern nails and bolts. The frames had different spacing from the original, and the hull wasn't sealed by sinking it and allowing the wood to swell. The gaps between the planks were sealed with caulking. The finished product was another close approximation to the original ship, and it was primarily designed to promote Cypriot tourism. This second sea-going replica gained international attention when it carried from Cyprus to Athens copper from which medals for the 2004 Olympics were forged.

Kerynia Liberty's sturdy modern construction also made it ideal for seeking answers to some of the nagging questions regarding the original ship's cargo. Michael Katzev died suddenly of a stroke in 2001, and in the wake of his death, Susan vowed to complete the final study of the Kyrenia Ship. Unlike with *Kyrenia II,* she would provide the new replica with a full complement of amphoras, made to conform precisely to ancient specifications of size and weight. By the time the sea tests began, *Kerynia Liberty* carried a cargo that was as heavy as the one borne in 300 B.C., based on the best estimates of the original cargo, including the wine in the amphoras, the iron ingots and the millstones, which were also recreated. The results were stunning.

The ship, as presented by Dick's original lines drawings, would have been dangerously overloaded had it sailed with the cargo that was found covering the hull on the sea floor. "It was pretty clear to Dick that somewhere there had been a miscalculation in the height of the ship, and that the original ship, the ship that sank, had to have been higher," Susan Katzev said.

What had he missed? How, three decades after he completed the reconstruction, had he failed to understand the messages that Aristides had sent him? It was as if he were back in the castle once again, the shadows of the Crusader hall extending around him as he struggled to understand. His old friend seemed to be laughing at him once more. Modern man, indeed. Dick was certain that his earlier calculations of the basic dimensions were correct. He had rechecked everything he'd done in Cyprus before *Kyrenia II* was built, and again after she had retired, as he prepared his textbook. Somewhere in the giant jigsaw puzzle of ancient technology, he was missing a clue.

By then, in 2004, Dick was eighty years old. Mounting health issues made it difficult to travel, but he never stopped thinking about the ship. It was still trying to tell him something, something he'd missed in all his years of study. He went over each of the fragments again, reviewing the questions he'd never been able to answer after all the years of study. There was the curious shift of the mast step—it had been turned around and moved forward about 30 centimeters later in the ship's life. The step had what seemed to be an extra notch that never fit properly. Then there were the frames. Some of them never seemed to align quite right on their upper ends, yet the lower sections, nearest the keel, fit perfectly. The upper ends had shims and wedges, a seemingly shoddy bit of workmanship for Aristides, the man of pride.

In some ways, this newest puzzle from the past was like a tonic for his health issues. He might not have been able to travel, but by late 2005, he was still plugging away on his Kyrenia Ship research, still adding to his database of ship data, and he had begun developing a new system for on-site recording and research that would streamline the Steffy Method for future generations of reconstructors. At the same time, he became fascinated by signs that the ancients may have used mathematics in their designs in ways scholars never thought possible. The kid who flunked high school math was now pouring over mathematics texts and collaborating with his longtime friend and scholar Patrice Pomey to trace the origins of geometry in shipbuilding.

But it was the recurring whispers from Aristides, once again beckoning across the ages, that would keep him going. The mystery was never far from his mind. He kept reviewing the clues—the amphoras, the mast step, the frames. Were they all related? What was the ship, his oldest friend, trying to tell him? The answer would come to him in the most unlikely of places.

15 : THE VOYAGE ENDS

I didn't notice the end when it began. Looking back on my father's final years, I'm stunned and embarrassed by my obliviousness. Perhaps that is the lament of all children who watch their parents slowly descend into death. We do not want to confront the truth, and then once it's forced upon us, we question why we didn't recognize it sooner. What might I have done? Even after the time that's passed, I still wrestle with the ghosts of regret.

In truth, my failure to see or accept what was happening was fueled by my father's quiet obstinacy about his health and by his overarching desire not to burden his children with his problems. His health had been slipping for more than a decade. When I was growing up, he'd seemed like a medical wonder. He ate what he wanted and never gained weight, always a steady 165 pounds. During his years in the electrical business, when the work was long and physical and done six days a week, his biceps bulged from the daily workout of earning a simple living. His smoking habit, begun after entering the Navy as a teenager, continued until retirement, but even that seem to leave him unaffected. Compared with my mother, whose health was always fragile and interfered with ordinary activities, my father seemed to me like some modern, gentle Hercules.

Perhaps I chose to be blind to the effects of age. In the early 1990s, he visited my wife and me in the Dallas area, as we moved from one suburb to another. I'd decided to move everything myself, and though my father offered to help, I noticed he quickly got out of breath and couldn't carry as much as he used to. He was seventy by then, but still active and traveling widely.

My mother's death, however, had been a wake-up call. He no longer took his health for granted. The first problems were with his heart. He became dizzy while driving, and because he was near a hospital, he pulled into the emergency room. After a series of tests, doctors found several arteries almost blocked, and he underwent a quintuple bypass. He handled it with his usual nonchalant demeanor. With a shrug, he said years of Pennsylvania Dutch cooking had finally caught up with him. As he went through the surgery, I was overcome by a painful déjà vu. He was having heart surgery, as my mother had, in the same unit of the same hospital. Now, I was the one sitting in fearful reverie in the waiting room, spending hours tracing the patterns of the wallpaper with my eyes, unable to concentrate, as I awaited the next five-minute visit in the intensive care unit.

He recovered from that surgery, surprisingly, as if nothing had happened. He resumed regular walks in College Station's only shopping mall, logging as much as 3 miles a day. On a follow-up visit, though, a heart specialist made passing reference to his emphysema. I interrupted him and made him repeat what he had said. "Yeah," my father said with a nod, as if he were surprised by my surprise. I was shocked only because my father hadn't told me. After fifty years of smoking, the diagnosis wasn't surprising, and yet it was one more blow to my vision of my father as Hercules.

The heart problems were followed a few years later by a bout with prostate cancer, which again my father weathered as if he were dashing through the rain to catch a bus—a minor inconvenience, but nothing that slowed him noticeably. He continued his research, working on the massive database of shipwreck information, and he continued to publish on a regular basis. He traveled to Venice and Turkey and other old haunts, but as the years wore on, he had several bouts with pneumonia, to which he'd grown susceptible because of the emphysema. Traveling became more difficult.

In 2001, he wrote a letter to my brother and me, telling us that the doctors had found his lungs were severely and irreversibly damaged. He talked to us almost weekly by phone, and the letter was an odd formality that drove home the seriousness, even though its tone was upbeat. "I do not want you to be concerned about this because I am certainly not going to let it bother me," he wrote. "In a nutshell, I have a problem but I am not surrendering."[1] I called him, and he deflected my concerns with his usual good-natured chuckle. He just thought we should know. "Well," I said slowly, "is this degenerative? Is it going to get worse?"

"I don't know," he said. "I didn't ask about that."

My father came from a family that didn't talk about their ailments. His parents were more bothered by complaints than aches and pains.

Sometimes their silence was maddening, and other times, downright unfathomable. I suspected my father had in fact been told whether his lungs would get worse, but he chose to keep that to himself. My brother and I referred to this process as the "Dad Filter." My father was self-sufficient and through his final days remained mentally alert, so we didn't pry. We tried to respect his privacy.

And so it went. For a good four years, my father had occasional bouts of pneumonia, and he'd cut back on travel, even on trips to Virginia to see my brother's family. But each week, on the phone, he gave us up-dates about how far he'd walked and how well he was doing compared with some of the other people his age that he knew. This happens when you get old, he would say.

In the spring of 2006, what had been a slow decline accelerated. At home one morning, my father felt tightness in his chest, and he buckled over in pain. It took me several weeks to get the full account of what had happened from him. He called 911, and a few minutes later, the doorbell rang. Thinking it was the ambulance and unable to stand, he crawled to answer the door. In the doorway stood a UPS driver delivering ink cartridges for his computer printer. My father quickly assured the driver he was fine, signed for the cartridges, and proceeded to sit on the floor and wait for the ambulance. He needed the cartridges, he explained later when I asked what he was thinking.

He spent eight days in intensive care with heart arrhythmia. Though I visited him, he shooed me away. He was fine. There was nothing I could do. I should go home to my family. The Dad Filter was running at full tilt. My father, like his parents before him, refused to inconvenience any-one, even a package delivery driver, at a moment of crisis. His mother, Zoe, when she was well into her seventies, would insist on waiting in the snow for her ride to church, rather than standing just inside the door in the warmth. If someone were kind enough to give her a ride, she didn't want to keep that person waiting. Even for a few seconds. Even if she'd been a member of the church for sixty years and was so well regarded in town that almost anyone would have carried her to church on their backs.

Certainly, then, my father was not going to inconvenience his own family. He didn't want us to worry, and he didn't want to interfere with our lives. Besides, he knew it was a busy time for me. The fallen leaders of Enron, Ken Lay and Jeffrey Skilling, were on trial, and for the *Houston Chronicle* it was the story of the year. As the business columnist, I sat in court every day, blogging and writing about the proceedings. During brief recesses, I called the ICU on my cell phone from the hallway of the courthouse, checking in with my father twice a day. My brother would call too, and at night we'd compare notes by e-mail, looking for clues that had slipped through the Dad Filter.

To outsiders, even to the medical professionals involved with his care, it probably seemed crazy. They, however, didn't understand my father's insistence that he would not be a burden on anyone, even in intensive care. Some of the doctors questioned me about his living alone, but none said directly that he shouldn't. You don't realize, I told them, how important his independence is and how much he wants to get back to work. The ships—especially the Kyrenia Ship—still called to him.

During his eight-day stay in ICU, he had an unexpected visitor: Aristides. Laid up in bed, unable to even read, he began thinking about "his" ship, his greatest accomplishment. He'd been looking over his old lines drawings just before he'd been rushed to the hospital, and, of course, he knew every splinter of the hull better than he knew his own house. All the hours of study had etched them in his mind, and he could see her lines as clearly as if he were standing in front of her. In his mind, he was in the castle again, studying that long graceful arc of the hull.

And suddenly, he knew. In one flash of epiphany, thirty years of nagging details aligned to reveal the answer. The amphoras were the key. For years, Dick had teased archaeologists like George Bass about their fascination with pottery, about how they missed the most important part of a ship—the wood. How ironic, then, that it would be the clay jars and other cargo that revealed one of the more startling discoveries to come out of the Kyrenia Ship. With only the beeps of the heart monitors and medicine dispensers to herald the revelation, he lay between the bed rails while his mind raced. The Kyrenia Ship, his oldest friend, was actually *two* ships. The hull had been modified, most likely by reusing timbers from another vessel. Some later craftsman had taken Aristides' handiwork and modified it, much as the boat builder on the Sea of Galilee, only with better tools and skills. In a way, it seemed so obvious, and yet, in the study of shipwrecks, it was unprecedented. No wreck had ever yielded enough data to show signs of such major overhaul. But that *had* to be the answer. Sometime, probably in the ship's later years, someone had raised the sides of the hull.

Dick returned home like a man reborn and immediately went to work on a new set of drawings. He set up a drafting table in the living room, and the dining table, so rarely used for dining over the years, once again became a storage area for ship plans. Suddenly, everything made sense. Those sloppy upper frames weren't the work of Aristides at all. Years later, someone had come along and extended them, giving support to additional planks. The ancient repairman had tried to reshape them, but they didn't fit properly, and that explained the shims and wedges. Then there were those bizarre cuts in the floor planking around frame forty. It had bothered him for years. Why had it been done? The central portion of the flooring over the keel and along the bilge lines had been cut away. That meant the low point of the hull had been changed, moved forward from under the aft cabin to just below the mast step. The low point of the hull was where water collected, and the crew had to have access to it so they could routinely bail the water out. With the low point moved forward, the flooring had been cut away to allow access to the bilge. That also explained the extra notch in the mast step. It too had been moved forward. "Originally, she had been designed as a lighter ship, capable of carrying less cargo than she was eventually carrying when she sank," Laina Swiny said.

The work brought with it a new vigor, an energy that rivaled the old days. For months, it seemed as if he had made a remarkable recovery, and he talked about his findings like a schoolboy talking about the new girl in class. When he spoke of the ship and his epiphany, his eyes glinted with their familiar twinkle.

Though it may seem routine or even logical in modern times, ancient shipbuilders tended to favor craftsmanship over pragmatism. Wooden ships of the time lasted little more than a decade, according to the common wisdom. If they broke, if they sprung a leak, perhaps the ancient mariners simply scuttled them and built anew. No shipwreck had revealed evidence of a hull being, essentially, bulked up and adapted to a different purpose. The Kyrenia Ship proved once again she was no routine wreck. From within her limestone chamber in Cyprus she had sent a message to a hospital room in Bryan, Texas, revealing more details that would cause yet another review of the Kyrenia Ship reconstruction. Now my father had the chance to learn not just how the ancient Greeks built ships, but how they altered them. Artisans to the end, the changes were so good, the clues so scant, it had taken the ancient vessel's surrogate shipwright more than thirty years of listening to hear what the ship was telling him.

Although the energy of his discovery propelled him, even my father's passion couldn't override the effects of his declining health. As quickly as he had seemed to rebound, he began to slide again. By Thanksgiving, we were worried. His breathing was labored, he'd been losing weight, and he seemed to lack the stamina he'd had just months earlier. But his good humor remained, and he assured us he was fine. The Dad Filter was working overtime, and not just for family members. Susan Katzev and Laina Swiny, sharing the excitement of the new discovery, were working in Maine and calling frequently to share ideas with him.

"I didn't want him to be sick," Swiny said. "I didn't want to see it. We were so involved in this. He was extremely good at hiding it. We'd call him up on the phone. We'd discover something and we'd say, 'We've got to get Dick's opinion,' and he'd say, 'Yes, yes—I'll look into it.' And his heart was totally into it."

But by November, he was unable to do any drafting. His hands weren't steady enough, and he didn't have the stamina to stand at the table. None of us, though, caught on right away. I was so used to seeing ship's drawings spilling across the dining room table that when I'd visit, I assumed the ink on them was fresh. A few days after New Year's, my mother-in-law paid him a visit. My in-laws and my father had become good friends in the years since my mother died, and that bond would prove vital in my father's final months. He wound up back in the hospital, although the diagnosis was vague. His breathing became more difficult, his heartbeat irregular. He stayed there for almost a month, and when he was released, his lung specialist urged me to consider a nursing home.

My father wouldn't hear of it. He had plans to get back to work, and the only place to do that was at home. He reminded me of the research library in his study, of the ship plans on the table, of the drafting board in the living room upon which his latest Kyrenia Ship drawings remained half finished. Still shrouded in my own denial, I dismissed the doctor's concerns. He didn't understand my father and his need to be productive. I compromised. We opted for around-the-clock in-home care.

It seemed the perfect solution, but it didn't work. He was supposed to move around, to walk about the house and sit at the table for meals, but he wouldn't. He began to make excuses, like a teenager avoiding homework. Because I lived only an hour and a half away, I was making trips to his house most weekends. My brother, who lived in Virginia and traveled frequently, came when he could. I spent hours sitting in a chair near my father's bed, talking with him, spending more time with him than I had since I was a young boy. In some ways, it reminded me of my childhood, of those nights in Kyrenia when he would come home from the castle, sit beside me on the couch, and read *Crooked Aleppo.* I could almost feel—perhaps I desperately wanted to feel—the sea breeze on the back of my neck.

I cherished the conversations but dreaded the reason for them. I knew he was dying, but I refused to acknowledge it. The ship plans, still on the dining room table, remained untouched. Some were carelessly pushed aside by the care givers who needed a place to set things and who obviously had never seen the inside of a ship lab.

In his study, I kept piling the mail on his desk. When I would take it to him, he'd tell me he would look at it later, but he never did. He grew weaker, eating less and less. Even the physical therapists couldn't get him out of bed. Still, I embraced my own denial. I sorted the mail into piles and paid the bills, but the stack for him to review continued to grow. I threw out the junk mail, but kept the pile of letters from colleagues and other seemingly important correspondence. It became a monument to my emotional blindness. My father wasn't going to get better. If he stayed at home, he might never get out of his bed, and the ship plans, like the monument of mail, would remain as he left them.

After three months of close calls and general apprehension, my father was back in the hospital and the pulmonologist was more emphatic. He wouldn't release my father until I agreed to move him to a nursing home. By then, my denial had crumbled under the weight of my own anxiety and fear. The Dad Filter had long since broken down. I had seen my father—Hercules with the bulging biceps, the handyman who could fix anything, the quiet genius who did what no one else in the world did—afraid.

He was scared by his own frailty and frightened by the uncertainty beyond the edge of the bed. There had been moments when our roles reversed, when I was the parent and he the child, frightened and helpless. He looked to me for comfort, for reassurance, for the decisions he seemed no longer able to make. I kept trying to push those decisions back on him, telling myself I was fighting for him to keep control of his life. But I was fighting myself, unable to face the truth that had been bedridden in front of me for weeks. My father was now dependent on me. We both knew it, but years of his refusal to be a burden prevented either of us from saying it.

One decision, however, he made easy for me. Before I could tell him about the nursing home, he told me he didn't want to go home again. My brother and I found him a nice place with a private room. We got him a high-speed Internet connection, and Wayne Smith, a colleague from the nautical program who was working on a virtual reality program to show how the Kyrenia Ship broke apart when she sank, brought him a laptop computer. For a few months, he again had a remarkable resurgence. He ate better; his strength returned; he got out of bed and even walked with assistance. He began again thinking about ships. He talked with old colleagues on the phone, and students from the university came to see him. He even talked about collaborating on one more publication.

"I am becoming much stronger and feeling a lot better, although I will be confined to a wheelchair for the rest of my life," he wrote to Susan Katzev. He was anxious for Smith's program to be completed. "I can hardly wait to see a ten-thousand-piece Kyrenia Ship dissipate into six thousand pieces on the seabed."[2] We sold the three-bedroom "dream house" he and my mother had built soon after I left home, and he directed the removal of his library and research to the nautical program, telling Katzev that once that was done, "I hope to begin working on Kyrenia once again."[3]

As the months wore on, the peaks in activity grew shorter and the valleys of decline grew deeper. As the doctors came to his room, they would see the pictures I'd hung on the walls, one of Kyrenia Harbor as it was in the early 1970s, the other of my father rebuilding the ship. They would get him talking again about that magical vessel, the one that had transformed our lives.

The ship was always there, even in the final days, from her sturdy keel—Crooked Aleppo—to the ragged edges of her ancient reassembled hull. She was a presence in that tiny room just as much as she had been in our lives for more than thirty years. My father never stopped thinking about her, and I wondered later, after I'd discovered the essay in which he referred to Aristides, if the ghost of the old shipwright wasn't there too, looking over his friend as he prepared for his final voyage.

My father bristled at not being productive or, as he liked to put it, at "not being worth anything to anybody." He never understood—or at least he underestimated—the value of his own presence. Even in his final days, nurses would come to his room and watch football with him on Sunday afternoons. He was a favorite patient, amusing the staff with his good-natured heckling. My father's good humor and humility, even amid great pain, continued to enthrall.

In early November, his health failing, he still managed to receive a busload of colleagues, including old friends such as Patrice Pomey and Lucien Basch from Europe, who were in town attending a conference. Susan Katzev had arrived a few days early, waiting for the right time, when Dick would feel strong enough to see her. When she entered his room, she found him prepared for the visit. He was sitting upright in his bed, the deep creases of his face framing eyes that still sparkled. The small talk was upbeat—TV, football, and his hopes for a student project involving the Kyrenia Ship. As talk turned to the ancient hull, Susan pumped him for his latest thoughts, which he'd been too weak to type in e-mails. "He had anticipated all my questions and presented me with a red spiral notebook with his handwritten answers, telling me this humble merchant ship was by far his favorite of all the ships he had dealt with and that he foresees it giving up many more secrets to those who will study her in generations to come."[4] Rather than a single scholar like himself working alone to crack the ship's secrets, Dick envisioned a renewed team effort, using the latest in scientific analysis and computer imaging. "Our old vessel has a lot of secrets to unlock," he told her.[5]

When the end came, it came quickly, though not surprisingly. He'd had a series of late-night trips to the emergency room, and after the third one it became clear there was nothing more that could be done. The biceps that once seemed to me as if they could lift the world were now thin as twigs. An oxygen tube was ever present and when he did get out of bed, he was upright only long enough to swing into a wheelchair.

My wife, our kids, and her family took him Thanksgiving dinner at the nursing home. We watched football, but he returned to bed exhausted. I stayed through the weekend, but he shooed me back to Houston with his usual pronouncements about work and family. Two days later, I got a call from a hospice worker. I'd better come back as soon as possible. He'd taken a turn for the worse. I filed my column and left, racing through the darkness of the back roads that had become uncomfortably familiar. When I arrived, he could barely speak. Each word was a whisper, each syllable an exertion. He told me, as he always did, that I didn't need to be there, but it was half-hearted. For the first time, I felt he didn't want me to leave.

The next morning, George Bass and Cemal Pulak, his former teaching assistant, paid a visit. Pulak had just returned from Turkey, where his team was working on an amazing find uncovered in the Yenikapi neighborhood of modern Istanbul. While digging a tunnel for a subway line between Europe and Asia, construction crews uncovered the ancient harbor of Theodosius, one of Constantinople's trading ports.[6] Pulak was excavating two Byzantine galleys from the tenth century. For years, archaeologists had debated the spacing of the oars on such vessels, but because the bulwarks and upper hull portions of wrecks rarely survived the ages, no one knew for sure how much room the Byzantines left for their rowers.

Galleys, by their nature, are long, powerful ships, but their design came with certain compromises. Allow too much room for the rowers and the hull would sag in the middle under the weight of the oarsmen. Squeeze the rowers in too closely to strengthen the hull and the oarsmen couldn't get their full stroke, leaving the vessel underpowered. A replica of a Greek trireme, or three-tiered galley, had shown that an earlier estimate that the oars were 88 centimeters apart wasn't right. The ship couldn't reach the speed to which galleys were believed to have traveled.

The Theodosius galleys hadn't been rotting on the seabed; they'd been preserved on land, much like the Sea of Galilee boat. The hulls were preserved to the bulwark, providing the first proof of oar spacing— about 95 centimeters. It was a unique and exciting discovery, and Pulak could barely contain his enthusiasm as he recounted it. I looked at my father. Was it too much for him? Would it exhaust him?

I saw something I hadn't seen in weeks. The old glimmer in his hazel eyes, the excitement of hearing about ships. A faint smile crept across his face. After they left, he uttered his final three words, so barely audible I had to put my ear almost on his lips: "That was nice."

He drifted off after that, and although he lived until the early hours of the next morning, he never regained consciousness. His final waking moments had been spent with Bass—the man who had enabled the dream, who'd opened the door to opportunity—and with Pulak, who's among the next generation of nautical archaeologists my father helped train. They stood before his bed, talking of the newest discovery from the ancient world that would bring the past a little closer to the present, unpacking another piece of the cargo of knowledge, talking of ships until the end.

As we filed out of the funeral home, my oldest son, Ben, turned to me. "Dad," he said, "we really should go to Cyprus." He'd just heard some of the tributes to his grandfather, including one from Susan Katzev, read by Laina Swiny, and he was both surprised and proud that people came from as far away as Israel to attend the service. He'd grown up hearing stories of Kyrenia and seeing pictures of the ship, but he'd never seen her in person. For that matter, *I'd* never seen the completed reconstruction. He was right. We needed to go. For years, I'd toyed with the idea of returning to Kyrenia, but the political situation made it difficult. I wasn't sure I wanted to take my children when they were young, yet it didn't seem right to go without them. Now, they were older and the political divide on Cyprus more stable. I did a little checking and was assured that crossing the "green line" into the Turkish side of the island, a "country" unrecognized by the international community, was safe.

As the plane landed in Larnaca, I was unsure what to expect. I realized I was returning to an island of ghosts, reliving my memories of a place and a time long gone. Yet by the time we got to Kyrenia and stood before the ship, time and doubts melted away. She remains displayed in all her splendor, one of the sea's greatest puzzles, solved by a small-town electrician.

I found myself thinking of my indecision as a teenager, unsure what I wanted to do with my life and debating whether I should even bother going to college. My father tried to persuade me, and I quickly pointed out that he hadn't gone to college, and everything had worked out. It had, he acknowledged, but it hadn't been easy. He hadn't done himself any favors. Later, after winning the MacArthur grant and with his new career well established, he reflected on that struggle, on those difficult years of transition from electrician to ancient ship reconstructor. It had, indeed, worked out fabulously well. "Perhaps," he wrote to a former student, "it has been better this way, since I worked harder and enjoyed it more in trying to make up for lost time."[1]

A few days after my father's death, I was going through some things that I had brought from his house months earlier. I found an old steno notebook with a few pages left in it. I looked at the faded beige cover and smiled. It had various titles crossed out from different projects over the years: "Notes from Catalog K-S," "Defence Info" (a reference to the summer project in Maine) and "4/75." Embossed on the cover were the words "Evangelismos Bookshop Famagusta," Cyprus. Three decades old, my father kept reusing the notebook as long as it had pages in it. I smiled the way you do when grief suddenly mingles with fond memories. I flipped open the cover. Scrawled at the top of the first page was once sentence: "Predict the KS will be revealing secrets for many years to come."

It was probably the last thing he wrote about his beloved ship. It was his introduction of Aristides to future generations. Others are already building on his latest discoveries, finding evidence of additional repairs and modifications made to the hull. If my father read ships' hulls like a newspaper, as Shelley Wachsmann so eloquently put it, then the Kyrenia Ship is his encyclopedia, a tome exemplifying his greatest discoveries, now preserved amid its ancient fragments.

As I stare down the length of the hull, I can't help but think of the career that flowed from the ancient planks and frames, and the impact it had around the world. Dozens of former students now lead projects in countries as far-flung as Egypt, Sweden, and Australia, and they are recognized the world over as being some of the best at what they do.[2] A world of friendships endure too. The following fall, on the Greek island of Hydra—Dick's favorite—his friend Harry Tzalas convened a conference in Dick's honor attended by ship scholars from around the globe. Likewise, signs of my father's achievements can be found from the eastern Mediterranean to the plains of central Texas.

About a month after his death, on January 1, 2008, Cyprus officially adopted the euro as its currency. Of the eight new coins minted, three bear the image of the Kyrenia Ship, immortalizing his work and linking the island's past to the present. In Turkey, in the Byzantine chapel at the center of Bodrum's castle, a half model of the seventh-century ship from Yassi Ada is on display, one of the few models that my father didn't destroy in the course of his research. He finally finished it almost two decades after he'd first written to Bass in 1964.

At Texas A&M, his long-time friend and colleague George Bass erected a plaque outside the ship lab naming it in Dick's honor. INA announced the J. Richard Steffy Scholarship, giving support to future students in the name of a man who never went to college himself. It's an enduring testament to the message of my father's life: Sometimes, the best ideas come from the most unlikely places. Sometimes, they start in a landlocked town, with some scrap paper and homemade glue.

"In my memory, I see that boy, my big brother, on the floor of our Denver home, cutting from paper the parts of ships and fitting them together, gluing them with flour paste," his sister, Muriel, wrote. "He certainly did fulfill the dream of his life."[3]

Now I stand once again before that dream, before the rebuilt hull of the Kyrenia Ship, and I ponder the course of my father's life from that corner of Main Street in tiny Denver, Pennsylvania, to a Crusader castle half a world away. I think of his improbable journey that led him to the thoughts of a shipwright who lived more than two thousand years ago and from there to a professorship in Texas in a field that he created from his own mind. Near the bow, Laina Swiny is explaining my father's accomplishment to his grandchildren, telling them about his ability to transform the flattened remains into the three-dimensional reconstruction before them. As we're getting ready to leave, my daughter tells me she can feel his presence in the room, and she's right. We all feel it.

If, as John Steinbeck once said, the relationship between men and boats is unique among inanimate objects, if the building of ships results in the ship receiving "a man-shaped soul,"[4] then a piece of my father's soul resides here among the timbers of his favorite hull.

As we turn to leave, I take one last glance down the worm-eaten surface of the keel, wiggling, detached, underneath the hull. Good-bye, Crooked Aleppo.

ACKNOWLEDGMENTS

The list of people without whom this project wouldn't have happened is long enough to be a book unto itself. My gratitude begins with my wife, Laurie, who was a constant source of encouragement, support, and tolerance, and my children, Ben, Daniel, and Annie, who put up with a father who spent too many weekends hunched over a keyboard or traveling to places like Greece and Turkey without them.

Special thanks must also be given posthumously to my mother, Lucille Steffy, whose natural secretarial skills resulted in boxes of well-organized documents that preserved vital research material years after her death.

My brother, David, my aunt, Muriel Steffy Lipp, and my uncle, Milt Steffy, all graciously shared personal insights and memories and reviewed the manuscript.

The Institute of Nautical Archaeology has been generous in opening its archives and supporting this project from the beginning, thanks to its former and current presidents, James Delgado and Deborah Carlson.

Shelley Wachsmann gave not only his time and some rare recordings of my father discussing his work, but also provided the impetus for this book to find a publisher. Fred van Doorninck provided insights into the early days of nautical archaeology and his collaborations with my father.

George Bass deserves special mention, not just for the time he took to assist with this effort, but for taking the time to listen to an amateur ship modeler those many years ago. Without him, none of this would have been possible.

Laina Swiny offered her memories and insights into my father's work and provided my family with a VIP tour of the Kyrenia Ship during our visit to Cyprus in 2008. It was there, in the shadow of Crooked Aleppo, that this project began, though I didn't fully realize it at the time.

Amid the sharing of many fond memories and some amazing lobster Newburg, Susan Katzev put up with me digging through her well-organized files for a weekend and draining her printer ink. Later she spent hours scouring the manuscript to ensure the ship details were correct.

The cooperation, insights, hospitality, and translation skills of Harry Tzalas also were invaluable. Both he and Manolis Psaros took time away from their businesses to help me understand construction of *Kyrenia II*.

I must offer special acknowledgment to Wayne Smith, who provided hours of unsolicited support and friendship to my father in his final years. His careful transport of my father's files to the INA archives ensured the records needed for this project were preserved.

I also want to thank those who took time to field phone calls, sit through interviews, or respond to my pestering e-mails: Maureen Atwell, Beth Braznell, Vaughn Bryant, Kevin Crisman, Fred Hocker, Paul Johnston, Gregg Kreutz, Cemal Pulak, and Cheryl Ward.

I am indebted to friends in the Bodrum area. Robin Piercy dug through reams of old files and gigabytes of digital photos, and he and his wife, Sula, were wonderful hosts. Don and Suzanna Frey showed me Bodrum as only they can. I appreciate Sheila Matthews's willingness to spend hours with me despite a hectic travel schedule.

My time in Bodrum was made more enjoyable by Maya and Omer, who were more than just hotel managers. Omer, in particular, shuttled me all over the Bodum area, and I appreciate all his help. I also must compliment their boss, Malone Mitchell, for the delightful accommodations.

Dick Jefferis provided some vital fact checking on the USS *Wyffels*.

I am grateful to my editors at the Houston Chronicle—Jeff Cohen, George Haj, and Laura Goldberg—who were flexible and understanding in allowing me to juggle this project with my column-writing duties. I appreciate the support of numerous colleagues who offered encouragement, and I am especially indebted to David Kaplan, who made it his mission to find the perfect title.

Mary Lenn Dixon and her staff at the Texas A&M University Press deserve special thanks for their enthusiasm and support of this project.

NOTES

CHAPTER 1

1. J. Richard Steffy, "Shipwrecks Reveal Early Technology," unpublished manuscript, 1975, originally written for *Scientific American.*

2. One of the earliest representations of a sail-powered Greek merchant ship on the Attic cup, British Museum B436, dates to c. 510 B.C.

3. Susan Wormer Katzev, "The Ancient Ship of Kyrenia, Beneath the Cyprus Seas," in *Great Moments in Greek Archaeology,* ed. Panos Valavanis (Los Angeles: The J. Paul Getty Museum, 2007), 291–99.

4. Susan W. and Michael L. Katzev, "Last Harbor for the Oldest Ship," *National Geographic* 146 (November 1974): 620 (inset).

5. Michael L. Katzev, "Resurrecting the Oldest Known Greek Ship," *National Geographic* 137 (June 1970): 841–57.

6. J. R. Steffy, "A Cargo of Knowledge, *INA Quarterly* 28 (Spring 2001): 10–12.

7. J. R. Steffy, "Nautical Archaeology Construction Techniques of Ancient Ships," *Naval Engineer's Journal,* October 1975: 85–91.

8. J. R. Steffy, untitled handwritten essay, about 1984 (presented by Loren C. Steffy at the Tropis X International Symposium on Ship Construction in Antiquity, Hydra, Greece, Aug. 27–Sept. 2, 2008).

9. Susan W. Katzev, eulogy for J. Richard Steffy, 2007.

10. John Noble Wilford, "Civilization and Sail, an Ancient Marriage," *The New York Times,* July 3, 1992, arts section, metro edition.

CHAPTER 2

1. Naval records on the Atlantic crossings may be incomplete. Dick wrote that the ship made twenty-eight Atlantic crossings, but he didn't cite his source. J. Richard Steffy, "The Saga of Lucy and Dick Steffy," (self-published, 2000), 3.

2. Muriel Steffy Lipp, "Sweeping Up the Heart," (self-published, 2003) 107–108.

3. U.S. Census, 1879; "nickname Dawdy": Lipp, "Sweeping," 108–109.

4. Fietta's lineage was determined by histories of Berks County, Pennsylvania, and personal correspondence.

5. Lipp, "Sweeping," 109.

6. J. R. Steffy, "Saga," 2.

7. Lipp, "Sweeping," 7.

8. J. R. Steffy, "Saga," 2; Lipp, "Sweeping," 7.

9. Lipp, "Sweeping," 4.

10. J. R. Steffy, "Saga," 3–6.

11. J. R. Steffy, letter to Michael Katzev, May 24, 1989.

12. Steffy, "Saga," 15–16.

13. Ibid, 18.

14. Ibid, 19.

15. J. R. Steffy, letter to Muriel Steffy (Lipp), Sept. 22, 1945.

16. J. R. Steffy, letter to M. Steffy, Oct. 12, 1945.

17. J. R. Steffy, U.S. Navy service records; *The Dictionary of American Naval Fighting Ships.* (DANFS Online), |FCO|Hyperlinkwww.hazegray.org/danfs/escorts/de6.htm|FCC|.

18. J. R. Steffy, letter to M. Steffy, Sept. 27, 1945.

19. John Steinbeck, *Once There Was a War* (New York: Penguin Books, 1994) (originally published by Viking Press, 1958).

20. J. R. Steffy, letter to M. Steffy, Aug. 18, 1945.

21. DANFS online, "Wyffels," www.hazegray.org/danfs/escorts/de6.htm.

22. J. R. Steffy, letter to M. Steffy, Sept. 16, 1945.

23. Navsource Online: Destroyer Escort Photo Archive, |FCO|Hyperlinkwww.navsource.org/archives/06/006.htm|FCC|.

24. J. R. Steffy, letter to M. Steffy, Sept. 27, 1945.

25. J. R. Steffy, letter to M. Steffy, Oct. 23, 1945.

CHAPTER 3

1. Franklin and Marshall College Veterans Administration Guidance Center report, Lancaster, Pennsylvania, Aug. 7, 1946.

2. Milwaukee School of Engineering grade reports, 1947–48.

3. J. Richard Steffy, "The Saga of Lucy and Dick Steffy," (self-published, 2000), 21.

4. Ibid, 24.

5. Lucille Koch, "My Autobiography," tenth-grade class paper, Nov. 14, 1940.

6. Aquila, Royersford High School, 1943, 19.

7. J. R. Steffy, "Saga," 23–27.

8. Milton G. Steffy Jr., e-mail message to author, Aug. 20, 2009.

9. Federal tax returns of J. R. Steffy and Lucille Steffy, 1965–69.

10. Milton Steffy e-mail, Aug. 20, 2009.

11. The visit was before the partial core meltdown of a reactor unit in 1979 that would change the nation's views on nuclear power.

12. J. R. Steffy, "Saga," 28–29.

13. Lucille Steffy medical records and history, 1967–68.

14. Federal tax returns, J. R. Steffy and L. Steffy, 1965.

15. J. R. Steffy, "Saga," 30.

16. Milton Steffy e-mail, Aug. 20, 2009.

17. J. R. Steffy, sermons to St. John's UCC Church, Denver, Pennsylvania, 1962–74.

18. J. R. Steffy, "Saga," 30.

CHAPTER 4

1. National Geographic Society membership certificate, Jan. 1, 1953.

2. Institute of Nautical Archaeology, "Key Figures: George Fletcher Bass," |FCO|Hyperlinkhttp://inadiscover.com/about/key_figures/bass/.|FCC|

3. Even then, Dick didn't see models as keepsakes. Both the collier and the skuta wound up in my room as toys and were eventually thrown away.

4. Mystic Seaport, Charles G. Davis Collection: Biography of Charles G. Davis," |FCO|Hyperlinkhttp://library.mysticseaport.org/manuscripts/coll/co 11253.cfm#head39200688|FCC|.

5. Charles G. Davis, *The Built-Up Ship Model,* (Salem, Mass.: Marine Research Society, 1933), v. At this time, Dick noted in pencil on the inside cover when he began reading a book.

6. J. Richard Steffy, letter to *Proceedings,* U.S. Naval Institute, April 4, 1961.

7. William M. Weise, "Marine Research Hobby of Lancaster Countian," *The Reading Eagle,* July 7, 1963, Sunday Eagle Magazine supplement, 2–3.

8. Ibid.

9. Cheryl Ward, e-mail message to author, Feb. 2, 2010. Ward said she was unaware that Dick had built an Egyptian model early in his career. Dick later gave the model to the University of Pennsylvania museum and eventually recommended it be discarded because it had no value as a research model.

10. J. R. Steffy, "The Saga of Lucy and Dick Steffy," (self-published, 2000), 30.

11. J. R. Steffy, letter to Fred van Doorninck, Jan. 4, 1965.

12. J. R. Steffy, audio recording of an interview by Shelley Wachsmann, 1994.

13. J. R. Steffy, letter to George F. Bass, April 1, 1964.

14. Ibid.

15. G. Bass, letter to J. R. Steffy, April, 6, 1964.

16. J. R. Steffy, letter to Fred van Doorninck, Aug. 26, 1968.

17. J. R. Steffy, *Wooden Shipbuilding and the Interpretation of Shipwrecks* (College Station, Texas: Texas A&M University Press, 1994), 221.

18. Shelley Wachsmann, *The Sea of Galilee Boat* (College Station, Texas: Texas A&M University Press, 2009), 126.

19. J. R. Steffy, *Wooden Shipbuilding,* 232–33.

CHAPTER 5

1. Glenn Darrington, taped interview with Richard Steffy (transcript), Jan. 15, 1999.

2. J. Richard Steffy, "The Saga of Lucy and Dick Steffy," (self-published, 2000), 31.

3. Michael L. Katzev, "Resurrecting the Oldest Known Greek Ship," *National Geographic* 137 (June 1970): 841–57.

4. Vasamuseet, "Vessel," |FCO|Hyperlinkwww.vasamuseet.se/sitecore/content/Vasamuseet/Skeppet.aspx|FCO|.

5. M. Katzev, handwritten notes, 1971.

6. M. Katzev, letter to J. R. Steffy, Jan. 21, 1971.

7. J. R. Steffy, letter to M. Katzev, Feb. 1, 1971.

8. Susan W. and Michael L. Katzev, "Last Harbor for the Oldest Ship," *National Geographic* 146 (November 1974): 618–25.

9. M. Katzev, letter to J. R. Steffy, April 29, 1971.

10. J. R. Steffy, "Saga," 31–32.

11. J. R. Steffy, letter to Lucille Steffy, July 26, 1971.

12. J. R. Steffy, "Remembering Michael L. Katzev," *INA Quarterly* 29 (Fall/Winter 2002): 11.

13. J. R. Steffy, letter to Lucille Steffy, Oct. 17, 1973.

14. J. R. Steffy, letter to Lucille Steffy, Aug. 5, 1971.

CHAPTER 6

1. J. R. Steffy, "Remembering Michael L. Katzev," *INA Quarterly* 29 (Fall/Winter 2002): 11.

2. Susan Langston, "Shipwreck Ashore," *AINA Newsletter* 1 (Winter 1975): 1–4.

3. Jesse Langston, "West Windsor Woman Inspires Nautical Chronicle," *The Trenton Times,* Sept. 25, 1988.

4. J. R. Steffy, letter to Lucille Steffy, July 28, 1971.

5. Income tax returns for J. R. and Lucille Steffy, 1971 and 1973.

6. J. R. Steffy, letter to M. Katzev, Nov. 17, 1971.

7. J. R. Steffy, "The Saga of Lucy and Dick Steffy," (self-published, 2000), 32.

8. Ibid.

9. J. R. Steffy, letter to M. Katzev, March 8, 1972.

10. J. R. Steffy, letter to M. Katzev, Jan. 12, 1972.

11. J. R. Steffy, letter to Robin C. M. Piercy, March 27, 1972.

12. J. R. Steffy, condensed log of work submitted to M. Katzev, 1972–73.

13. J. R. Steffy, letter to M. Katzev, March 8, 1972.

14. J. R. Steffy, correspondence with M. Katzev, May 24, 1971–March 29, 1972. Recent research by Laina Swiny suggests that the yo-yos were more likely used as quick releases for a fabric or skin cover over the cargo hold. They also may have been used for adjusting tension on lines.

15. J. R. Steffy, letter to M. Katzev, March 24, 1972.

16. Laina Swiny, letter to J. R. Steffy, Feb. 18, 1972.

17. Connie Grzelka, "Denver Man to Rebuild 2,400-Year-Old Ship," *Lancaster New Era,* March 20, 1972.

18. L. K. Steffy, personal diary, 1972.

19. Bill O'Boyle, "Agnes Now a Flood of Memories," *The (Wilkes-Barre) Times Leader,* June 21, 2009.

CHAPTER 7

1. J. R. Steffy, "Remembering Michael L. Katzev," *INA Quarterly* 29 (Fall/Winter 2002): 11.

2. J. R. Steffy, unpublished manuscript on the Kyrenia Ship, 2005. An earlier, interim report on the hull was published in the *American Journal of Archaeology* in 1985. I have chosen to use the later manuscript my father had completed before his death because it contains revisions to his earlier work.

3. J. R. Steffy, untitled handwritten essay written in about 1984 (presented by Loren C. Steffy at the Tropis X International Symposium on Ship Construction in Antiquity, Hydra, Greece, Aug. 27–Sept. 2, 2008).

4. Ibid.

5. Ibid.

6. J. R. Steffy, Kyrenia Ship manuscript.

7. J. R. Steffy, Kyrenia Ship notes on the fiberglass test replica, test number one, undated.

8. J. R. Steffy, Kyrenia Ship manuscript.

9. Ibid.

10. Ibid.

11. J. R. Steffy, condensed log of work submitted to M. Katzev, 1972–73.

12. J. R. Steffy, letter to Lucille Steffy, Aug. 26, 1973.

13. J. R. Steffy, handwritten notes on Kyrenia Ship reconstruction, May 4, 1975.

14. J. R. Steffy, Kyrenia Ship manuscript.

15. Ibid.

16. Ibid.

17. Ibid.

18. J. R. Steffy, letter to M. Katzev, June 8, 1973.

19. J. R. Steffy, letter to Lucille Steffy, July 13, 1973.

20. J. R. Steffy, letter to Lucille Steffy, July 17. 1973.

21. J. R. Steffy, letter to Lucille Steffy, Sept. 26, 1973.

22. J. R. Steffy, letter to Lucille Steffy, Oct. 3, 1973.

23. J. R. Steffy, letter to Lucille Steffy, Oct. 23, 1973.

24. J. R. Steffy, letter to Lucille Steffy, Oct. 11, 1973.

25. J. R. Steffy, Kyrenia Ship manuscript.

26. J. R. Steffy, letter to Lucille Steffy, Nov. 9, 1973.

27. J. R. Steffy, letter to Lucille Steffy, Nov. 14, 1973.

28. J. R. Steffy, letter to Lucille Steffy, Nov. 23, 1973.

29. J. R. Steffy, letter to M. Katzev, Jan. 28, 1974.

30. J. R. Steffy, letter to M. Katzev, Feb. 25, 1975.

31. J. R. Steffy, Kyrenia Ship manuscript.

CHAPTER 8

1. Kyriacos C. Markides, *The Rise and Fall of the Cyprus Republic* (New Haven, Conn.: Yale University Press, 1977), 1.

2. Frank McLynn, *Lionheart and Lackland, King Richard, King John and the Wars of Conquest* (London: Vintage Books, 2007), 201.

3. Cypnet, "Kyrenia Castle," |FCO|Hyperlink|FCO|Hyperlinkwww.cypnet .co.uk/ncyprus/city/kyrenia/castle/index.html|FCC||FCC|.

4. Nicholas Farrell, "Paradise for Pirates," *Scotsman,* June 12, 1999.

5. Lucille Steffy, family calendar, 1972.

6. Lucille Steffy, letter to Muriel Steffy Lipp, July 10, 1972.

7. J. Richard Steffy, "The Saga of Lucy and Dick Steffy," (self-published, 2000), 33.

8. George Bass, letter to J. R. Steffy, Sept. 15, 1972.

9. G. Bass, letter to Michael L. Katzev, Sept. 21, 1972.

10. M.Katzev, letter to G. Bass, Nov. 21, 1972.

11. G. Bass, letter to J. R. Steffy, May 23, 1973.

12. J. R. Steffy, letter to Lucille Steffy, Aug. 30, 1973.

13. J. R. Steffy, letter to Lucille Steffy, Sept. 8, 1973.

14. J. R. Steffy, letter to Lucille Steffy, July 12, 1973.

15. Lucien Basch, letter to J. R. Steffy, Feb. 14, 1976.

16. J. R. Steffy, letter to Lucille Steffy, July 14, 1973.

17. J. R. Steffy, letter to Lucille Steffy, Oct. 10, 1973.

18. Hellenic Institute of Maritime Archaeology, letter to J. R. Steffy, May 14, 1974.

19. J. R. Steffy, letter to Lucille Steffy, June 20, 1974.

20. J. R. Steffy, letter to Lucille Steffy, Oct. 16, 1973.

21. J. R. Steffy, letter to Lucille Steffy, July 14, 1973.

22. J. R. Steffy, letter to Lucille Steffy, Oct. 24, 1973.

23. J. R. Steffy, letter to G. Bass, Jan. 11, 1974.

24. G. Bass, letter to J. R. Steffy, Feb. 2, 1974.

25. J. R. Steffy, letter to G. Bass, March 21, 1974.

26. G. Bass, letter to the AINA board, May 14, 1974.

CHAPTER 9

1. J. Richard Steffy, letter to Lucille Steffy, May 15, 1974.

2. J. R. Steffy, letter to Michael L. Katzev, March 12, 1974.

3. Kyriacos C. Markides, *The Rise and Fall of the Cyprus Republic* (New Haven, Conn.: Yale University Press, 1977), 189.

4. The events of Cyprus in the summer of 1974 remain a divisive issue. The politics behind the war have filled entire books, and I have purposely provided only a cursory overview of the events. My father never took sides in the conflict, noting with some pride that he continued to work on projects with permits from both the Greek and Turkish governments for the rest of his career.

5. J. R. Steffy, letter to Lucille Steffy, July 2, 1974.

6. J. R. Steffy, letter to Lucille Steffy, July 10, 1974.

7. Ibid.

8. J. R. Steffy, telegram to Lucille Steffy, July 18, 1974.

9. "Area Man Stranded in Turkey by Cyprus War," *Lancaster Intelligencer-Journal,* July 29, 1974.

10. J. R. Steffy, letter to George Bass, Aug. 25, 1974.

11. "Area Archeologist Flees Cyprus," *The Reading Times,* July 29, 1974.

12. Laina Swiny, interview with author, Oct. 26, 2009.

13. Susan Katzev, letter to J. R. Steffy, Nov. 12, 1974.

14. J. R. Steffy, letter to Michael L. Katzev, Feb. 6, 1974.

15. J. R. Steffy, presentation for INA board of directors annual meeting, Dallas, Texas, 2001.

16. George Bass, letter to Claude Duthuit, Aug. 21, 1974.

CHAPTER 10

1. George Bass, interview with author, Sept. 5, 2009.

2. Vaughn Bryant, interview with author, Jan. 22, 2010.

3. Clausen left Texas before AINA completed its move to Texas A&M. He returned to Florida, and in 1997 he was arrested for killing his wife. He is serving a fifty-year prison sentence (Greg Retsinas, "Manhunt Continues for Suspect," *Sarasota Herald-Tribune,* July 26, 1997, and Florida Department of Corrections inmate records).

4. G. Bass, letter to John Brown Cook, April 7, 1975.

5. J. Richard Steffy, handwritten notes on Kyrenia Ship reconstruction, May 5, 1975.

6. David C. Switzer, "Excavating the *Defence," INA Newsletter* 2.2 (Summer 1975); and Barbara Ford and David C. Switzer, *Underwater Dig: The Excavation of a Revolutionary War Privateer* (New York: William Morrow and Co., 1982), 13–25.

7. J. R. Steffy, "The Institute's Model Shop," *AINA Newsletter* 3 (Spring 1976): 1–4.

8. J. R. Steffy, letter to G. Bass, Feb. 10, 1976.

9. J. R. Steffy, letter to G. Bass, Dec. 15, 1975.

CHAPTER 11

1. J. Richard Steffy, letter to Michael Katzev, Nov. 14, 1976.

2. J. R. Steffy, "The Brown's Ferry Vessel: A Sunken Time Capsule," Rice Museum, Georgetown, South Carolina: |FCO|Hyperlink|FCO|Hyperlinkwww .ricemuseum.org/vessel.php|FCC||FCC|.

3. J. R. Steffy, letter to Michael and Susan Katzev, May 21, 1979.

4. George Bass, interview with author, Sept. 5, 2009.

5. Frederick H. van Doorninck, "The Glass Wreck at Serçe Limani," *INA Newsletter* 15 (September 1988): 1–9.

6. J. R. Steffy, letter to Alan Albright, Oct. 15, 1985.

7. J. R. Steffy, "Reconstructing the Hull," *INA Newsletter* 15 (September 1988): 14–21.

8. J. R. Steffy, letter to Lucille Steffy, June 9, 1974.

9. Cemal Pulak, interview with author, Feb. 12, 2010.

10. F. Hocker, tribute to J. R. Steffy, *The INA Newsletter* 15 (September 1988): 14–21.

11. J. R. Steffy, "Ship Models as Tools for Reconstructing Shipwrecks," (paper presented at the Western Ship Modelers Association annual conference, Long Beach, California, 1998).

12. J. R. Steffy, Anthropology 616 course description, Texas A&M University, Spring 1984.

13. G. Bass, letter to MacArthur Foundation, Jan. 31, 1985.

14. J. R. Steffy, Anthropology 616 course description, Texas A&M University, Spring 1990.

15. Ken Cassavoy, handwritten notes for Anthropology 616, Texas A&M University, undated.

16. Shelley Wachsmann, *The Sea of Galilee Boat* (College Station, Texas: Texas A&M University Press, 2009), 167.

CHAPTER 12

1. This chapter offers only a cursory view of these projects. The Athlit Ram and the Sea of Galilee boat have been written about extensively, and the Herculaneum boat to a lesser extent. See the Selected Bibliography for more information on these vessels.

2. J. Richard Steffy, untitled handwritten essay, about 1984 (presented by Loren C. Steffy at the Tropis X International Symposium on Ship Construction in Antiquity, Hydra, Greece, Aug. 27–Sept. 2, 2008).

3. Lionel Casson and J. R. Steffy, ed., *The Athlit Ram* (College Station, Texas: Texas A&M University Press, 1991), 3.

4. J. R. Steffy, "The Athlit Ram, A Preliminary Investigation of Its Structure," *The Mariner's Mirror* 69 (August 1983): 229–247.

5. J. R. Steffy, letter to Lucille Steffy, Aug. 21, 1982.

6. J. R. Steffy, letter to Lucille Steffy, Aug. 23, 1982.

7. Casson and Steffy, *The Athlit Ram,* 6–39.

8. J. R. Steffy, "The Athlit Ram," *Mariner's Mirror,* 244.

9. J. R. Steffy, untitled essay.

10. J. R. Steffy, letter to Lucille Steffy, Aug. 26, 1982.

11. Rick Gore, "After 2,000 Years of Silence, the Dead Do Tell Tales at Vesuvius," *National Geographic* 165 (May 1984): 557–613.

12. Shelley Wachsmann, *The Sea of Galilee Boat* (College Station, Texas: Texas A&M University Press, 2009), 133–34.

13. J. R. Steffy, "The Herculaneum Boat: Preliminary Notes on Hull Details," *American Journal of Archaeology* 89: 519–21.

14. Wachsmann, *Galilee Boat,* 135.

15. J. R. Steffy, report to Dott. M. Giuseppina Cerulli Irelli. Aug. 9, 1983.

16. Gore, *Geographic,* 606.

17. J. R. Steffy, letter to Joseph Judge, Sept. 1, 1982.

18. Gore, *Geographic,* 606.

19. J. R. Steffy, letter to Irelli.

20. Gore, *Geographic,* 606.

21. J. R. Steffy, letter to Irelli.

22. J. R. Steffy, "The Saga of Lucy and Dick Steffy," (self-published, 2000), "Ship Studies" addendum, 10.

23. J. R. Steffy, letter to Michael Katzev, May 14, 1986.

24. J. R. Steffy, "Saga," "Ship Studies" addendum, 12.

25. Wachsmann, *Galilee,* 7–33.

26. Ibid., 136–40.

27. J. R. Steffy, "Saga," "Ship Studies" addendum, 12.

28. Wachsmann, *Galilee,* 136–40.

29. Ibid.

30. Ibid.

31. Ibid, 301–304.

32. Wachsmann, tribute to J. R. Steffy,|FCO|Hyperlinkhttp://blogs.tamu .edu/steffy/|FCC|.

33. Wachsmann, *Galilee,* 141.

34. Ibid., 141–47.

35. J. R. Steffy, letter to Karen Sullivan, March 21, 1986.

36. J. R. Steffy, "Saga," "Ship Studies" addendum, 8–11.

37. Ibid.

CHAPTER 13

1. Cheryl Ward, interview with author, Feb. 1, 2010.

2. Paul F. Johnston, interview with author, Jan. 29, 2010.

3. Beth Braznell, interview with author, March 8, 2010.

4. Maureen Atwell, interview with author, Feb. 19, 2010.

5. MacArthur Foundation, "About the Fellows Program," |FCO|Hyper link|FCO|Hyperlinkwww.macfound.org/site/c.lkLXJ8MQKrH/b.4536879/ k.9B87/About_the_Program.htm|FCC||FCC|.

6. The MacArthur Fellows nomination process is anonymous, and the author of the letter did not want to be identified.

7. J. R. Steffy, letter to George Bass, Jan. 31, 1980.

8. Summary report on J. R. Steffy, Oct. 30, 1987.

9. Joe Drape, "Banking on Brains, Foundation's Cash Gives the Gifted a Chance to Excel," *The Dallas Morning News,* Aug. 10, 1986.

10. George Bass, email message to author, March 11, 2010.

11. Ibid.

12. G. Bass interview with author, Sept. 5, 2009.

13. The MacArthur Foundation confirmed that the nominator was a single individual; at one point in our discussion the pronoun "she" was used. Kreutz's son, Gregg, said he and his sisters found no records in his mother's papers indicating she nominated Dick. However, I have come to the conclusion, as has George Bass, that she did.

14. J. R. Steffy, "The Saga of Lucy and Dick Steffy," (self-published, 2000), 23.

15. J. R. Steffy, memorandum to Vaughn Bryant, Jan. 18, 1990.

16. Teresa Francis, letter to J. R. Steffy, Feb. 12, 1992.

17. J. R. Steffy, *Wooden Shipbuilding and the Interpretation of Shipwrecks* (College Station, Texas: Texas A&M University Press, 1994), xii.

CHAPTER 14

1. Harry Tzalas served as translator for my interview with Manolis Psaros, conducted at his shipyard in Perama on Nov. 3, 2009.

2. J. Richard Steffy, cost estimate prepared for Michael Katzev, January 1976.

3. J. R. Steffy and M. Katzev, correspondence, Feb.–April 1979.

4. H. Tzalas, letter to J. R. Steffy, March 22, 1983.

5. J. R. Steffy, letter to H. Tzalas, March 31, 1983.

6. H. Tzalas, interview with author, Nov. 3–4, 2009.

7. J. R. Steffy, letter to H. Tzalas, March 31, 1983.

8. J. R. Steffy, letter to Owain Roberts, Jan. 21, 2002.

9. Henry Kamm, "New Model of Ancient Vessel Resuming Trip of 2,300 Years," *The New York Times,* June 23, 1985.

10. H. Tzalas, letter to J. R. Steffy, Dec. 2, 2004, with handwritten notes by J. R. Steffy.

CHAPTER 15

1. J. Richard Steffy, letter to Loren C. Steffy, Aug. 20, 2001.

2. J. R. Steffy, e-mail to Susan Katzev, May 23, 2007.

3. Ibid.

4. S. Katzev, e-mail to colleagues telling of J. R. Steffy's death, Nov. 29, 2007.

5. Ibid.

6. Institute of Nautical Archaeology, "Yenikapi Byzantine Shipwrecks Exca-

vation and Study—Turkey," |FCO|Hyperlinkhttp://inadiscover.com/projects/
all/southern_europe_mediterranean_aegean/yenikapi_harbor_wrecks_tur
key/introduction/|FCC|.

EPILOGUE

1. J. Richard Steffy, letter to Steve Ross, Jan. 10, 1986.

2. George Bass, interview with author, Sept. 5, 2009.

3. Muriel Steffy Lipp, "Sweeping Up the Heart," (self-published, 2003), 40.

4. John Steinbeck, *The Log from the Sea of Cortez* (New York: Viking Press, 1941), 18.

GLOSSARY OF SHIP TERMS[1]

adze An axe-like tool with its blade at right angles to the handle, used for shaping and dressing wood. Also called *adz.*

amidships The middle of the vessel, either longitudinally or transversely.

ballast Heavy material, such as iron, lead, or stone, placed low in the hold to lower the center of gravity and improve stability.

batten A thin plank or strip of wood used to determine hull curvatures or to temporarily connect timbers during construction.

bilge The area of a hull's bottom on which it would rest if grounded; generally the outer end of the floor. When used in the plural, especially in contemporary documents, *bilges* refers to the various cavities between the frames in the floor of the hold where bilge water tends to collect.

boat An open vessel, usually small and without decks, intended for use in sheltered water.

bow The forward part of the hull, specifically, from the point where the sides curve inward to the stem.

bulwark The side of a vessel above its upper deck.

buttock The convex part of the hull beneath the stern deck.

buttock lines Projections on a lines drawing that reveal vertically oriented longitudinal hull shapes.

caprail A timber attached to the top of a vessel's frames. Also called *main rail* or *cap.*

ceiling The internal planking of a vessel.

cutwater The forward-most part of the stem; the stem piece or nosing that parts the water.

dowel A cylindrical piece of wood, with a constant diameter, used to align two members by being sunk into each. Unlike treenails and pegs, dowels served an alignment function only, additional fastenings being necessary to prevent separation of the joint.

draft The depth to which a hull is immersed; also, a drawing or plan. Also called *draught.*

1. Excerpted from *Wooden Shipbuilding and the Interpretation of Shipwrecks,* by J. Richard Steffy (College Station, Texas: Texas A&M University Press, 1994).

floor The bottom of a vessel between the upward turns of its bilges.

floor timber A frame timber that crossed the keel and spanned the bottom; the central piece of a compound frame.

forecastle Variously, a short, raised foredeck; the forward part of the upper deck between the foremast and the stem; or the quarters below the foredeck.

frame A transverse timber, or line or assembly of timbers, that described the body shape of a vessel and to which the planking and ceiling were fastened. Frames were sometimes called *timbers* or, erroneously, *ribs.* Ancient ships often had frames composed of lines of unconnected timbers; later ships usually had compound frames composed of *floor timbers, futtocks,* and *top timbers.*

futtock A frame timber other than a floor timber, half-frame, or top timber; one of the middle pieces of a frame.

galley A seagoing vessel propelled primarily by oars, but usually one that also could be sailed when necessary. Also, a name given to a vessel's kitchen.

garboard strake The strake of planking next to the keel; the lowest plank. Also, the lowest side strake of a flat-bottomed hull. Also called *garboard.*

gunwale The upper edge of a vessel's side. In sixteenth-century vessels, the wale against which the guns rest. Also called *gunnel.*

half-frame A frame whose heel began at or near one side of the keel or deadwood and spanned part or all of that side of the hull; half-frames were normally used in pairs.

hatch A rectangular opening in a vessel's deck. Also called *hatchway.*

helm The tiller or steering wheel; in a general context, the wheel, tiller, and rudder.

keel The main longitudinal timber of most hulls, upon which the frames, deadwoods, and ends of the hull were mounted; the backbone of the hull.

keelson An internal longitudinal timber or line of timbers, mounted atop the frames along the centerline of the keel, that provided additional longitudinal strength to the bottom of the hull; an internal keel.

lines The various shapes of a hull; expressed graphically, a set of geometric projections, usually arranged in three views, that illustrates the shape of a vessel's hull. Also called *hull lines.*

mast step A mortise cut into the top of a keelson or large floor timber, or a mortised wooden block or assembly of blocks mounted on the floor timbers or keelson, into which the tenoned heel of a mast was seated.

mold A pattern used to determine the shapes of frames and other compass timbers. Molds were usually made from thin, flexible pieces of wood. Also called *mould.*

mold loft A protected area or building in a shipyard where the hull lines, from which the molds were produced, were drawn full size on a specially prepared flat surface. (On the Kyrenia ship project, the mold lofts line two of the walls on either side of the reconstructed hull.)

mortise-and-tenon joint A union of planks or timbers by which a projecting piece (tenon) was fitted into one or more cavities (mortises) of corresponding size.

peg A tapered wooden pin driven into a pre-drilled hole to fasten two members or lock a joint. Pegs came in a variety of sizes and tapers; they could have square, round, or multisided cross sections. The important difference between dowels and pegs in ancient construction was that the former were of constant diameter and lightly set, whereas the latter were tapered and driven with appreciable force. The most common use of pegs in ancient construction was the locking of mortise-and-tenon joints. Also called *tenon peg.*

planking The outer lining, or shell, of a hull.

port The left side of a vessel when facing forward. Also called *port side.*

rabbet A groove or cut made in a piece of timber in such a way that the edges of another piece could be fit into it to make a tight joint. Generally, the term refers to grooves cut into the sides of the keel, stem, and sternpost, into which the garboards and hooding ends of the outer planking were seated.

ram A strong projection on the bow of an ancient warship, usually sheathed in metal, used as a weapon to strike another vessel. Specifically, the ram included the ramming timber, the forward bow timbers configured to reinforce the ramming timber, and a metal sheath; in actual practice, the metal sheath is usually called the ram. Rams were also used, with little success, on iron warships after the middle of the nineteenth century.

rib A small transverse member, often flexible and composed of one or several pieces, that stiffened the outer skin of a hull. Although often a layman's term for *frame,* rib is more properly applied to small craft, such as canoes, small boats, and certain heavy frames that ran from gunwale to gunwale in clinker-built vessels or vessels whose skin is made of material other than wood.

rockered keel A keel that is curved longitudinally so that it is deeper at its middle than at its ends. The term also refers to keels that are molded to a greater dimension amidships than at their ends. *Rocker* should not be confused with *sag,* which is an accidental rocker.

rudder A timber, or assembly of timbers, that could be rotated about an axis to control the direction of a vessel underway. Until the middle of the medieval period, the practice was to mount rudders on one or both stern quarters; these were known as *quarter rudders.* By the late medieval period, however, it appears that most vessels of appreciable size were steered by a single rudder hung at the sternpost; these were known as *stern-hung rudders.*

sag The accidental rocker formed in a keel and bottom due to insufficient timbering or improper loading. Also called *sagging.*

scarf An overlapping joint used to connect two timbers or planks without increasing their dimensions. Also called *scarph.*

seam The longitudinal joint between two timbers or planks; the term usually refers to planking seams, the longitudinal juxtaposition of the edges of planks in the sides or decks, which were made watertight.

sheathing A thin covering of metal or wood to protect hulls from marine life or fouling, or to stabilize and protect surface material applied for that purpose. Sheathing was most commonly used in the form of copper, lead, zinc or alloy sheets, or thin wooden planks known as *furring* or *deals.*

shell The external planking of a vessel.

shell-first construction A modern (sometimes misleading) term used to describe the process by which all or part of the outer hull planking was erected before frames were attached to it. In pure shell-built hulls, outer planking was self-supporting and formed the primary structure; the framework fastened to it formed the secondary, or stiffening, structure. Also called *shell-built.*

shim A thin piece of wood used to fill a separation between two timbers or a frame and a plank.

shipwright A master craftsman skilled in the construction and repair of ships. In many instances, the person in charge of a ship's construction, including the supervision of carpenters and other personnel, control of expenditures, schedules, and acquisition of materials. Probably in many more areas and periods than have been documented, the term designated a formal title, such as the shipwrights to the English monarchs, or a level of expertise qualifying admission to a guild or association.

skeletal construction A modern (sometimes misleading) term used to describe the procedure in which hulls were constructed by first erecting frames and then attaching the outer skin of planking to them. Also called *frame-first construction.*

stanchion An upright supporting post, including undecorated supports for deck beams and bulkheads.

starboard The right side of a vessel when facing forward.

stem A vertical or upward curving timber or assembly of timbers, scarfed to the keel or central plank at its lower end, into which the two sides of the bow were joined. Also called *stempost.*

stern The after end of a vessel.

sternpost A vertical or upward curving timber or assembly of timbers stepped into, or scarfed to, the after end of the keel or heel.

strake A continuous line of planks, running from bow to stern. Also called *streake.*

tenon A wooden projection cut from the end of a timber or a separate wooden piece that was shaped to fit into a corresponding mortise.

tiller A wooden or metal level fitted into the rudder head, by which the rudder could be moved from side to side.

timbers In general context, all wooden hull members; specifically, those members that formed the frames of a hull.

top timber The uppermost member of a frame.

treenail A round or multisided piece of hardwood, driven through planks and timbers to connect them. Treenails were employed most frequently in attaching planking to frames, attaching knees to ceiling or beams, and in scarfing of timbers. They were used in a variety of forms: with expanding wedges or nails in their ends, with tapered or square heads on their exterior ends, or completely unwedged and unheaded. When immersed, treenails swelled to make a tight fit. Also called *trunnel* or *trennal.*

turn of the bilge The outboard part of the lower hull where the bottom curved toward the side.

SELECTED BIBLIOGRAPHY

Bass, George F. *Archaeology Beneath the Sea.* New York: Walker & Co., 1975.

Bass, George F. (ed). *Beneath the Seven Seas: Adventures with the Institute of Nautical Archaeology.* London: Thames & Hudson Ltd., 2005.

Bass, George F., Sheila Matthews, J. Richard Steffy, and Frederick H. van Doorninck Jr., *Serçe Limani: An Eleventh Century Shipwreck Vol. 1, The Ship and Its Anchorage, Crew and Passengers.* College Station, Texas: Texas A&M University Press, 2004.

Casson, Lionel and J. Richard Steffy (ed). *The Athlit Ram,* College Station. Texas: Texas A&M University Press, 1991.

Davis, Charles G. *The Built-Up Ship Model.* Salem, Mass.: Marine Research Society, 1933.

Davis, Charles G. *The Ship Model Builders Assistant.* New York: Edward Sweetman, 1955.

Deiss, Joseph Day. *Herculaneum: Italy's Buried Treasure.* New York: Harper & Row, 1985.

Durrell, Lawrence. *Bitter Lemons.* London: Faber and Faber Ltd., 1964.

Hill, George. *A History of Cyprus, Vol I: To the Conquest of Richard the Lion Heart.* Cambridge, England, Cambridge University Press, 1940.

Hocker, Frederick and Cheryl Ward (eds). *The Philosophy of Shipbuilding: Conceptual Approaches to the Study of Wooden Ships.* College Station, Texas: Texas A&M University Press, 2004.

Johnson, Gene. *Ship Model Building.* Centerville, Md.: Cornell Maritime Press, 1944.

Markides, Kyriacos C. *The Rise and Fall of the Cyprus Republic.* New Haven, Conn.: Yale University Press, 1977.

McLynn, Frank. *Lionheart and Lackland, King Richard, King John and the Wars of Conquest.* London: Vintage Books, 2007.

Steffy, J. Richard. *Wooden Shipbuilding and the Interpretation of Shipwrecks.* College Station, Texas: Texas A&M University Press, 1994.

Steinbeck, John. *The Log from the Sea of Cortez.* New York: Viking Press, 1941.

Valavanis, Panos (ed). *Great Moments in Greek Archaeology.* Los Angeles: J. Paul Getty Museum, 2007.

Wachsmann, Shelley. *The Sea of Galilee Boat.* College Station, Texas: Texas A&M University Press, 1995.

INDEX

academic career at A&M
   achievements/promotions, 132–34
   associate degree, electrotechnol-
      ogy, 22
   course structure, 107–8
   and failure, teaching value of, 116
   Israel, professorship in, 117
   MacArthur Foundation award,
      130–32
   publication, 128–29
   teaching style, 108–9, 114, 115
   thesis committee involvement, 115
   workload as professor, 110
acanthus wood, 35
adze, shaping with, 35, 66, 67, 143,
   gallery section
air conditioning, lack of, 70, 98, 103
Aleppo pine, 7, 141
almonds, Kyrenia Ship, 3, 43, 81
American Institute of Nautical
   Archaeology (AINA)
   and Cyprus war, 100
   Defence project, 103–4
   Dick joining, 89–90
   formation of, 84–85
   Galilee boat, 122–28
   launch of A&M program, 105–6
   move to new building at A&M,
      109
   name change to INA, 128
   Serçe Limani project, 111–14
   space issues at A&M, 107
   university affiliation, quest for,
      100–102
   See also gallery section

American Journal of Archaeology, 128
amphoras, Kyrenia Ship, 4, 43, 146–
   47, 148, 153
   See also gallery section
A&M University. *See* Texas A&M
   University
The Ancient Mariners (Casson), 108
ancient ship reconstruction, Steffy
   Method development, 40–41,
   55–57, 76, 127–29
apprentice's marks *vs.* Aristides'
   marks, Kyrenia Ship, 67–68
Archaeological Institute of America,
   42
Aristides, 7, 67–68, 153
artistic talents of family, 13, 15
Athlit battering ram, 117–19, *gallery
   section*

banking business, 13
Basch, Lucien, 61, 86–87, 118
basement
   flooding of, 63, 85
   as modeling shop, 32, 40, 47,
      48–49
Bass, George F.
   1974 coup in Cyprus and move
      to United States, 98–99
   and dedication of ship lab to
      Steffy, 162
   at Dick's death, 158–59
   and Dick's desire for nautical
      archaeology as career, 55–56
   Dick's first communications with,
      37–38

failure, value of in reconstruction
process, 116
fame and recognition
for Kyrenia project, 82, 87–88
MacArthur Foundation award,
130–32
move to Cyprus, 61
farm, Steffy, 11, 12
fiberglass replica, Kyrenia Ship, 69,
gallery section
flashlight bulb, ship model in, 33
flaws in construction, Kyrenia Ship,
68
flexible fastening system for Kyrenia
Ship, 70, 74
"floaters," 103
fragments, numbers of, 52, 66, 111
frame-first *vs.* shell-first construction, 61, 77, 86–87, 139, 143
frames, Kyrenia ship
distortion of, 51, 60
fitting and placement, 72–74
original construction methods,
66
frame *vs.* plank hull shaping, 66, 71,
72–73
Franklin & Marshall school, 22, 43
Franzén, Anders, 133–34
Free Chinese Navy, 21
freshwater immersion in wood conservation, 45–46, 47, 66, 70, 118,
128
Fritz, B. Scott, 25
Fry, Richard, 13, 14
Fry, Zoe (mother), 13–14

Galilee boat, 122–28, *gallery section*
garage ship lab (Zoe's), 98, 105
garboards, 125
garboard strakes, 72
"genius" grant, 130–32, 134
George R. Skolfield (ship), 54

German ancestry of Steffy, 11
Girne (Kyrenia), 139
glass, Islamic, 111, 112, *gallery
section*
grandchildren, 135
Great Depression, 10, 13, 14, 23–24
Greek Cypriots, 50, 79, 93–97
Greek shipbuilding, 138–39
Grill, Eliza (grandmother), 12, *gallery
section*
grinding stones, Kyrenia Ship, 3, 6,
43, 75

half models, 39
hawk's nest, 39
health issues
Dick, 148–49, 150–59
Lucille, 24, 28–29, 58, 135–36
Lucille's mother, 62, 83
Milton G., 88, 92
Zoe, 13
Hellenic Institute for the Preservation of Nautical Tradition, 138
Hellenic Institute of Marine Archaeology, 87
Herculaneum boat, 119–22, 124,
gallery section
Hocker, Fred, 109, 113–14, 115, 136
homelife and family
1960s Denver, PA, 29
Kyrenia, 80–81
Milt and Zoe, 14–15
outings, 16, 27–28, 82, 135
religion, 12, 28, 30, 126–27
Houston Chronicle, 152–53
hull, *Defence,* 104
hull, Galilee boat, 124–26
hull, Herculaneum boat, 120–21
hull, Kyrenia Ship
condition of at excavation, 4
construction, original, 5, 66, 67–
68

pastimes in Kyrenia, 81
pedestal for Kyrenia Ship keel, 61, 67, 71
PEG (polyethylene glycol), 47, 51–52, 71, 128
    See also wood, conservation and restoration of
Pennsylvania Dutch, 11, 12
"Pepsi," 17
Perama, Greece, 139, 140
personality/character
    ambition, 21, 30, 56
    humility, 157
    humor, 15, 17, 26, 50, 60, 115–16, 126, 157
    insecurity, academic, 133
    meticulousness, 27
    patience, 27
    patriotism, 20
    physical appearance, 2, 15, 17, 18, 150
    posthumous honors, 161–62
    recruitment by Katzev, 44–48
    on running the business, 25
    shyness, 18–19
    stoicism, 20, 151–52
    on teachers, 17
    war, abhorrence of, 20, 119
    on women, 19
Philadelphia Inquirer, 61
Piercy, Netia, 65
Piercy, Robin
    and 1974 coup in Cyprus, 98
    as assistant director of Kyrenia project, 65
    on Dick's approach, 51
    on display options for Kyrenia Ship, 69–70
    on emergence of wood from PEG, 71
    on living conditions in Kyrenia, 80

    on Lucien Basch, 86
    Mombasa wreck, 111
    and "the Tank," 49, 50
    on working with Dick, 50
pine species, 7, 141
pirate attack hypothesis, 3, 147
planking, 52, 59–60, 74, 120
    See also gallery section; hulls
plank *vs.* frame hull shaping, 66, 71, 72–73
pneumonia, bouts with, 151, 152
political issues affecting projects (foreign), 93–97, 121–22, 146
politics, campus, 133
polyethylene glycol (PEG), 47, 51–52, 71, 128
    See also wood, conservation and restoration of
polyurethane encasement, 127–28
Pomey, Patrice, 149
pre-Revolutionary wreck, 110
preservation of wood. *See* wood, conservation and restoration of
Princess Matoika (ship), 10–11
Prizer-Painter Company, 24
prostate cancer, 151
Protestant religion, 12
Psaros, Manolis, 139–44
Psaros Shipyard, 140–41, *gallery section*
Pulak, Cemal, 113, 158–59

reconstruction
    computers in, 98, 114–15, 135, 149, 151, 157
    Steffy Method development, 40–41, 55–57, 76, 128–29
    See also Kyrenia Ship, reconstruction; *individual projects*
"The Reconstructor," 78, 124
recording data, Dick's technique for, 109